# Great Depression and New Deal
## Almanac

# Great Depression and New Deal
## Almanac

Sharon M. Hanes
and
Richard C. Hanes

Allison McNeill,
Project Editor

Detroit • New York • San Diego • San Francisco • Cleveland • New Haven, Conn. • Waterville, Maine • London • Munich

# THOMSON
™
## GALE

## Great Depression and New Deal: Almanac
Sharon M. Hanes and Richard C. Hanes

**Project Editor**
Allison McNeill

**Permissions**
Lori Hines

**Imaging and Multimedia**
Dean Dauphinais, Christine O'Bryan,
Robert Duncan

**Product Design**
Pamela Galbreath, Cynthia Baldwin

**Composition**
Evi Seoud

**Manufacturing**
Rita Wimberley

**LIBRARY OF CONGRESS CATALOGING-IN-PUBLICATION DATA**

Hanes, Sharon M.
Great Depression and New Deal almanac / Sharon M. Hanes and Richard C. Hanes;
 Allison McNeill, editor.
 p. cm.
 Includes bibliographical references (p. ) and index.
Contents: Causes of the Depression–New Deal–Agriculture/Farm Relief–Banking and
 housing–Ethnic populations–Education–Everyday life–Entertainment and news
 media–Riding the rails (Youth on the move)–Rural Electrification–Social Security–Women in public life–Works Progress Administration–Employment and industry–Prohibition and crime–End of Depression/World War II mobilization.
 ISBN 0-7876-6533-9
1. United States–History–1933-1945–Juvenile literature. 2. United States–History–1919-1933–Juvenile literature. 3. Depressions–1929–United States–Juvenile
 literature. 4. New Deal, 1933-1939–Juvenile literature.  [1. United
 States–History–1933-1945. 2. United States–History–1919-1933. 3. Depressions–1929. 4. New Deal, 1933-1939.]  I. Hanes, Richard Clay, 1946-  .
 II. McNeill, Allison. III. Title.
 E806.H315 2002
 973.917–dc21

2002011133

# Contents

# Introduction

Embedded within the timeline of a nation's history are certain extraordinary events that spur rapid change within the society and impact the political life and thinking of the people for decades thereafter. In the timeline of the United States, such events include the American Revolution (1775–83), the Civil War (1861–65), World War II (1939–45), and perhaps the Vietnam War (1954–75). Aside from wars, other momentous and highly influential events include the industrial revolution (roughly nineteenth century), the civil rights movement of the 1950s and 1960s, and the Great Depression (1929–41). The Great Depression was the longest and worst economic crisis in U.S. history. It was not only economically devastating for millions, but was a personal tragedy for Americans from the very young to the very old.

What could cause such a dramatic economic downturn in the United States? To most Americans it seemed the prosperity of the "roaring" 1920s would go on forever. Yet, throughout the 1920s economic difficulties in certain segments of the American economy began to surface. Industrialization, that is, the development of industries that mass-produced consumer goods such as washing machines and automobiles, dramatically affected the United States. Rolling off assembly lines at ever increasing rates, goods were touted by advertisers who encouraged consumers to borrow money to buy the goods, a practice known as buying on credit. In the 1920s American values of thrift and saving money increasingly gave way to accumulating debt as Americans bought the latest products on "credit" just as soon as the products appeared in the stores. Banks eagerly made loan after loan. However, by 1929 this buying had slowed. It seemed consumers could only buy so much.

The major share of wealth in the nation rested in the hands of a tiny percentage of individual families. The very wealthy could not sustain enough buying power to make up for the slowdown in buying by the rest of the population. Goods began to accumulate on store shelves forcing factories to slow down production and lay off workers.

Another sector of the U.S. economy experiencing difficulty was the agriculture sector. Farmers had been overproducing since the end of World War I (1914–18) even after the drop in overseas demand for their products. The glut of farm products had driven farm prices so low that farmers could barely earn a living much less buy consumer goods. Farm families still accounted for 25 to 30 percent of the U.S. population, so a significant number of Americans were already struggling.

Although these various signs of economic trouble began emerging in the 1920s, hardly anyone paid attention. The majority of Americans were enjoying prosperity as never before. So, when in October 1929 the U.S. stock market crashed, the American public was shocked. They suddenly realized the economic health of the nation was not as good as it had seemed. Billions of dollars were lost and small investors were wiped out. Although the stock market crash was only one of a number of factors leading to the Great Depression of the 1930s, in the public's mind it has always marked the start of the worst economic crisis in U.S. history. By 1932 twelve million workers, amounting to over 25 percent of the workforce, were jobless. Industrial production had dropped to 44 percent of the average in the 1920s. For those who kept their jobs, incomes dropped an average of 40 percent between 1929 and 1932.

For the first time many citizens questioned the U.S. system of democracy and capitalism (an economic system in which goods are owned by private businesses and price and production is decided privately). They also questioned the notion of individualism, the American belief that people can successfully make their own way in society without government intervention. The prevailing mood of the nation moved from opportunity to despair; from progress to survival. A philosophical tug of war raged between big business, who wanted to work out the country's economic woes voluntarily, and those who wanted government to begin regulating business. President Herbert Hoover (served 1929–1933) was unable to halt the economic slide.

The inauguration of Franklin D. Roosevelt as the thirty-second president of the United States in March 1933 signaled the beginning of a new relationship between Americans and their government. For the first time in U.S. history the people began to look to the government to aid in their economic well-being. For many Americans, President Roosevelt's introduction of an incredible variety of social and economic programs, known as the New Deal, brought hope again. People believed they had a leader who actually cared about their welfare and establishing economic safety nets. The New Deal programs were designed to first bring relief (food, clothing, monetary payments) to Americans hardest hit by the Depression. Next came the recovery and reform programs to stimulate the economy and put into place plans that would lessen the danger of future depressions. Government became intricately involved in business regulation, labor organizations, public support of the arts, social security, resource conservation, development of inexpensive and plentiful energy sources, stock market reform, farming reform, photodocumentary journalism, housing reform, public health programs, and increasing the number of minorities and women in public life. Business leaders and the well-to-do despaired that the atmosphere of *laissez-faire* (in which industries operated free of government restraint) was over. Government regulations and higher taxes ended the long tradition of industry voluntarily regulating itself.

As the Depression lingered on through the 1930s, various segments of American society were affected differently. Those in the middle classes learned to "make do," creating meals from simple ingredients, making their own clothes, finding entertainment at home with board games and listening to the radio, and helping other family members who had lost their jobs. The extreme competitiveness and consumption-oriented values of the 1920s gave way to cooperativeness and neighborly help. Those Americans already considered poor or part of a minority group suffered mightily during the Depression. In contrast America's wealthiest families, for the most part, seemingly ignored the Depression and continued their luxurious lifestyle.

Roosevelt's New Deal did not lead directly to major economic recovery for the United States. By the mid to late 1930s President Roosevelt hesitated to spend the amount of money necessary to push the economy into complete recovery. While the New Deal programs did not stop the Depression, they did end the dramatic plunge in the economy and gave food and shelter to those most in need. The Great Depression did not fully end until 1941, as the United States prepared for World War II. The mobilization of industry to manufacture massive quantities of war materials and the growth of the armed forces at last ended the Great Depression.

The extraordinary event of the Great Depression brought major change in how Americans view government. Historically the federal government was viewed as detached from the everyday activities of Americans. The severity of the Depression made Americans consider, even demand, that the federal government act to enhance and insure the well-being of its citizens. At the beginning of the twenty-first century debate continues over how far the government should go in guaranteeing the financial security of its citizens. Debates still rage over government regulation of business, individualism versus cooperation for the common good, and over specific issues such as the Social Security system, the role of labor unions in business, and the welfare system providing aid to the nation's poorest.

We have, in *Great Depression and New Deal: Almanac*, concentrated on the actual event of the Great Depression rather than simply relating all general happenings of the 1930s. The volume covers the major events, themes, and effects of the Depression on different segments of U.S. society and U.S. popular culture. Its chapters cover the causes of the Depression, the New Deal programs, and the impact on the everyday life of Americans. Our goal throughout is to provide a clear, accurate account of a highly complex and difficult decade in American history that continues to impact the United States in the twenty-first century.

*Sharon M. Hanes and Richard C. Hanes*

# Reader's Guide

The Great Depression, which took place between 1929 and 1941, was the deepest and most prolonged economic crisis in United States history. It is a story of great human suffering for many and the inspiring rise of some to meet the challenge. President Franklin D. Roosevelt introduced a diverse series of new federal programs, known collectively as the New Deal, that revamped the nation's governmental system. From the strife came the modern bureaucratic state providing economic safeguards for its citizens. America emerged as a profoundly different nation by 1941 than it had been in 1929. The New Deal did not end the Great Depression and lead to full economic recovery, but it did end the dramatic economic plunge, gave those most affected food and shelter, and reestablished hope in the future and faith in the U.S. economic system.

*Great Depression and New Deal: Almanac* presents a comprehensive overview of the period in American history known as the Great Depression, from the crash of the U.S. stock market in October 1929 until the end of the Depression in 1941 that came as a result of mobilization for World War II

(1939–45). During this time the role of the United States government expanded to protect its citizens from unpredictable economic fluctuations and to provide an economic safety net for future times of trouble. Government became involved in business regulation, labor organizations, public support of the arts, social security, federal law enforcement, resource conservation, development of inexpensive and plentiful energy sources, stock market reform, farming reform, photodocumentary journalism, housing reform, public health programs, and increasing the number of minorities and women in public life. The volume covers the causes of the Depression; all the major legislation and programs of the New Deal; how the general public, including minorities, was affected by the Depression; and governmental changes that made society more comfortable.

### Features

*Great Depression and New Deal: Almanac* is divided into sixteen chapters, each focusing on a particular topic, such as banking and housing, electrification, farming, industry and labor, social security, Works Progress Administration, news and entertainment, crime, education, and everyday life. The chapters contain sidebar boxes that highlight people and events of special interest, and each chapter offers a list of additional sources students can go to for more information. Ninety-five black-and-white photographs help illustrate the material. The volume begins with a timeline of important events in the history of the Great Depression; a "Words to Know" section that introduces students to difficult or unfamiliar terms (terms are also defined within the text); and a "Research and Activity Ideas" section. The volume concludes with a general bibliography and a subject index so students can easily find the people, places, and events discussed throughout *Great Depression and New Deal: Almanac*.

### Great Depression and New Deal Reference Library

*Great Depression and New Deal: Almanac* is only one component of the three-part U•X•L Great Depression and New Deal Reference Library. The other two titles in this set are:

- *Great Depression and New Deal: Biographies* (one volume) presents the life stories of twenty-nine individuals who played key roles in the governmental and social responses to the Depression. Profiled are well-known figures such as Franklin D. Roosevelt, Eleanor Roosevelt, Will Rogers, Frances Perkins, and Woody Guthrie, as well as lesser-known individuals such as Hallie Flanagan, head of the Federal Theatre Project, and Mary McLeod Bethune, educator and the first black American to head a federal agency.

- *Great Depression and New Deal: Primary Sources* (one volume) tells the story of the Great Depression in the words of the people who lived it. Thirty full or excerpted documents provide a wide range of perspectives on this period in history. Included are excerpts from presidential press conferences, inaugural speeches, addresses to Congress, and radio addresses; later reflections by key government leaders; oral histories of those who experienced the economic crisis, including youth who rode the rails; lyrics of songs derived from the Great Depression experience; and reflections by photographers who recorded the poverty and desperation of the time.

- A cumulative index of all three titles in the U•X•L Great Depression and New Deal Reference Library is also available.

## Advisors

A note of appreciation is extended to the *Great Depression and New Deal: Almanac* advisors who provided invaluable suggestions when the work was in its formative stages:

Frances Bryant Bradburn
Director of Educational Technologies
North Carolina Public Schools
Raleigh, North Carolina

Elaine Ezell
Media Specialist
Bowling Green Junior High School
Bowling Green, Ohio

## Dedication

To our son, Dustin, who endured numerous discussions and debates of New Deal policy and Great Depression issues over dinner and during car trips.

## Special Thanks

Catherine Filip typed much of the manuscript. Much gratitude also goes to the advisors who guided the project throughout its course.

## Comments and Suggestions

We welcome your comments on *Great Depression and New Deal: Almanac* and suggestions for other topics to consider. Please write: Editors, *Great Depression and New Deal: Almanac,* U•X•L, 27500 Drake Rd., Farmington Hills, Michigan 48331-3535; call toll-free: 1-800-877-4253; fax to (248) 699-8097; or send e-mail via http://www.gale.com.

# Great Depression Timeline

**January 17, 1920** The Eighteenth Amendment, known as Prohibition, goes into effect, banning the sale and manufacture of all alcoholic beverages in the United States.

**1921–1932** With every passing year, Prohibition is ignored more and more while the gangsters of organized crime become immensely wealthy from bootlegging illegal alcohol.

**1923** The value of stocks on the U.S. stock market begins a six-year upward climb.

**1928** "Amos 'n' Andy," a radio program, premieres and becomes the most popular radio show through the 1930s.

**November 1928** Republican Herbert Hoover is elected president of the United States. His policies would prove ineffective in fighting the Great Depression that struck in October 1929.

**October 24, 1929** Known as "Black Thursday," a record-breaking crash on the New York Stock Exchange be-

**The New York Stock Exchange Building, October 29, 1929.** *AP/Wide World Photo.*

gins several weeks of market panics. Many investors lose vast sums of money when the value of stocks plummets. Approximately 12.8 million shares of stock are sold in one day, most at prices far below their values only a few days earlier.

**October 29, 1929** Known as "Black Tuesday," the value of stocks on the New York Stock Market continues its dramatic decline. Approximately 16,410,000 shares, a record number, are sold. The nation's economy steadily erodes into the Great Depression, the worst economic crisis in U.S. history.

**1930–1932** Gangster movies are at their height of popularity.

**1930** Hostess food manufacturer creates the Twinkie, an inexpensive treat for economy-minded Americans.

**1930** Congress authorizes construction of Hoover Dam, known as Boulder Dam during the New Deal, on the Colorado River. Construction begins in 1930 and is completed in 1936. The project provides thousands of jobs.

**1931–1932** More than 3,600 banks suspend operations as the Depression deepens and thousands lose their jobs and incomes.

**1931** Sales of glass jars for preserving food at home increases dramatically. Preserving food decreases a family's food expenses.

**1931** A drought begins in the Eastern states during the summer and quickly spreads to the Midwest and Great Plains. The drought will continue throughout the decade resulting in "dust bowl" conditions.

**1931** New York City reports ninety-five cases of death by starvation as the number of unemployed and those going hungry increases.

**October 24, 1931** Alphonse Capone, the nation's most notorious gangster, receives an eleven-year prison sentence for income tax evasion.

**1932** Jigsaw puzzles are mass-produced for the first time and provide inexpensive entertainment.

**An approaching dust storm.** *AP/Wide World Photo.*

**1932**  Prices for farm produce hit bottom as farmer unrest rises.

**1932**  Sixty percent of the U.S. population still faithfully pay the few cents it costs to attend movies.

**1932**  The Depression spawns cuts in educational budgets affecting teacher salaries and programs offered and leads to school closures, especially in rural areas.

**January 22, 1932**  Congress establishes the Reconstruction Finance Corporation to provide federal financial support to the banking system.

**July 2, 1932**  Franklin Delano Roosevelt delivers a speech accepting the Democratic nomination for president pledging "a new deal for the American people."

**July 28, 1932**  Thousands of unemployed and financially strapped World War I veterans and their families, known as the Bonus Army, march on Washington, DC, seeking early payment of previously promised bonus pay, but are denied by Congress. Violence erupts, reflecting badly on the Hoover administration.

**November 1932**  Roosevelt handily wins the presidential election over incumbent Republican Herbert Hoover but will not be inaugurated until March 4, 1933.

**1933–1935**  Midwestern outlaws rob banks and kills citizens on wild rampages through the nation's heartland.

**1933**  Unemployment reaches 25 percent of the nation's workforce.

**1933**  Estimates reveal that well over one million Americans are homeless and almost one-fourth are riding the railroads in search of work or aimlessly drifting. Youth comprise 40 percent of that number on the rails.

**1933**  The number of marriages declines 40 percent from the 1920s level as couples, unable to earn a living wage, postpone marriage.

**1933**  The number of lynchings of black Americans in the United States during the Great Depression peaks at twenty-eight.

**Striking farmers dump milk on the road.** *Corbis Corporation.*

**World War I veterans march on Washington, D.C.** *AP/Wide World Photo.*

**An unemployed woman sells apples to make a living.** *AP/Wide World Photo.*

**Shirley Temple.**
*Popperfoto/Archive Photos.*

**1933** Membership in teachers' unions such as the American Federation of Teachers (AFT) increases rapidly in reaction to budget and staff cuts due to the Depression.

**1933** Big, splashy musicals become hit movies taking Americans' minds off the hard economic times.

**1933** Child actress Shirley Temple is introduced to movie audiences.

**1933** The Chicago World's Fair opens.

**March 4, 1933** With the U.S. banking system all but paralyzed, Franklin D. Roosevelt is inaugurated as president declaring "there is nothing to fear but fear itself."

**March 6, 1933** At 1:00 A.M. President Roosevelt orders a nationwide "bank holiday" from Monday, March 6 through Thursday, March 9, and then extends it through March 12.

**March 6, 1933** First Lady Eleanor Roosevelt begins her weekly news conferences open only to women journalists.

**March 9, 1933** Congress begins a special session to approve legislation aimed at economic relief and recovery. Congress passes the Emergency Bank Act in a successful effort to restore public confidence in the banking system.

**March 12, 1933** President Roosevelt delivers his first radio "fireside chat," explaining to the American people what has happened in the U.S. banking system.

**March 13, 1933** Most U.S. banks successfully reopen.

**Mid-March 1933** President Roosevelt begins the first of his informal and informative presidential news conferences.

**March 31, 1933** The Civilian Conservation Corps (CCC) is established providing jobs in conservation activities for young Americans replanting forests, soil conservation, and flood control.

**May 12, 1933** Congress passes the Agricultural Adjustment Act (AAA), designed to raise farm prices by encouraging farmers to reduce production.

**Eleanor Roosevelt.** *AP/Wide World Photo.*

**May 12, 1933** Congress passes the Emergency Farm Mortgage Act to provide loans to farmers in heavy debt.

**May 12, 1933** Congress passes the Federal Emergency Relief Act (FERA), providing funds to assist state relief programs helping the unemployed, aged, and ill.

**May 17, 1933** The Tennessee Valley Authority (TVA) is created to bring economic development to the Southeast through construction of numerous dams and hydropower plants.

**May 27, 1933** Congress passes the Federal Securities Act requiring companies and stockbrokers to provide full information about new stocks to potential investors.

**The Bank of United States reopens on March 13, 1933.** *AP/Wide World Photo.*

**June 13, 1933** Congress passes the Home Owners' Refinancing Act, which creates the Home Owners' Loan Corporation (HOLC) to provide loans to homeowners facing the loss of their homes because they cannot make payments.

**June 16, 1933** Congress passes the Farm Credit Act. It formalizes the earlier-created Farm Credit Administration, which established a system of banking institutions for farmers.

**June 16, 1933** Congress passes the Banking Act, also known as the Glass-Steagall Act, establishing the Federal Deposit Insurance Corporation (FDIC) insuring individual bank accounts against loss.

**June 16, 1933** Congress passes the National Industrial Recovery Act establishing codes of fair practice for industry and business and creating the National Recovery Administration (NRA).

**The Blue Eagle, symbol of the National Recovery Administration.** *Franklin D. Roosevelt Library.*

**June 16, 1933** The Public Works Administration (PWA) is created to distribute almost $6 billion between 1933 and 1939 for public works projects, including construction of roads, tunnels, bridges, dams, power plants, and hospitals.

**June 16, 1933** Congress finishes the special session, an intensive period of lawmaking that becomes known as the First Hundred Days.

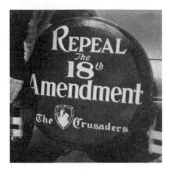

**The Eighteenth Amendment, Prohibition, is repealed in December 1933.** *Library of Congress.*

**November 9, 1933** Roosevelt establishes the Civil Works Administration (CWA) to assist unemployed workers through the winter months.

**December 5, 1933** The thirtieth state ratifies the Twenty-first Amendment ending Prohibition, which banned the sale of all alcoholic beverages.

**1934–1935** J. Edgar Hoover's Special Agents of the Federal Bureau of Investigation (FBI) capture or kill all of the famous Midwest outlaws and restore confidence in U.S. law enforcement.

**January 31, 1934** Congress passes the Farm Mortgage Refinancing Act providing $2 billion in loans to refinance farm loans.

**June 6, 1934** Congress passes the Securities Exchange Act that prohibits certain activities in stock market trading, sets penalties and establishes the Securities Exchange Commission (SEC) to oversee stock market trading.

**June 18, 1934** Congress passes the Indian Reorganization Act (Wheeler-Howard Act) establishing the cornerstone of New Deal Indian policy.

**June 19, 1934** Congress passes the Communications Act that creates the Federal Communications Commission (FCC) to oversee the nation's mass-communications industry.

**June 28, 1934** Congress passes the National Housing Act, creating the Federal Housing Administration (FHA) to assist homeowners in buying a new house in hopes of spurring the construction industry. This act is the last piece of legislation passed under the First New Deal that began with legislation in March 1933.

**1935** Warner Brothers' sensational hit movie *G-Men* immortalizes J. Edgar Hoover as America's number one cop, made his "government men," later known as FBI agents, famous, and helped restore a general respect for law enforcement.

**1935** In one week people buy twenty million Monopoly games, providing inexpensive entertainment.

**FBI chief J. Edgar Hoover, left.** *AP/Wide World Photo.*

**1935** More than 500,000 men are enrolled in 2,600 Civilian Conservation Corps camps across the United States.

**April 8, 1935** Congress passes the Emergency Relief Appropriation Act creating the Works Progress Administration (WPA) and providing almost $5 billion for work relief for the unemployed for such projects as construction of airports, schools, hospitals, roads, and public buildings. This act marks the beginning of the Second New Deal

**April 27, 1935** Congress passes the Soil Conservation Act establishing the Soil Conservation Service (SCS) to aid farmers suffering drought and massive soil erosion.

**April 30, 1935** Roosevelt creates the Resettlement Administration (RA) to help poor farmers either improve the use of their lands or move to better lands. The agency's Historical Section begins a major photodocumentary project of the Depression.

**May 11, 1935** Roosevelt creates the Rural Electrification Administration (REA) to bring inexpensive electricity to rural areas.

**May 27, 1935** In one of several rulings against New Deal programs, the U.S. Supreme Court in *Schechter Poultry Corporation v. United States* rules the National Industrial Recovery Act is unconstitutional thus removing legal protections for labor unions. This day becomes known as "Black Monday."

**June 26, 1935** Roosevelt creates the National Youth Administration (NYA) to provide part-time jobs to high school and college students and other unemployed youth.

**July 1, 1935** The Federal Deposit Insurance Corporation (FDIC) begins operation providing stability to the banking system by insuring bank deposits.

**July 5, 1935** Congress passes the National Labor Relations Act, better known as the Wagner Act, to support the right of workers to organize and bargain collectively with employers over working conditions, benefits,

**The WPA marks the beginning of the Second New Deal.** *AP/Wide World Photo.*

**Power lines are erected to bring electricity to a rural area.** *Library of Congress.*

**Students learning auto mechanics in a National Youth Administration program.** *Library of Congress.*

**Frances Perkins was instrumental to the passage of the Social Security Act.** *AP/Wide World Photo.*

and wages. The act also bans certain unfair business practices.

**August 2, 1935** Created as part of the WPA, the Federal One program is established to provide jobs for the unemployed in music, theater, writing, and art.

**August 14, 1935** Congress passes the Social Security Act establishing a program of social insurance to aid the unemployed, the elderly in retirement, needy children and mothers, and the blind.

**August 23, 1935** Congress passes the Banking Act strengthening the Federal Reserve System.

**August 30, 1935** Congress passes the Wealth Tax Act creating higher tax rates for the wealthy and corporate and inheritance taxes.

**November 1935** The Federal Surplus Commodities Corporation is established to continue distributing food to the needy.

**November 9, 1935** Labor leader John L. Lewis establishes the Committee of Industrial Organizations to represent semi-skilled and unskilled laborers of the mass production industries.

**1936** Mary McLeod Bethune is named head of the Division of Negro Affairs of the National Youth Administration becoming the first black American to head a government agency.

**January 6, 1936** The U.S. Supreme Court in *United States v. Butler* rules the Agricultural Adjustment Act is unconstitutional.

**June 16, 1936** Congress passes the Flood Control Act in response to massive floods in the Ohio and Mississippi River areas.

**November 1936** Franklin Roosevelt wins a landslide reelection capturing a record 61 percent of the vote.

**December 30, 1936** Sit-down strikes shutdown seven General Motors plants in Flint, Michigan. The company will give in to worker demands by February 11, 1937.

**1937** Roosevelt appoints attorney William Hastie as the first black American federal judge in U.S. history.

**Sit-down strikers at an auto plant in Flint, Michigan.** *UPI/Corbis-Bettmann.*

1937   Author Erskine Caldwell and photographer Margaret Bourke-White publish *You Have Seen Their Faces*.

1937   Kraft introduces the "instant" macaroni and cheese dinner and Hormel introduces Spam meat. The low cost of both items helps feed families who are on a tight budget.

**February 5, 1937** Roosevelt introduces a proposal, known as the "court packing plan," to reorganize the U.S. Supreme Court. The plan attracts substantial public opposition.

**May 24, 1937** The U.S. Supreme Court upholds the constitutionality of the Social Security Act.

**July 22, 1937** Congress passes the Bankhead-Jones Farm Tenancy Act making low interest loans available to tenant farmers, farm laborers, and small landowners, many of whom are victims of the Dust Bowl, to purchase or expand their own lands.

**August 20, 1937** The Bonneville Power Act establishes the Bonneville Power Administration to market public power in the Pacific Northwest.

**September 1, 1937** Roosevelt creates the Farm Security Administration, absorbing the Resettlement Administration including the photography project.

**September 3, 1937** Congress passes the National Housing Act, known as the Wagner-Steagall Housing Act, creating the U.S. Housing Authority to oversee construction of low-cost housing.

**October 1937** An economic "recession" begins as industrial production and farm prices fall and unemployment rises. In hopes of never again using the term "depression," President Roosevelt coins the term "recession."

**February 16, 1938** Congress passes the new Agricultural Adjustment Act providing new price supports for farmers and promoting conservation practices.

**June 24, 1938** Congress passes the Food, Drug, and Cosmetic Act.

**June 25, 1938** The Fair Labor Standards Act places legal protections over child labor, minimum wages, and maxi-

**A homeless mother and her two children in California.** *Franklin D. Roosevelt Library.*

**Hooverville shacks are home to many during the Depression.** *Corbis Corporation.*

**Radio keeps Americans informed and entertained in the 1930s.** *Franklin D. Roosevelt Library.*

mum hours. This act is the last legislation of the Second New Deal.

**October 30, 1938** Orson Welles' *Mercury Theatre of the Air* broadcasts a radio adaptation of H.G. Wells' 1898 novel *The War of the Worlds* causing widespread panic.

**1939** Eighty percent of American households own radios.

**1939** The Golden Gate International Exposition opens in San Francisco and the New York World's Fair opens in New York City.

**1939** The Federal Writers Project publishes *These Are Our Lives* and John Steinbeck publishes *The Grapes of Wrath.*

**1939** Drought comes to an end as rains return to the Great Plains in the fall.

**1939** Reporter Edward R. Murrow broadcasts from London, England, during the German bombing raids on the city shifting public concerns away from domestic economic issues to foreign issues.

**1939** World famous American opera singer Marian Anderson is denied the opportunity to perform in a private concert hall in Washington, DC, because she is black, leading to a major public backlash against racism.

**May 16, 1939** The Food Stamp program begins.

**August 10, 1939** Congress passes the Social Security Act Amendments adding old age and survivors' insurance benefits for dependents and survivors.

**1941** Roosevelt signs an executive order prohibiting racial discrimination in the defense industry, the first such proclamation since Reconstruction in the 1870s.

**1941** Author James Agee and photographer Walker Evans publish *Let Us Now Praise Famous Men.*

**July 9, 1941** President Roosevelt announces extensive preparations in case of U.S. entrance into World War II.

**December 7, 1941** Japan bombs U.S. military installations at Pearl Harbor, Hawaii, leading the United States to enter World War II in both Europe and the Pacific.

**Dust storms and drought come to an end by 1939.** *AP/Wide World Photo.*

**January 16, 1942** The War Production Board is established to direct war mobilization.

**April 1942** The War Manpower Commission is created to help allocate manpower to industries and military services.

**April 12, 1945** Franklin Roosevelt suddenly dies at sixty-three years of age from a cerebral hemorrhage.

**Thousands of wandering youth find employment once the U.S. enters World War II.** *National Archives and Records Administration.*

# Words to Know

## A

**abstinence:** A voluntary decision not to drink alcoholic beverages.

**activist:** One who aggressively promotes a cause such as seeking change in certain social, economic, or political conditions in society.

**amortize:** To allow a loan to be repaid with stable monthly payments that include both principal and interest; amortizing mortgages allow buyers to gradually repay the principal balance until the loan is paid back in full.

**appraisal:** The set value of a property as determined by the estimate of an authorized person.

**appropriations:** Money authorized by Congress to an agency for a special purpose.

**atomic bomb:** A bomb whose explosive force comes from a nuclear splitting apart of atoms releasing a large amount of energy.

**attorney general:** The chief law officer of a state or country and head of the legal department. In the United States, the person is head of the U.S. Department of Justice and is a member of the president's cabinet.

# B

**bank holiday:** The legal suspension of bank operation for a period of time.

**bank run:** A sudden demand to withdraw deposits from a bank; bank runs occurred after the stock market crash of 1929, when depositors feared that their banks were unstable.

**benefits:** Financial aid (such as insurance or retirement pension) in time of sickness, old age, or unemployment. Also holidays, vacations, and other privileges provided by an employer in addition to hourly wages or salary.

**big business:** Large and influential businesses such as industries or financial institutions.

**Black Cabinet:** An informal organization of black Americans serving in various federal positions that advised President Franklin Roosevelt on black issues through the late 1930s.

**bootlegger:** A person who illegally transports liquor.

**boycott:** A refusal by a group of persons to buy goods or services from a business until the business meets their demands.

**breadlines:** During the Depression, long lines of unemployed people waiting to receive a free meal of soup and a chunk of bread from a charity or soup kitchen.

**broker:** One who buys or sells a stock for an investor and charges a fee for the service.

**budget:** The amount of money a person or family has to spend on food, clothing, shelter, and other necessities.

**buying on margin:** The purchase of stock by paying some cash down and borrowing the rest of the purchase price.

# C

**cabinet:** An official group of advisors to the U.S. president including the heads of the various major governmental departments such as Department of Commerce.

**capital:** Money invested in a business and used to operate that business. Capital is the amount banks owe their owners.

**capitalism:** An economic system in which goods are privately owned and prices, production, and distribution of goods are determined by competition in a free market.

**chain gangs:** Groups of convicts chained together while working outside the prison.

**collective bargaining:** Negotiation between representatives of an employer and representatives of labor, with both sides working to reach agreement on wages, job benefits, and working conditions.

**collectivism:** Shared ownership of goods by all members of a group; a political or economic system in which production and distribution are controlled by all members of a group.

**commercial bank:** A bank that offers checking accounts, savings accounts, and personal and business loans.

**communism:** A theory calling for the elimination of private property so that goods are owned in common and available to all; a system of government in which a single party controls all aspects of society, as in the Union of Soviet Socialist Republics (U.S.S.R.) from 1917 until 1990.

**conservation:** The planned management of natural resources, such as soil and forests.

**conservative:** A person who holds traditional views and who seeks to preserve established institutions; a conservative approach to education, for example, stresses traditional basic subject matter and traditional methods of teaching.

**cooperative:** A private, nonprofit enterprise, locally owned and managed by the members it serves and incorporated (established as a legal entity that can hold property or be subject to lawsuits) under state law.

**corporate volunteerism:** To encourage business to support a public program or goal through voluntary actions rather than by government regulation.

**craft union:** A type of union that represents workers having a particular skill, regardless of their workplace.

**cutting lever:** The device on rail cars that can uncouple or detach rail cars from each other.

# D

**default:** Failure to meet the payment terms of a legal contract, such as failure to make payments to repay a home loan; in cases of default, lenders may begin foreclosure proceedings to regain their losses.

**dependents:** People who must rely on another person for their livelihood; generally applied to children age eighteen and younger.

**deportation:** The removal of immigrant noncitizens from a country.

**desegregation:** To stop the practice of separating the races in public places such as public schools.

**direct relief:** Money, food, or vouchers given to needy people by the government for support. This term is not commonly used in the United States anymore; the current term is "welfare."

**dividend:** A payment made from a corporation's profits to its stockholders.

**documentary literature:** Articles or books describing actual events or real persons in a factual way.

**documentary photograph:** A photographic image in black and white or color that is realistic, factual, and useful as a historical document.

**domestic goods:** Goods related to home life; also, goods produced within the nation as opposed to foreign-made goods.

**drought:** A long period of little or no rainfall.

**drug trafficking:** Buying or selling illegal drugs; drug dealing.

# E

**electrification:** The process or event in which a house, farm, industry, or locality is connected to an electric power source.

**entrepreneur:** An individual willing to take a risk in developing a new business.

**eviction:** To force a tenant from their home by legal process.

**executive order:** A statement written and issued by the president that uses some part of an existing law or the U.S. Constitution to enforce an action.

**exposure:** Being unsheltered and unprotected from the harsh weather elements, such as wind, rain, or cold, to an extent leading to illness or death.

# F

**foreclosure:** A legal proceeding begun by a lender, usually a bank, to take possession of property when the property owner fails to make payments; in a home or farm foreclosure the lender seizes and auctions off the borrower's property to pay off the mortgage.

# G

**genre:** A category of entertainment, such as radio comedy, drama, news, or soap operas.

# H

**hobo:** A tramp, vagrant, or migratory worker.

**holding companies:** A company that controls one or more other companies through stock ownership.

**Hoovervilles:** "Towns" of shacks and other crude shelters put up by homeless people; sarcastically named after President Herbert Hoover, whom many felt did nothing to help Americans devastated by the Great Depression.

**hopper cars:** Rail cars that can readily dump their loads out the bottom.

**humanitarian:** One who helps others improve their welfare.

**hydroelectric power:** Electricity generated from the energy of swift-flowing streams or waterfalls.

# I

**immigration:** Legal or illegal entry into a country by foreigners who intend to become permanent residents.

**incentives:** Something that encourages people to take action such as a guarantee of substantial profits for business leaders.

**industrial mobilization:** To rapidly transform or change an industry from one manufacturing household or peace-time goods to production of war materials in the time of war for government service.

**industrial union:** A union that represents all workers, skilled and unskilled, in a particular workplace.

**infrastructure:** Basic facilities and developments that form a foundation of an economic system including roads, airports, power plants, and military installations.

**installment buying:** Purchasing items on credit; making a down payment and, after taking possession of the item, paying off the rest of the cost with monthly payments.

**interest:** Money paid to a lender (in addition to the principal amount borrowed) for use of the lender's money.

# L

**labor leader:** An individual who encourages workers to formally organize so as to more effectively negotiate better working conditions and wages from the employer.

**labor movement:** The collective effort by workers and labor organizations to seek better working conditions.

**labor unions:** Employee organizations established to seek improved working conditions and wages from employers.

**laissez-faire (les-ā-fair):** A French term that describes the general philosophy of a government that chooses not to intervene in economic or social affairs; in French the term means "let people do as they choose."

**leftist:** A person promoting radical or socialistic politics in the form of liberal reform or revolutionary change.

**lobby:** A group of persons attempting to influence lawmakers.

**lynching:** The murder of an individual, most commonly a black American by a mob of white Americans, with no legal authority, usually by hanging.

# M

**making do:** Using items on hand to stretch a budget. For example, sewing one's own clothes instead of buying them at a store, or using leftovers and other simple ingredients to stretch meals over several days.

**maldistribution:** An uneven distribution of income or wealth; if the distribution is too unbalanced, it can cause general economic problems.

**mass media:** Various means of communication such as radio, movies, newspapers, and magazines that reach large numbers of people.

**migrant workers:** Laborers who travel from place to place to harvest farm crops for various farmers as the crops mature through the seasons.

**missions:** A place to aid the needy and preach the gospel, often located in poorer city areas.

**mobilization:** Preparations for war, including assembling of materials and military personnel.

**mortgage:** A legal document by which property is pledged as security for the repayment of a debt; when a buyer takes out a loan from the bank to purchase a home, the buyer pledges the home as security; if the buyer defaults on the loan, the bank takes the home to pay the debt.

**municipal:** A local government of a town or city.

**mural:** A painting applied directly onto a permanent wall.

# N

**New Dealers:** Influential members of President Roosevelt's administration who promoted economic and social programs designed to lead the nation to economic recovery.

**newsreels:** Short films presenting current events.

# O

**old-age insurance:** Assurance of cash payments, generally made monthly, to retired workers; also called a pension plan.

**oral history:** The memories of an event or time, captured in the words of the person who lived it.

**organized crime:** A specialized form of crime carried out by loosely or rigidly structured networks of gangs with certain territorial boundaries.

# P

**principal:** The original amount of money loaned; a buyer must repay the principal and also pay the lender interest for the use of the money.

**private sector:** Businesses not subsidized or directed by the government but owned and operated by private citizens.

**productivity:** The rate at which goods are produced.

**progressive tax:** Taxing the income of wealthy individuals at a higher rate than those with lower incomes.

**Prohibition:** The period from 1920 to 1933 during which a legal restriction against the manufacture, sale, or distribution of alcoholic beverages was in effect in the United States. Officially known as the Eighteenth Amendment.

**proletarian literature:** Writing about the working class largely for working class consumption.

**public utility:** A government-regulated business that provides an essential public service, such as electric power.

**public works projects:** Government funded projects often for providing jobs for the unemployed such as construction of roads, bridges, airfields, and public buildings.

**pump priming:** Federal government spending designed to encourage consumer purchases; during the Depression the federal government spent money to create jobs through work relief programs, reasoning that if enough people received wages and began buying goods and services, the economy would improve.

# R

**racketeering:** A person who obtains money through fraud or bribery. In the 1930s, gangsters worked their way into positions of authority in regular labor unions and then stole money from the union's pension and health funds.

**recession:** A slump in the economy; another term for "depression."

**reclamation:** A program of converting land unsuited for farming to agricultural production by providing water through irrigation systems.

**refinance:** To set up new terms for repayment of a loan that are beneficial to the borrower.

**relief:** Easing the strife of the needy by providing food, money, shelter, or jobs. (See also direct relief and work relief.)

**reservations:** Tracts of public land formally set aside for exclusive use by American Indians.

**retrenchment:** Cutbacks in school budgets, including cuts in teacher salaries, number of classes, and number of teachers.

**run:** Unexpected numerous withdrawals from a bank by depositors fearful of the soundness of the bank.

# S

**scab:** A person who refuses to join a strike and fills the job of a striking worker.

**school board:** A local committee in charge of public education in their area.

**school district:** A region or locality within which the public schools share an overall budget and common leadership through a school board.

**securities:** Stocks or bonds.

**sharecroppers:** Farmers who rent the land that they work and who use the landowner's tools; sharecroppers give part of the harvest to the landowner.

**shysters:** Lawyers who use questionable or unprofessional methods.

**sit-down strike:** A refusal to work conducted by laborers who stay at their workstations and block employers from replacing them with other workers.

**slum:** An overcrowded urban area characterized by poverty and run-down housing.

**social insurance:** A broad term referring to government-sponsored social well-being programs, such as old-age pensions, unemployment support, workers' compensation for those injured on the job, and health care programs.

**social legislation:** Laws that address social needs such as assistance for the elderly, retirement payments, unemployment support, workers' compensation, and health care programs.

**social reconstructionism:** A radical philosophy in education that calls for a new, more equitable social order to be established through classroom instruction in public schools.

**soup kitchen:** A place where food is offered free or at a very low cost to the needy.

**speakeasy:** A place where alcoholic beverages were sold illegally during Prohibition.

**speculation:** Buying stocks and/or other high-risk investments with the assumption that they can always be sold at a higher price.

**standard of living:** The level of consumption by individuals or a society as reflected by the quality of goods and services available.

**strike:** An organized effort by workers to gain official recognition, better working conditions, or higher wages by refusing to work.

**suburb:** A community on the outskirts of a city.

**suffrage:** The right to vote.

**survivor benefits:** Monthly cash benefits paid to the surviving family members of a worker who has died. Survivors may include a spouse, dependent children under eighteen years of age, and a dependent parent age sixty-two or older.

**syndicate:** An association or network of groups that cooperate to carry out certain business or criminal activities.

**syndication:** An agency that buys articles or photographs and sells them for publication at the same time in numerous newspapers.

# T

**temperance:** Moderation or abstinence in the use of alcoholic beverages.

**tenant farmers:** Farmers who rent the land they work but who use their own tools; tenant farmers give part of the harvested crops to the landowner.

**tenement:** A large housing structure containing apartment dwellings that barely meet minimum standards of sanitation, safety, and comfort.

**trade unions:** Labor unions in which the workers share a common craft in contrast to general labor unions in which workers share a common employment in a common industry.

**transient:** A person traveling around, usually in search of work.

# U

**underworld:** The world of organized crime.

**unemployment insurance:** Cash payments made for a limited period of time to workers who involuntarily lose their job; workers must be able and willing to work when a new job is available.

**union:** An organized group of workers joined together for a common purpose, such as negotiating with management for better working conditions or higher wages.

**U.S. Mint:** The place where U.S. money is produced.

# V

**vocational education:** Providing instruction or training for a particular trade.

# W

**welfare:** The health and prosperity of an individual or group; also financial assistance to those in need.

**white-collar workers:** Professional workers whose jobs do not normally involve manual labor.

**work relief:** A government assistance program that provides a needy person with a paying job instead of money, food, or vouchers (known as direct relief). Different from the twenty-first-century welfare-to-work program, work relief involves government-sponsored projects; the "work" in welfare-to-work is in the private sector. The term "work relief" is not commonly used anymore in the United States.

**workers' compensation:** A system of insurance designed to provide cash benefits and medical care to workers who sustain a work-related illness or injury.

# Research and Activity Ideas

The following ideas and projects might be used to supplement your classroom work on understanding the Great Depression and New Deal era in United States history:

**Exploring the Internet:** Many sites on the Internet facilitate understanding of life in the 1930s, New Deal programs, and the lives of Franklin and Eleanor Roosevelt. The following list gives general sites and sites specific to a particular topic such as the history of Social Security. Explore the sites, select one, and report to the class what can be found at a particular website.

1. http://newdeal.feri.org—*The New Deal Network: The Great Depression, the 1930s, and the Roosevelt Administration.* This site is sponsored by the Franklin and Eleanor Roosevelt Institute and the Institute for Learning Technologies and funded partly by the National Endowment for the Humanities. The New Deal Network offers students pathways to view documents and photographs of the 1930s; a calendar of month-to-month important events related to the 1930s; and many varied features such as a selection of letters

from young people written to Eleanor Roosevelt, the stories of New Deal agencies that brought electricity to rural areas of the United States, and dolls made by Works Progress Administration workers in Milwaukee, Wisconsin.

2. http://memory.loc.gov/ammem/fsowhome.html—*The Library of Congress's American Memory Project. America From the Great Depression to World War II: Photographs from the FSA-OWI, 1935–1945.* One of the many interesting pathways at this site starts with selecting Black and White Photos, then click on Geographic Location Index. See if photographs exist from your home state, county, or town. You will find many areas represented.

3. http://www.fdrlibrary.marist.edu—*Franklin D. Roosevelt Library and Digital Archives.* Among many pathways be sure to click on New On-Line Photos.

As part of the 1930s New Deal programs, many federal government departments began or expanded into departments familiar to Americans in the twenty-first century. Department homepage sites are available on the Internet. To explore a department's development, look for a history section. Here are a few to get you started:

1. http://ssa.gov—Social Security Administration. Go to history of Social Security.

2. http://www.fbi.gov—Federal Bureau of Investigation. Go to Library and Reference, then click on History of the FBI.

3. http://doi.gov—Department of Labor. Go to About DOI and click on History.

**The Crash:** Old issues of local newspapers are likely available at your public library, a nearby public university or college library, or from the local newspaper itself. Locate and review newspapers for the days between October 24 and the early part of November 1929. Assess if reporters grasped the seriousness of the stock market crash. Choose interesting accounts to read to the class.

**Visual Diagram of the Causes of the Depression:** Create a visual diagram illustrating the causes that led to the

Depression. Place the word Great Depression at the center of the diagram and surround it with words or pictures that convey the various causes.

**Political Debates:** Democrat Franklin D. Roosevelt ran for and won four presidential elections, in 1932, 1936, 1940, and 1944. The Republican candidates that ran against him included: in 1932 the incumbent President Herbert Hoover; in 1936 Governor Alfred M. Landon of Kansas; in 1940 Wendell L. Wilkie, a corporate president from Indiana; and in 1944 Governor Thomas E. Dewey of New York. President Roosevelt was wildly popular in the first few years of his presidency and remained popular with the majority of Americans the entire twelve years of his presidency. Nevertheless, as with any sitting president, he had his critics who opposed his policies. Explore the issues in each of the elections focusing on the arguments against Roosevelt's reelection. Divide the class into Democrats supporting Roosevelt and Republicans supporting their party's candidate. Have a rousing debate of the issues.

**Eleanor Roosevelt's Press Conferences:** Within a few days of President Franklin Roosevelt's March 4, 1933, inauguration, Eleanor Roosevelt began to hold weekly press conferences for women reporters. Most city and university libraries have old issues of magazines. Find the October–November 1984 issue of *Modern Maturity* and in the article "Eleanor Roosevelt and the Female White House Press Corps" learn from accounts related by women who actually attended the conferences. How do you think these women-only press conferences impacted opportunities for women desiring careers in journalism? Do you think having a woman's perspective on news was meaningful to America's women of the 1930s? Remember women had gained the right to vote in 1920. Report your findings on Roosevelt's press conferences to the class.

**Cartoon Creation:** Cartoons were common features in newspapers and magazines. Used to illustrate the artist's viewpoint of a happening or common issue of the day, cartoons drew reactions from readers ranging from laughter and agreement to howls of disagreement.

Use your imagination and artistic skills to create a cartoon about some aspect of the Great Depression. Topics might include the stock market crash of 1929, the effect of the Depression on farmers or consumers, President Herbert Hoover's troubles trying to deal with the economic crisis, banks shutting their doors, President Franklin Roosevelt's actions to bring relief and recovery to the nation, or illustrate issues revolving around the many pieces of New Deal legislation. Be sure to convey an emotion such as humor, fear, or surprise. Write a caption for the cartoon that captures the essential message or spirit of the cartoon.

**Works Progress Administration (WPA):** The WPA touched almost every county in the United States. Research what buildings, art projects, theater productions, or other WPA projects impacted your community.

**Civilian Conservation Corps (CCC):** CCC camps were established in states throughout the country. Research and locate where camps were in your state. In some areas camps are being partially restored to provide educational experiences. Find out if any camps are restored near your home.

**New Deal Poster:** Many posters were created, printed, and distributed across the United States to give information about and win approval for New Deal programs. Study any one of the many New Deal programs such as the Civilian Conservation Corps (CCC) or National Youth Administration (NYA), then create a poster that could be used to draw attention to the program.

**Dust Bowl:** Imagine living on a farm within the Dust Bowl. Write an account of a major dust storm hitting your farm. Describe dust storm effects on your daily life, health problems, effects on livestock, and impact on the crops. Then make an important decision: would you choose to stay on your farm or pack all your belongings and head west to California. If you stay, what New Deal programs might aid you. If you move west, describe your journey and what you find in California.

**Everyday Life:** Make a list of persons who students know that either lived during the Depression or were children of those who lived through the Depression. Decide to interview the persons most likely to remember life or stories of life during the 1930s. Develop questions ahead of time. Tape record the interview and later transcribe the recording into written notes. This process is known as taking and recording an oral history. Share the oral history with the class.

**Cost of Everyday Items:** In the Everyday Living chapter refer to the sidebar boxes that list the prices of store-bought items. These prices seem very low. Choose seven or eight items and compare 1930s prices to modern day prices. Also, compare several earning levels in the 1930s to modern day earning levels. Remember in the 1930s there was generally only one wage earner in the family.

**The Movies:** At the depths of the Great Depression from 1930 to 1933 sixty to seventy-five million Americans, representing 60 percent of the U.S. population, still faithfully attended the movies. The few cents it cost to gain admission was an extravagance for many but it seemed Americans had to have their movies. Watch one of the many classic films of the 1930s. Suggestions include gangster movies *Little Caesar* (1930) or *Public Enemy* (1931); comedian Charlie Chaplain's or the Marx Brothers' 1930s films; musicals such as *42nd Street* (1933), *Gold Diggers of 1933,* and *Footlight Parade* (1933); Shirley Temple movies from the 1930s; the law and order film *G-Men* (1935); and a film that told the story of refugees from the Dust Bowl, *The Grapes of Wrath* (1939). Applying your knowledge of the hardships Americans faced during the Depression, why do you think the movie you chose appealed to Depression audiences? Did they identify with the characters in some way or were they escaping reality?

**Riding the Rails:** You are a teenage member of a family of three children, a father, and a mother. Your father has lost his job and has been looking unsuccessfully for a new job for months. There is barely enough food to feed everyone. You decide to leave home and ride the trains across America in search of work. Write a diary about leaving home, your hopes, dreams, and fears. Describe your experiences riding the rails.

Go to an Internet search engine and enter the key words: hobo signs. Investigate what various signs stood for. Many of the signs and symbols pictured on the Internet are similar to those found along railways in the 1930s. The symbols were usually drawn with chalk or coal on fences, train yard structures, sidewalks, or buildings. They conveyed information or warnings about the areas. For instance, one symbol indicated a safe camp near the rail yard, another would indicate whether the water was safe to drink. Use signs from the Internet plus create your own signs to describe your present-day community.

**Rural Electrification:** Imagine a day in your life without electricity. List the ways in which your daily activities would be different from today. Follow your home's electricity to its source: where does it come from; how is it generated, distributed, and transmitted? When was electric service in your community first available? Did the New Deal influence the development of power sources for your community?

**Into the Twenty-first Century:** Identify many federal government programs that were first developed as New Deal programs and, although perhaps greatly expanded or changed, are still important to Americans in the twenty-first century. Choose one, study its origin, and follow its development into the twenty-first century. Report to the class.

# Great Depression and New Deal
# Almanac

# Causes of the Great Depression

The period from 1920 to 1929 is known as the Roaring Twenties. Those years were exciting, fascinating, and entertaining for the U.S. population, whose sons had just fought and won World War I (1914–18), the war that had promised to end all wars. Everyone was enthralled with the new gasoline automobiles that Henry Ford (1863–1947) had made affordable. Women had gained the right to vote, and some had acquired new electric machines that made life easier, such as washing machines and vacuum cleaners. Every day more Americans brought a radio into their homes; the radio brought music and news that thrilled listeners. The new moving pictures captivated audiences in palace-like movie houses. Businesses and manufacturing industries continuously expanded. The prices of their stocks steadily increased through the 1920s, going on a wild ride upward between 1926 and October of 1929. Stock prices went far beyond realistic values and had little basis in the health of the companies. These skyrocketing stock prices signaled trouble for the U.S. economy.

As early as March 1929 a few financial experts warned that banks were making too many loans for stock speculation

## What Is Stock?

Stocks are shares in the ownership of a corporation. The sale of stock raises capital, or operating money, for the corporation. Buying stocks makes the purchaser a part owner of the corporation, a stockholder. For every share owned, the purchaser gets one vote at stockholder meetings, thus influencing to some degree major company decisions. The more shares owned, the greater the influence a person holds.

When stocks are bought and sold, the transactions are reflected on the New York Stock Exchange. Theoretically the price of a stock is determined by the overall worth and health of the corporation. However, stock prices often go up and down rather unpredictably.

If a corporation is healthy and profitable, it pays a certain amount of money per stock share to the stockholders. These payments are called dividends and can be taken in the form of more stock rather than cash if the stockholder desires.

(the buying and selling of stock without regard for its actual value or the strength of the individual company). The Federal Reserve, the U.S. central bank, tried to rein in the country's banks but with no success. Several leaders of industry also noticed that unemployment was quietly on the rise. Nevertheless, despite a few warnings, the stock market headed up and up.

In September an economist for the *New York Herald Tribune,* Roger Babson, predicted the market was headed for a crash. After his speech stocks wavered and declined a bit. The Federal Reserve again tried to curb the out-of-control pace at which banks were making loans to buy stocks. Though the first seed of doubt had been planted, most investors chose to listen to Charles E. Mitchell, head of New York's National City Bank; John Raskob, financial giant; and J. P. Morgan and Company: These leaders in finance announced that the market's future was overwhelmingly positive. The market's behavior was a bit erratic in early October but nevertheless reached its all-time high on October 10, 1929.

On Wednesday, October 23, a block of General Motors stock was sold at a loss, and the market headed down. Orders to sell came in too fast for brokers to keep up with. Bankers tried to stabilize the market at the end of the day, but on Thursday, October 24, the market nose-dived. Financial losses were in the billions of dollars, and small investors were wiped out. On Friday, October 25, and Monday, October 28, bankers tried to revive the market by finding new big investors. But late on Monday they announced they could no longer support the market. On Tuesday, October 29, 1929—which became known as "Black Tuesday"—stock prices plunged even lower.

The Dow-Jones Industrial Average, an average overall measure of stock values based on the stock prices of thirty leading U.S. companies, was at an all-time high of 353 on October 10, 1929. It then dropped for the next four years, reaching a low of 41 on July 8, 1933. Not until 1954 did the Dow-Jones average again climb to 353.

## Overview: Causes of the Great Depression

The crash of the New York Stock Exchange on October 29, 1929, signaled the start of the Great Depression, the worst economic crisis in U.S. history. This period would last until 1941, when the United States began preparations to enter World War II (1939–45). When the stock market began to spiral downward, many looked on in disbelief. However, others recognized that the plummeting prices were a confirmation of severe economic problems long in the making. For much of the 1920s the United States seemed prosperous. Many Americans were employed, and goods such as automobiles, appliances, and furniture flowed out of factories. Yet an undercurrent of unhealthy factors ran through the American economy—factors that all came together and surfaced in late 1929.

During the 1920s there was no national economic planning or any significant watchdog agency to monitor the U.S. economy. The Republican administrations of Presidents Warren G. Harding (1865–1923; served 1921–23), Calvin Coolidge (1872–1933; served 1923–29), and Herbert Hoover (1874–1964; served 1929–33) followed a laissez-faire approach. *Laissez-faire* refers to the deliberate absence of government regulation. None of these presidents attempted to regulate the buying or selling of stocks and bonds; they exercised no controls over banking, manufacturing, or agricultural production. Likewise, no attempt was made to gather or analyze statistics that would have pointed to increasing problems in stock investing and overproduction of agricultural products and consumer goods. This approach to government was a major contributing factor in the Great Depression.

Another general factor that contributed to the Depression was the "get rich quick" mentality that developed during the 1920s. Many Americans believed their fortune was just around the corner. This belief was fueled by the mass production of consumer goods, mass advertising in magazines and newspapers, and exotic silent movies telling tales of riches and success. With this "get rich quick" attitude, many Americans began to recklessly spend what little money they had. Hoping to look like glamorous movie stars, they bought a vast array of beauty products. On a larger scale many Americans purchased, sight unseen, parcels of land in Florida and southern California. When some investors went to visit the lots that had been purchased, they found swamps or desert. Realizing they had made a poor investment, many turned to the roaring stock market to overcome their losses. Focused on their own individual situations, these people did not recognize that their actions would soon combine with a number of other factors to produce the Great Depression.

Historians at the beginning of the twenty-first century recognize a number of causes for the Great Depression, including the following:

- Chronic agricultural overproduction and low prices for farm products

- Overproduction of consumer goods by manufacturing industries

- Concentration of wealth in the hands of a few (often referred to as maldistribution or unequal distribution of wealth; *mal-* means bad)

- The structure of American business and industry itself, which included several large holding companies

- Investors' speculation (buying stocks with the assumption that they can always be sold at a profit)

- The lack of action by the Federal Reserve System

- An unsound banking system

## Agricultural woes

U.S. agriculture did not share in the prosperity of the booming 1920s. U.S. farmers had been overproducing since World War I (1914–18). During that war Herbert Hoover was the federal government's food administrator. He encouraged large increases in American agricultural production during the war because European production was greatly disrupted and the United States needed to supply its European allies with food. Before the war U.S. farmers produced less than 690,000 bushels of wheat yearly, but by the war's end they were producing 945,000 bushels per year. After the war U.S. farmers went on producing vast amounts of food each year. The use of machinery improved farm technology. Tractors replaced horses and mules. American agriculture employed 25 to 30 percent of the U.S. workforce in the 1920s, and it relied on income from food exports to European countries. But European countries had resumed their own food production after the war. Many of the European nations were troubled with postwar economic problems, so even though they still needed some U.S. food, they had no money to purchase it. U.S. producers had competition from Argentina, South Africa, and other nations, and this made it more difficult to sell meat

and cereal crops on the world market. Nevertheless, U.S. agricultural production remained high. Farmers were still producing 800,000 bushels of wheat a year in 1930, and they were generally growing more crops of various kinds than they could sell. Because of the large U.S. crop and meat surpluses, prices for farm products fell dramatically.

**Herbert Hoover inspects a food shipment bound for Europe, circa 1921.** *Archive Photos. Reproduced by permission.*

President Calvin Coolidge took little interest in the farmers' problems. He dismissed the difficulties, saying that farmers never made money. Efforts in Congress to protect U.S. farmers from foreign competition failed. As a result the farmers' situation worsened throughout the 1920s. Farmers had to borrow to buy seed and equipment. Most took out loans against their land and homes. But food prices continued to fall, and by the late 1920s many U.S. farmers were

## The Securities and Exchange Commission

Expanding on the Securities Act of 1933, which required companies and stockbrokers to provide information on stock offered to the public, the Securities Exchange Act of 1934 established the Securities and Exchange Commission (SEC). The purpose of the SEC is to work with Congress and other federal agencies to enforce securities (stocks and bonds) laws and protect investors. The creation of the SEC ensured that the stock market would not be a free-for-all, but rather a more closely monitored and regulated industry than in the 1920s. Congress hoped to restore the faith of investors and prevent another market crash as severe as the one of 1929.

Because investors have no guarantees that securities (stocks and bonds) will not lose value, the SEC requires public companies to disclose meaningful infor-

mation to the public so that investors can judge to the best of their ability whether a company's securities are a good investment. The SEC requires almost all companies selling stocks publicly to provide financial reports to the public. Companies are required to tell the truth about their business, their stocks, and what risks might be involved in investment. The SEC also oversees the stock exchanges, brokers, and investment advisers.

The SEC is composed of five commissioners appointed by the U.S. president. No more than three commissioners may belong to the same political party. The first chairman of the SEC, appointed by President Franklin Roosevelt, was Joseph P. Kennedy (1888–1969), father of future president John F. Kennedy (1917–1963; served 1961–63).

hopelessly in debt. They began to miss payments on their loans, weakening their local banks. Between 1921 and 1929 an average of more than six hundred banks failed every year (compared to sixty-six a year between 1910 and 1919). Almost all of the failures were small rural banks. By 1929 farming families—roughly a quarter of the U.S. population—were desperately struggling.

## Manufacturing overproduction

Although farmers were losing ground throughout the 1920s, manufacturing rolled along at top speed. By 1929 stores and warehouses in America were bulging with goods. Between 1923 and 1929 worker output of manufactured goods increased by 32 percent. Assembly lines and new machinery boosted production. As manufacturers saw it, the more goods produced and sold, the more profit there was to be had. Homes in U.S. cities were being electrified, which created a market for new, timesaving electric appliances. Appeals to buy were everywhere. Advertisers touted their products, and movies teased Americans with images of movie stars living with luxuries all around. Although most Americans had little money left over after paying for necessities such as housing and food, they found a way to buy the new automobile, the electric washing machine, and the radio: It was called credit, or installment buying. A small first payment (down payment) was made; then the rest of the price was paid over time. This system worked well as long as the buyer had a job. Installment buying had never been used in America before the late 1920s. Previously, if the total cash price could not be paid up front, the purchase was not made.

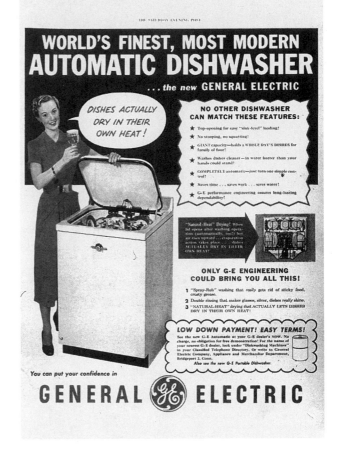

Timesaving appliances were a must-have in the 1920s, even if the consumer could not afford to pay for them. *The Advertising Archive. Reproduced by permission.*

Even with the installment plan, there were limits on how much Americans would or could buy; there were only so many kitchen appliances or cars a person needed. Buying slowed down. By 1929 the stores had built up huge inventories of goods and stopped ordering from factories. Manufacturers had overproduced, and they had to begin cutting back. Factories began laying off substantial numbers of workers, even before the stock market crash. When the crash came, many more people lost not only their jobs but their savings, too. The growing number of unemployed people bought only bare necessities. Goods sat on shelves in warehouses and stores. Manufacturing ground to a halt, and more and more people were laid off as a result. It was a vicious spiral downward.

# Concentration of wealth

Despite the general appearance of prosperity in the 1920s, Americans did not share wealth equally. Historians speak of a growing maldistribution of wealth in the 1920s. *Maldistribution* means a very uneven distribution of wealth. Maldistribution has characterized much of human history: Many people have only a few material goods and have no way to change their position; a few people have a great deal of wealth and are determined to keep that wealth for themselves. Such was the case in America in 1929 prior to the Great Depression. The top 0.1 percent of American families had a combined income equal to the total income of the bottom 42 percent of the population. Between 1920 and 1929 the disposable income (money beyond what is needed for necessities) per person rose by 9 percent for most Americans, but the top 1 percent of the population saw a 75 percent increase. Concerning wealth (not income, but all forms of material goods that have money value), the maldistribution was even greater than it was for income: The top 2.3 percent of families with incomes of over $10,000 held 66 percent of all savings. In 1929 just prior to the stock market crash, of America's 27.5 million families, 78 percent—21.5 million— were not able to save anything after necessities were purchased. These 21.5 million earned under $3,000 a year. Six million earned less than $1,000 yearly.

The reason for the gap between rich and poor had much to do with wages. Although worker productivity (the rate at which goods are produced) increased 32 percent between 1923 and 1929, wages increased only 8 percent in the same period. At the same time, prices remained stable, and the costs of production fell as items were mass-produced. As a result, profits soared. Corporate profits increased by 62 percent, and those profits went to the factory owners, not to the workers. American workers were increasingly less able to purchase the vast amount of goods they were producing, even with installment buying. Of course, the wealthy spent money on luxury items, but this spending could not counteract the mounting financial distress of the masses in America.

The government did little to address the growing maldistribution of wealth. In fact, government action worsened the problem. Andrew Mellon (1855–1937), secretary of the treasury under Presidents Harding, Coolidge, and Hoover, was one of America's richest men. He saw to it that tax cuts for the wealthy passed through Congress in the 1920s, helping the rich retain even more of their wealth. When workers tried to organize and use unions and strikes to improve their wage and health benefits, the government was hostile to such activities. For a time the wealthy offset problems by investing in businesses, factories, and new beautiful buildings. But when Wall Street crashed, they pulled back, ceasing all investing. The wealth of the richest families was not based on the soaring stock market but on decades of banking and ownership of manufacturing companies. So, unlike the newly rich whose money was all in stocks, these families did not lose everything in the market crash.. Nevertheless, in late 1929 they retreated from investing and conserved their vast wealth.

## Holding companies

The unregulated structure of American business and industry created a series of huge holding companies. Holding companies own operating companies (companies that produce a product to sell). Holding companies provide overall direction and management advice, but produce no product or service themselves. To raise money to buy up operating companies, the holding companies sold stock and bonds to Americans, promising them that they were making the soundest investment possible—investment in American businesses. The holding companies used the money from stock and bond sales to buy large amounts of stock in many operating companies (companies that actually produce goods or services) so that they could control those companies. This practice was especially prevalent in utility, railroad, and entertainment industries. Part of the operating company's income went to its holding company. The holding company in turn used part of this money to pay stock dividends (cash distribution of profits) and interest on bonds to the investing public. If the directors of holding companies wanted more investment money, they simply formed another holding company that would buy out the first holding company. Eventually a house of cards developed, one holding company on top of another. When the stock market crashed, there were no more cash investors, and people could not afford to

A once-prosperous businessman is forced to sell his car after losing his money to the stock market.
*UPI-Corbis Bettmann. Reproduced by permission.*

buy the goods of the operating companies. The operating companies could not make enough profits to support the various levels of holding companies. Therefore, the holding companies could not get enough cash to pay dividends and interest to the public investors. The whole house of cards collapsed, wiping out the public's investments. It was only after the stock market crash that Americans realized how many holding companies had been formed and how much power and control they had wielded.

## Stock speculation

Speculation in stock means to buy stock with the assumption that it can always be sold at a profit. Businesses needed to sell stock to raise money to expand. By the mid-1920s only 2 percent of Americans were purchasing stock. But as manufacturing continued to expand, stock prices climbed upward and investors made money. Word got around, and by the late 1920s nearly everyone who had a decent income saved to buy a share of stock. It appeared to be an especially safe way to make easy money. However, investors were not protected from misleading information about stocks. It was difficult for investors to know exactly what they were buying. Companies told the public that they were doing well, but the public had no means of confirming that the companies' financial reports were reliable. To make matters worse, a dangerous way of buying stock developed. It was called "buying on margin."

Buying on margin means that a person purchases a stock by using a bit of his or her own money and borrowing the rest. It is similar to buying on credit. For example, to purchase a $100 stock the buyer might put up $20 and borrow $80 to make up the entire price. Investors worked with investment brokers to borrow money and then buy a stock. Investment brokers got their loan money from banks; brokers and banks alike believed that the stock market was on a permanent upward climb. The brokers set a margin limit. In the example the margin limit was 20 percent, meaning that the investor had to keep 20 percent of his or her own cash invested in the stock. If the stock value increased to $130, then the investor paid back the $80 borrowed and was left with the $20 originally invested and $30 profit. All $50 could be reinvested in a similar manner. The $30 profit represented a 150 percent profit. Such large profits were common as the market continued to rise. Investors, using their increasing profits and borrowed money, continued to buy stocks. This growing demand for stocks pushed stock prices up until they were dramatically higher than the stocks' real worth based on the particular company's profits and overall worth. When stock prices are steadily rising, the market is called a "bull" market. When the market steadily drops, it is a "bear" market. The market in mid-1929 was a raging "bull" market.

Consider what would happen if the investor in the previous example saw the price of his or her stock drop rather than rise. If the $100 price of the stock dropped to $70, then selling the stock at $70 would not even pay back the loan from the broker. The investor, owing $80 but having only $70, would have to come up with more cash. This is what happened not to one share but to millions of shares when the market dropped in October 1929. Investors could not come up with enough cash to meet their "margin calls," demands by the brokers for more cash. In only a few days several million investors lost all the money they had invested, as the market turned into the worst "bear" market of the twentieth century. One day these investors had been wealthy; the next, they wondered how they would survive.

## A meek Federal Reserve System

The Federal Reserve, established in 1913 as the nation's central bank, could possibly have controlled the wild speculation in the stock market and prevented the crash, but the bulls of Wall Street (investors who wanted to drive prices up) overpowered it. The Federal Reserve controlled the loaning of money to banks by raising and lowering interest rates. (Interest is what a borrower pays a lender for the use of the money.) If the Federal Reserve loaned $1,000 to a bank at 5 percent yearly interest, then the bank would have to pay the Federal Reserve $50 yearly in interest for use of that $1,000 loan. If the Federal Reserve raised the interest rate to 10 percent, then on $1,000 the bank would have to pay $100 yearly in interest. Raising the interest rate caused banks to borrow less from the Federal Reserve, because the money was more costly.

In the spring of 1929 several prominent financial experts warned against the widespread speculation in stocks. They knew the price of stocks had been driven up by margin buying, until prices were well above any real value based on the company's profits and overall worth. They called for the Federal Reserve to raise interest rates so banks would not borrow as much. If the banks borrowed less, they would have less money to loan to investment brokers, and those brokers would have less to lend to individual investors who wanted to buy stock on margin. This would slow stock speculation. However, in March 1929, the Federal Reserve decided not to raise interest rates but to merely warn banks to reduce the amount of money they were loaning for stock speculation. Ignoring the Federal Reserve's advice carried no penalty. Hoping stocks would continue to rise, the banks went on lending to investment brokers. The investment brokers went on lending out the money to the general public to invest in stocks. And the public went on buying stocks on margin. The Federal Reserve meekly backed down and let the speculation continue. When the market crashed, investors could not pay back brokers. Hence the brokers could not pay the bank interest on their loans, much less pay back the loan money. Thus by mid-1929 the banks had set themselves up for a big fall.

## An unsound banking system

In 1900 there were roughly twelve thousand commercial banks, banks where services included savings deposits and personal and business loans. By 1920 the number had risen to thirty thousand. With little banking supervision many one-office banks had opened in rural areas, using only a small amount of start-up money (sometimes as little as six thousand dollars). However, because of the surplus of U.S. farm products and plummeting crop prices, farmers were unable to make loan payments to these rural banks and bank failures resulted. Most bank failures between 1921 and 1929 occurred in communities of twenty-five hundred or fewer residents and with capital funds (the accumulated worth) of twenty-five thousand dollars or less.

Banks that were not damaged by the struggling agricultural industry aggressively competed with one another for deposits. To win deposits from businesses and individuals, banks offered to pay higher and higher interest rates. To cover the expense of high interest rates paid out to customers, banks needed to make more income from the interest they charged on loans. Therefore, they made loans easy to obtain, readily lending money for business activities, real estate, and investments in stocks and bonds. Banks assumed the economic boom of the 1920s would go on forever. Depositors who wished to invest in stock could fund up to 90 percent of the stock price through bank loans or through investment brokers who had obtained bank loans for stock purchase. But by the end of the decade individuals and businesses would be unable to keep up with their payments on these loans. Without the funds from loan repayments, many banks were forced to close their doors.

By October 1929, the various economic problems in the United States collided and caused a massive slide in the

Crowds move past the New York Stock Exchange Building in New York City on October 24, 1929, the day the stock market plunged. *AP/Wide World Photo. Reproduced by permission.*

U.S. stock market. The slide signaled the start of the Great Depression.

## Catastrophe: the Great Depression

For most Americans the Great Depression began suddenly in October of 1929. Most thought the economy had

STAGE  BROADWAY  SCREEN

# *VARIETY*

PRICE 25¢·

VOL. XCVII. No. 3    NEW YORK, WEDNESDAY, OCTOBER 30, 1929    88 PAGES

## WALL ST. LAYS AN EGG

**Going Dumb Is Deadly to Hostess In Her Serious Dance Hall Profesh**

**DROP IN STOCKS ROPES SHOWMEN**

**Kidding Kissers in Talkers Burns Up Fans of Screen's Best Lovers**

Many Weep and Call Off Christmas Orders — Legit Shows Hit

MERGERS HALTED

Talker Crashes Olympus

been going along fine. There were those, of course, who could read the warning signs of economic trouble, but if they spoke out, no one took them seriously. For the general public the first indication came at the moment of disaster, a moment so shocking that it could be precisely placed—in New York City, on Wall Street, on October 24, 1929, the day the stock market plunged. The Great Depression would linger until intensive preparations for World War II (1939–45) began, shortly after the Pearl Harbor attack on December 7, 1941. The war created jobs, both civilian and military, and improved wages, and finally the Great Depression came to a close.

The worst years of the Depression ran from 1929 to 1933. President Hoover, holding to the belief that Americans should be self-reliant and not depend on government, took a very conservative approach to solving the economic difficulties. He called for cooperation of business and industry to solve unemployment. For relief for the needy he depended on private charities and asked Americans to donate

Headline of the *Variety* newspaper after Black Tuesday, October 29, 1929. "Wall Street" refers to the location of the New York Stock Exchange. *UPI-Corbis Bettmann. Reproduced by permission.*

## Bonus Army

In the summer of 1932, in the midst of the Great Depression, a ragged multitude of veterans of World War I appeared with their families at the Capitol in Washington, D.C. They were there to request a service bonus that the government had promised to disperse to them by 1945. The veterans, most of whom were unemployed and homeless, had arrived with the intention of petitioning Congress to award them the bonus thirteen years ahead of its scheduled date. The "Bonus Army," as it came to be called, was the brainchild of Walter W. Waters, a cannery worker from Portland, Oregon, who had served as a medic in the 146th Field Artillery. Earlier that spring Waters told an assembly at a meeting of the National Veterans Association that they should present their demands to Congress.

The bonus was to be $1 a day for each day served in the United States and $1.25 for each day served overseas during World War I. This amounted to four or five hundred dollars for many, an amount that could buy up to five months of food and shelter for the veterans' families. The "Bonus Expeditionary Force," as the veterans called themselves, marched eastward at the beginning of May and gradually picked up recruits. News of the marchers quickly spread. The Bonus Expeditionary Force gained popular support, and along

the route sympathetic townspeople generally offered what help they could. Most of the veterans had not worked for a few years, many had been homeless, and all were desperate for whatever assistance they could get from the federal government. The Depression had taken its toll.

At the end of May the first thousand or so veterans arrived in Washington, D.C. More arrived each day, and by mid-July there were twenty thousand men, women, and children (some estimates reach as high as twenty-five thousand) living in twenty-seven camps in and around the district. Several hundred veterans and their families were given permission to temporarily occupy a number of buildings slated for demolition.

A cooperative environment prevailed for several weeks, and by June it appeared to the bonus marchers that Congress would be sympathetic and grant the early bonus payments. However, on June 15, Congress voted sixty-two to eighteen for a defeat of the bill to pay early bonuses. Many senators expected that civil disorder would ensue, but the veterans took the news calmly. Spontaneously a man began to sing the song "America." Everyone joined in, and as the melody sung by over nineteen thousand voices rose into the summer night, the veterans headed back to their camps.

**World War I veterans make the long trek to Washington, D.C., to demand payment of the soldiers' bonus.** *AP/Wide World Photos. Reproduced by permission.*

the army, to the scene of disorder. MacArthur was specifically instructed to cooperate with the police in charge, to turn over prisoners to civil authorities, and above all, to be as humane as possible while executing his orders.

MacArthur blatantly ignored his orders. He massed troops, cavalry, and six tanks along Pennsylvania Avenue, the main roadway leading to the White House. As the troops advanced, the cavalry drew their sabers and the crowd scattered. MacArthur gave orders to set the veterans' tents and shacks on fire. The blaze spread quickly as marchers, hurried and confused, moved to gather their few belongings.

MacArthur later insisted that this was a necessary response. He confided to his assistant, Major Dwight Eisenhower (1890–1969), that his objective was to rescue the nation from revolution. The "Battle of Washington," as the event was soon labeled in the press, was splashed across the nation's newspapers. Americans saw photographs of the marchers, disheveled and weary, fleeing from soldiers who carried bayonets. They saw troops stamping through the smoking debris of the former camps, and they saw resisters, still weeping from tear gas, hauled to police wagons. For many Americans the photographs of U.S. soldiers attacking veterans were shocking images.

After the news many went home. When about eight to ten thousand were left, small demonstrations began to erupt. By July 27 President Herbert Hoover's patience was exhausted, and he ordered that the camps and buildings housing the bonus veterans be cleared the next day. Hoover insisted that no troops be used and that the police handle it. On the morning of July 28 the veterans resisted, and the situation was soon out of control. Hoover directed Patrick J. Hurley (1883–1963), secretary of war, to order General Douglas MacArthur (1880–1964), chief of staff of

**Unemployed men lined outside a soup kitchen in Chicago, Illinois.**

generously to the charities. Hoover viewed the Depression as a natural downturn in the business cycle of ups and downs. The U.S. economy had experienced a number of these declines before—in 1819, 1837, 1857, 1873, 1893, and 1914—and each one was followed by a period of growth. Hoover told Americans that the economy, if left alone, would turn around within days or months. He urged them to have a more optimistic attitude. But the decline of business continued in 1930, 1931, 1932, and 1933. According to Frances Perkins (1882–1965), secretary of labor under President Franklin Roosevelt (1882–1945; served 1933–45), the whole economy, including business, manufacturing, banking, and agriculture, declined 38 percent during those years. Factories closed and laid off workers. Approximately 70 percent of Americans managed to keep their jobs, but they saw their pay decrease an average of 40 percent. Prices of goods also declined but by much less, generally 25 percent. Those not counted in the regular labor force, such as the self-employed, artists, writers, and dancers, found no market for their services and talents.

Bank runs and bank closures were common in 1932 and early 1933. Depositors lined up at banks, demanding all their money. Since banks had already loaned out much of their money, those toward the rear of the lines got nothing—lifetime savings were wiped out. Many people lost their homes or farms since they could no longer make payments on loans.

The toll on families was great. Financial problems broke some families apart. Marriages were postponed, and couples had fewer children. Schools adjusted to the crisis by shortening school hours, decreasing the number of school days, and laying off teachers. Some schools closed altogether. With no school or work many young people became transients (persons traveling in search of work) and wandered about the country on the railroads.

Americans hardest hit were those who were poor before the Depression: farmers, minorities, and the elderly. Up to 75 percent of black Americans lived in the rural South and worked in farming. Most had almost no income. Blacks in cities fared no better; they were always the first laid off from their jobs. Many elderly people lost their life savings because of bank failures. With no hope of earning income, they either moved in with their children or became part of an army of desperately poor and hungry people. In the cities, breadlines snaked for blocks as the unemployed waited for a meal of bread, beans or soup, and coffee. Men, women, and children rummaged through restaurant garbage cans or in city dumps for scraps of food. There was remarkably little stealing; Americans believed that they were somehow responsible for their situation and that they had to endure it without resorting to such extremes.

By the time President Roosevelt took office in March 1933, the American public was exhausted. The only ray of hope came from the new president and his reassuring manner. Roosevelt and his closest advisers immediately set about to bring relief and then recovery to the population and the country. A series of revolutionary programs, collectively known as the New Deal, emerged. These programs brought the U.S. federal government into the everyday lives of Americans as never before. Americans looked to Roosevelt and his New Deal for answers.

## For More Information

Bordo, Michael D., Claudia Goldin, and Eugene N. White, eds. *The Defining Moment: The Great Depression and the American Economy in the Twentieth Century.* Chicago, IL: University of Chicago Press, 1998.

Galbraith, John Kenneth. *The Great Crash, 1929.* Boston, MA: Houghton Mifflin, 1954.

Hiebert, Ray, and Roselyn Hiebert. *The Stock Market Crash, 1929.* New York, NY: Franklin Watts, 1970.

McElvaine, Robert S. *The Great Depression: America, 1929–1941.* New York, NY: Times Books, 1993.

Meltzer, Milton. *Brother, Can You Spare a Dime? The Great Depression, 1929–1933.* New York, NY: Alfred A. Knopf, 1969.

Migneco, Ronald, and Timothy L. Biel. *The Crash of 1929.* San Diego, CA: Lucent Books, 1989.

Paradis, Adrian A. *The Hungry Years: The Story of the Great American Depression.* New York, NY: Chilton Book Company, 1967.

Parrish, Michael E. *Anxious Decades: America in Prosperity and Depression, 1920–1941.* New York, NY: W.W. Norton, 1992.

Phillips, Cabell. *From the Crash to the Blitz, 1929–1939.* New York, NY: Macmillan, 1969.

Terkel, Studs. *Hard Times: An Oral History of the Great Depression.* New York, NY: Pantheon Books, 1970.

# The New Deal

"I pledge you, I pledge myself, to a new deal for the American people. Let us all here assembled constitute ourselves prophets [dedicate ourselves to the development] of a new order of competence and courage." Franklin Roosevelt (1882–1945) spoke these words on July 2, 1932, at the Democratic National Convention. He was accepting the Democratic Party's nomination to be a candidate in the U.S. presidential election of 1932. The phrase "new deal," planted in the public's mind, became a label for the political and economic programs Roosevelt created to combat the Great Depression (1929–39) and return America to prosperity.

At the time of Roosevelt's speech, Herbert Hoover (1874–1964) was the U.S. president and the Republican candidate for reelection. Hoover (served 1929–33) had fallen into disfavor with the American public. He had not met the public outcry for economic relief during the early years of the Depression. In addition, with his cool and stern manner, he did not connect well with the public, and their resentment of him grew. In Roosevelt the public sensed hope and optimism. Desperate for a new approach to solve the economic hardships of the Great Depression, the American people elected Roosevelt to the presidency by a wide margin in November 1932. However, it would be four months between the November election victory and Roosevelt's inauguration as president in March 1933. The Twentieth Amendment to the U.S. Constitution, which changed the inauguration date to January, was in the process of being ratified (voted on by the states) and would not take effect until the 1936 election.

Nevertheless, president-elect Roosevelt, together with a group of brilliant, creative advisers known as the Brain Trust, immediately began to work on solutions to the Great Depression. With more businesses and banks closing daily and people losing their jobs, homes, and farms, Roosevelt and his advisers could not wait until March to begin tackling the problems. Task force groups were formed to work on specific areas of difficulty, such as agriculture, and to propose solutions. This level of activity prior to inauguration had never occurred before in U.S. history.

Roosevelt, the Brain Trust members, and the task force groups focused on the "three Rs": Relief for the needy, plans for economic Recovery, and permanent change with Reform. They designed relief programs to help people until recovery and reform measures could begin to take effect. The numerous measures passed between March 1933 and June 1934 were known as the First New Deal. Legislation passed between April 1935 and June 1938 became known as the Second New Deal.

The people of the United States had long held to a belief in self-reliance: They thought they should be able to meet all their own needs and never look to the government for help. However, by 1929 over 50 percent of Americans lived in cities and depended solely on wages from jobs. If jobs were lost, families found themselves in desperate situations. There were no government programs such as unemployment insurance to fall back on. In rural areas farmers had been struggling throughout the 1920s with low prices for their products. The Great Depression had only increased their troubles. In 1929 income levels were already very depressed; and by 1932 farmers' income was one-third of what it had been in 1929. In addition, severe dust storms began to

## Brain Trust

Searching for solutions to the complex economic and social problems posed by the Great Depression, Democratic candidate Franklin Roosevelt (1882–1945) gathered together a group of advisers to assist in his 1932 presidential campaign. This group was called the "Brain Trust" because they were considered the brightest minds of the day. These advisers would analyze all the options available to Roosevelt on specific issues and then draft policies he might pursue. The core group consisted of three men, all from Columbia University in New York City: Raymond Moley (1886–1975) was a political scientist who had frequently written speeches for and advised Roosevelt; Rexford Guy Tugwell (1891–1979) was an expert in agricultural issues; Adolf Berle Jr. (1895–1971)

was the expert on business and economic affairs. Also part of the elite group were Basil O'Connor, Roosevelt's law partner prior to his presidential terms; Samuel Rosenman, Roosevelt's general counsel (attorney) in New York; and William Woodin, a New York businessman and former director of the New York Federal Reserve Bank.

The advice of this group led to the National Industrial Recovery Act of 1933 and the Agricultural Adjustment Act of 1933. Congress enacted both pieces of legislation soon after Roosevelt's inauguration as president in March 1933. The members of the original "Brain Trust" group played significant roles in the New Deal throughout the 1930s.

blow across the Great Plains in 1932. The once proud and independent American agriculture industry was in dire straits and clearly needed government help.

U.S. government leaders had long operated with the belief that government should have a very limited role in business activity, in agriculture, and in Americans' everyday lives. The misery of the Great Depression changed this attitude. With the New Deal legislation the federal government became for the first time a regular player in the private business world. The government would more closely oversee and control business activities. With legislation such as the Agricultural Adjustment Act of 1933 and the Social Security Act of 1935, the federal government entered into the everyday life of farmers and all Americans. The New Deal legislation set the foundation for government involvement and policies throughout the twentieth century.

# First New Deal: The first hundred days

On March 4, 1933, Franklin D. Roosevelt was sworn in as the thirty-second president of the United States. That evening Roosevelt called a special session of Congress to begin March 9. Congress would remain in session until June 16, one hundred days. Congress was to enact an emergency banking bill, an agricultural bill, and other proposed legislation worked out by Roosevelt's task force groups. Those one hundred days turned out to be perhaps the most amazing period in the federal government's history. Legislation poured out of Congress at a lightning-quick pace. Americans desperately needed help and hope, and their president and Congress did not disappoint. In this chapter the most important pieces of New Deal legislation are briefly described. The date each act was passed by Congress is also provided. If an act is discussed in more detail in following chapters, those chapters are identified for quick reference.

**Emergency Banking Relief Act (March 9, 1933):** The act authorized the U.S. Treasury Department to inspect the nation's banks to see which were strong enough to reopen after a nationwide closure of banks on March 6. (See Banking and Housing chapter.)

**Economy Act (March 20, 1933):** The act cut federal spending by combining programs, cutting jobs, and reducing certain payments to veterans. Many criticized President Roosevelt for trimming back government expenses while at the same time signing massive relief bills. Roosevelt tried to distinguish between the two by claiming that relief funds were an investment in the future. One year later Congress passed a bill, over Roosevelt's veto, largely negating the Economy Act.

**Beer Tax Act (March 22, 1933):** The act allowed the manufacture and sale of beer and light wines with no more than 3.2 percent alcohol. (See Prohibition and Crime chapter.)

**Civilian Conservation Corps Reforestation Act (March 31, 1933):** The act created jobs in conservation, including forestry work (such as planting trees), soil conservation projects, and flood control. This provided relief for young Amer-

icans, who were particularly hard hit by unemployment. (See Riding the Rails chapter.)

**Agricultural Adjustment Act (May 12, 1933):** The act was designed to raise farm prices by encouraging farmers to lower production. (See Farm Relief chapter.)

**Emergency Farm Mortgage Act (May 12, 1933):** To help farmers in heavy debt, the act provided farm loans with easier repayment options. (See Farm Relief chapter.)

**Federal Emergency Relief Act (May 12, 1933):** Creating the Federal Emergency Relief Administration (FERA), the act allocated direct aid to states so they could provide food and clothing to the unemployed, aged, and ill. The act provided $500 million for immediate relief. President Roosevelt named one of his closest advisers, Harry Hopkins (1890–1946), to direct FERA. The FERA program provided essential support and relief

**A cabinet-making class, sponsored by the Civilian Conservation Corps, held at Armstrong Night School in Richmond, Virginia, in 1933.** *Courtesy of the Franklin D. Roosevelt Library.*

while other programs were still being developed. Within a few years Roosevelt replaced FERA with programs that offered work, not just a handout. Harry Hopkins played an important role in developing and carrying out much of the New Deal legislation. (See Employment, Industry, and Labor chapter.)

**Tennessee Valley Authority Act (May 17, 1933):** Creation of the Tennessee Valley Authority (TVA) brought economic development to the southeast United States. The program built twenty new dams and renovated five old ones, bringing cheap hydroelectric power to the region. (See Electrifying Rural America chapter.)

**Securities Act (May 27, 1933):** The act required companies and stockbrokers to provide full information about new stocks to potential investors. (See "The Securities and Exchange Commission" sidebar in Causes of the Great Depression chapter.)

**National Employment Act (June 6, 1933):** This act created the U.S. Employment Service within the Department of Labor; the purpose of the new division was to set up a nationwide employment service network.

**Home Owners' Refinancing Act (June 13, 1933):** The act created the Home Owners' Loan Corporation (HOLC) to provide loans to home owners who were facing foreclosure (loss of a home caused by failure to make mortgage payments). (See Banking and Housing chapter.)

**Banking Act of 1933 (Glass-Steagall Act) (June 16, 1933):** Restoring confidence in U.S. banking, the act established the Federal Deposit Insurance Corporation (FDIC), which insured individual bank accounts against loss. (See Banking and Housing chapter.)

**Emergency Railroad Transportation Act (June 16, 1933):** The act attempted to help railroads reorganize to make them profitable again. However, the act met with resistance from railroad companies and railroad employees afraid of losing jobs and from railroad users who feared the loss of inexpensive freight fares. Congress allowed the act to die in 1936.

**Farm Credit Act (June 16, 1933):** The act formalized the Farm Credit Administration (FCA), which had been created

by an executive order from President Roosevelt on March 27, 1933. The act created a system of banking institutions for farmers. (See Farm Relief chapter.)

**National Industrial Recovery Act (NIRA) (June 16, 1933):** The act established codes of fair practice for industry and businesses. (See Employment, Industry, and Labor chapter.)

Workers sort packages of nonperishable food for needy New York City families as part of the Federal Emergency Relief Administration (FERA). *AP/Wide World Photo. Reproduced by permission.*

**Public Works Administration (PWA) (June 16, 1933):** Created under the authority of the NIRA, the PWA distributed almost $6 billion (the amount originally appropriated was $3.3 billion) between 1933 and 1939 for public works projects. PWA projects included roads, tunnels, bridges, dams, power systems, hospitals, the Mall in Washington, D.C., and many other improvements. The projects put the unemployed to work and were a means of pump priming. *Pump priming* means spending federal funds in ways that quickly put money into the hands of consumers, so that consumers will buy more goods and stimulate the economy. (See Employment, Industry, and Labor chapter.)

## A growing government

After being in session one hundred days, Congress wrapped up its special session on June 16. During the remainder of 1933 President Roosevelt established many boards and councils by executive order; these were intended to carry out the relief and recovery programs created by the new legislation. Although the economy slowly began improving, consumers still could not afford to buy goods, and more layoffs resulted by late fall. To help the unemployed through the winter of 1933–34, Roosevelt created the Civil Works Administration (CWA) on November 9. By February 1934 over 4.2 million workers were employed constructing streets, schools, and airports. The CWA also provided for fifty thousand rural schoolteachers' salaries. As part of the CWA, the Public Works of Art Project (PWAP) was established in December 1933. Over thirty-six hundred artists were employed by PWAP to create murals and sculptures for public buildings. PWAP was the first federally funded nationwide art program in the United States. Although PWAP was discontinued (along with all CWA programs) in the spring of 1934, support of the arts would reappear in the Second New Deal as part of the Works Progress Administration. Congress passed several new pieces of legislation in 1934. Together, the following acts and the legislation of the first hundred days constituted the First New Deal.

**Farm Mortgage Refinancing Act (January 31, 1934):** This act created the Federal Farm Mortgage Corporation, which

The Public Works Administration (PWA) provided $38 million in 1934 for the construction of Hoover Dam; the total construction cost was $114 million. Here, President Franklin Roosevelt (center) tours the construction site of the Hoover Dam. *Corbis Corporation. Reproduced by permission.*

would issue $2 billion to refinance farm loans. (See Farm Relief chapter.)

**Securities Exchange Act (June 6, 1934):** The act prohibited certain activities in stock market trading and set penalties for violations. It established the Securities and Exchange Commission (SEC) to oversee stock market trading. (See "The Securities and Exchange Commission" sidebar in Causes of the Great Depression chapter.)

**Corporate Bankruptcy Act (June 7, 1934):** This act made it easier for troubled companies to reorganize and start hiring again.

**National Housing Act (June 28, 1934):** With the intention of spurring the construction industry, this act created the Federal Housing Administration (FHA) to help Americans buy new houses. (See Banking and Housing chapter.)

## Critics of the First New Deal

Opposition to President Roosevelt's new government measures began to emerge in 1934. Different groups had different reasons for their opposition: Conservatives thought that the First New Deal went beyond the limit of governmental power allowed by the U.S. Constitution. On the other side, liberals believed that the federal government should go much further; they called for government ownership of banks and industry. Congress worried that the president was becoming too powerful and upsetting the balance between the executive, legislative, and judicial (court system) branches of government. Nevertheless, Roosevelt clearly had strong general public support during the early period of the New Deal. He could afford to ignore his critics. His confident, reassuring manner won over Americans who were desperate for relief from the severe hardships of the Great Depression.

## The Second New Deal

The Second New Deal lasted from April 1935 to June 1938, though most activity occurred in 1935 and 1936. Legislation passed during this period represented a clear political shift: While the First New Deal focused on national economic recovery through aid to businesses and large farm operators, the Second New Deal provided economic relief for families, common laborers, and small farmers.

By mid-1935 millions of employable people were still receiving unemployment relief. President Roosevelt was increasingly sensitive to outspoken critics who claimed that the New Deal ignored workers, the needy, and the aged. Through the first two years of his presidency, Roosevelt had tried to satisfy both big business and the common worker. By late 1934 Roosevelt had come to the conclusion that trying to please everyone in the nation was only leading to everyone's being dissatisfied to some degree. His political popularity was declining, and the presidential election of 1936 was looming.

Roosevelt decided to focus on the everyday American worker, small business, and small farmers. He dropped the ideas of national planning represented by the 1933 National Industrial Recovery Act (NIRA) and its industry codes that had given big business a dominating hand in regulating markets and wages. When, on May 27, 1935, the U.S. Supreme Court struck down the NIRA as unconstitutional (in other words, not in keeping with the U.S. Constitution), Roosevelt chose not to create a new version of the NIRA. Instead, with the Second New Deal legislation, Roosevelt and his advisers looked to supporting small companies and labor in reshaping U.S. economic policy. The Second New Deal also attempted to help small farmers, including tenant farmers, sharecroppers, and migrant workers. Tenant farmers rent farmland but have their own tools to do the work of farming. Sharecroppers work the land of a landowner who provides the sharecropper with tools. Both types of farmers give some of their harvested crops to the landowner. Migrant workers travel from place to place in order to harvest crops on a seasonal basis.

Roosevelt's support of American workers resulted in intense opposition to his programs from the business community, who felt that the president was neglecting business interests. Nevertheless, Roosevelt persisted with relief for workers, farmers, young Americans, and the unemployed.

## Unemployment relief

**Emergency Relief Appropriation Act (ERAA) (April 8, 1935):** Worker relief was the top priority of the Second New Deal. The Emergency Relief Appropriation Act (ERAA) directed $4.8 billion toward the creation of jobs. The Works Progress Administration (WPA), which was established under the act, became the biggest relief program of the Second New Deal. Recruited from among those already enrolled in relief programs, WPA workers built airports, schools, hospitals, roads, public buildings, and recreational facilities. Young people, women, and minorities were recruited for various projects. The WPA expanded its programs to include writers, artists, actors, musicians, and dancers by creating the Federal Writers Project, Federal Arts Projects, the Federal Theater Project (FTP), the Federal Music Project, and the Federal Dance Project. (See Works Progress Administration chapter.)

## Youth relief

**National Youth Administration (NYA) (June 26, 1935):** In early 1935 estimates placed the number of unemployed young people at five million. President Roosevelt wanted to give youths hope and faith in the U.S. economic system. The National Youth Administration provided high school and college students with part-time jobs and also provided jobs for those who had already dropped out. (See Riding the Rails chapter.)

## Farmer relief

**The new Agricultural Adjustment Act (February 16, 1938):** The new Agricultural Adjustment Act made the conservation provisions of the 1933 act permanent and included protection for farmers against lower prices caused by overproduction. In 1936 the U.S. Supreme Court had declared the original act (passed in May 1933) unconstitutional. (See Farm Relief chapter.)

**Soil Conservation Act (April 27, 1935):** Farmers in the middle section of the country, the Great Plains, were experiencing drought and massive soil erosion. The act established the Soil Conservation Service (SCS) to promote wide-ranging soil conservation practices. The Flood Control Act of 1936 was passed in response to flooding in areas near the Ohio and Mississippi Rivers. (See Farm Relief chapter.)

**Resettlement Administration (RA) (April 30, 1935):** Roosevelt created the Resettlement Administration (RA) under the authority of the Federal Emergency Relief Act. The goal of the RA was to help poor farmers either improve the use of their lands or move to better lands. (See Farm Relief chapter.)

**Rural Electrification Administration (REA) (May 11, 1935):** Roosevelt established the Rural Electrification Administration (REA) under the Federal Emergency Relief Act of 1933 to bring electricity to rural areas. (See Electrifying Rural America chapter.)

**Bankhead-Jones Farm Tenancy Act (July 22, 1937):** The act made low-interest loans available to tenant farmers, farm laborers, and small landowners so they could purchase or expand their own lands. Under authority of this act, Roosevelt created the Farm Security Administration (FSA) on September 1, 1937. The FSA absorbed the programs of the RA and replaced the RA. (See Farm Relief chapter.)

## Labor relief

**Fair Labor Standards Act (June 25, 1938):** This act replaced some standards set earlier in the no-longer-valid National Industrial Recovery Act and added new ones. Most important, the act set a minimum hourly wage and maximum weekly hours. (See Employment, Industry, and Labor chapter.)

**National Labor Relations Act (Wagner Act) (July 5, 1935):** The Wagner Act supported the right of workers to join unions and recognized the practice of collective bargaining. (Collective bargaining is negotiation that is conducted between representatives of employers and workers to reach an agreement on working conditions, wages, and job benefits.) In addition, the act prohibited various unfair business practices. (See Employment, Industry, and Labor chapter.)

**Social Security Act (August 14, 1935):** The Social Security Act set up a program of social insurance in the United States, in-

A road construction project is completed as part of the Works Progress Administration. *Corbis Corporation. Reproduced by permission.*

cluding unemployment insurance, old-age retirement payments, and aid to needy mothers and children, and the blind. (See Social Security chapter.)

**Wealth Tax Act (August 30, 1935):** The Wealth Tax Act included a small corporate tax and a small inheritance tax. The goal of the act was to redistribute some of the wealth concentrated among the very rich in order to benefit the vast majority of Americans who were not rich. The act made income taxes progressive, which meant that the wealthy would be taxed at a higher rate than those with lower incomes. (Progressive income taxes are still in effect in the United States in the twenty-first century.) The passage of this tax bill confirmed President Roosevelt as a representative of the working class.

# Election of 1936 and the Democratic Coalition

The Second New Deal programs of 1935 and 1936 proved extremely popular with most Americans. Roosevelt won the 1936 presidential election by a landslide—the largest margin of victory in U.S. history for a presidential election. (Roosevelt received 27.7 million votes; Republican presidential candidate Alfred Landon (1887–1987) received 16.6 million.) Democrats also swept into the U.S. Senate and House by large margins. An interesting group of Americans supported Roosevelt: It was the first presidential election in which the Democratic candidate won a majority of black Americans' votes. Support also came from other minorities and from laborers, Catholics, Jews, and big-city political organizations. The South also voted Democratic. This diverse group of supporters became known as the Democratic Coalition. The coalition would be highly influential in electing Democratic candidates for the next few decades.

# Court-packing bill

The excitement generated by Roosevelt's election and the expectation of more New Deal legislation was not long-lived. Before the election Roosevelt was greatly angered when the Supreme Court struck down two pieces of New Deal legislation—the first Agricultural Adjustment Act and the National Industrial Recovery Act. With a huge election victory behind him, Roosevelt boldly introduced a Supreme Court reform bill to Congress in 1937. Among other items, the bill proposed to add new judges to the Court, up to a total of fifteen judges. Roosevelt's proposal frightened the public and legislators alike; both felt he was trying to set up a Court friendly to his programs. Controversial hearings of the court reform bill dominated Congress for the next six months, and the bill failed to pass. As a result, momentum for more New Deal programs was lost.

## Recession of 1937

By spring of 1937 industrial production was at pre-Depression levels. Roosevelt decided it was time to see whether the economy could stand cutbacks of government relief support. Congress reduced funds for a number of relief programs, including a 25 percent decrease in the Works Progress Administration. By fall, industrial production fell, farm prices fell, and unemployment was on the rise. The recovery had come to a stop. Trying to keep public morale up, Roosevelt introduced a new term to refer to the economic downturn: *recession*. He desperately wanted to avoid the term *depression*, which evoked strong images of the dark times of the early 1930s. From that point on, and into the twenty-first century, the term depression was never again used to label an economic downturn; recession instantly became the preferred term.

## Last New Deal legislation

Despite the recession of 1937, Congress passed the Wagner-Steagall Housing Act on September 1, 1937. The act provided funds for public housing for the needy. Under the act the U.S. Housing Authority was established to oversee $500 million in loans for construction of low-cost housing (see Banking and Housing chapter). Another important New Deal act was a consumer protection bill, the Food, Drug, and Cosmetics Act, passed June 24, 1938. The act required that all ingredients in drugs be listed in their packaging, and it set higher standards for food labeling. Processing of food, drugs, and cosmetics was brought under federal control.

# End of the New Deal

The 1938 elections for the U.S. Senate and House marked the end of the New Deal. Increasing numbers of conservatives opposed to the New Deal programs took seats in Congress. President Roosevelt, by necessity, shifted his attention more and more to the brewing storm in Europe, soon to grow into World War II (1939–45).

The major push of New Deal legislation lasted only four years, from 1933 to 1937, but the total amount of legislation passed was staggering—more was passed than during any previous four-year period. For the first time in U.S. history the federal government played a role in the everyday lives of its people. Many of the programs established under the New Deal became cornerstones for programs lasting into the twenty-first century.

# For More Information

## Books

Conkin, Paul Keith. *The New Deal*. Arlington Heights, IL: Harlan Davidson, 1992.

Edsforth, Ronald. *The New Deal: America's Response to the Great Depression*. Malden, MA: Blackwell Publishers, 2000.

Leuchtenberg, William E. *Franklin D. Roosevelt and the New Deal, 1932–1940*. New York, NY: Harper & Row, 1963.

Moley, Raymond, and Eliot A. Rosen. *The First New Deal*. New York, NY: Harcourt, Brace & World, 1966.

Olson, James S., ed. *Historical Dictionary of the New Deal: From Inauguration to Preparation for War*. Westport, CT: Greenwood, 1985.

Reagan, Patrick D. *Designing a New America: The Origins of New Deal Planning, 1890–1943*. Amherst, MA: University of Massachusetts Press, 1999.

Roosevelt, Franklin D. *The Public Papers and Addresses of Franklin D. Roosevelt*. Vol. 2, 1933. New York, NY: Random House, 1938.

Schlesinger, Arthur M., Jr. *The Coming of the New Deal: The Age of Roosevelt*. Boston, MA: Houghton Mifflin, 1988.

Sternsher, Bernard. *Hope Restored: How the New Deal Worked in Town and Country*. Chicago, IL: Ivan R. Dee, 1999.

## Web Sites

*New Deal Network*. http://newdeal.feri.org (accessed on August 12, 2002).

Roosevelt University, Center for New Deal Studies. http://www.roosevelt.edu/newdeal (accessed on August 12, 2002).

# Banking and Housing

Franklin D. Roosevelt had been inaugurated as president of the United States on March 4, 1933, a day that found the U.S. banking system paralyzed. On March 6, Roosevelt declared a nationwide "bank holiday," closing all U.S. banks until March 13. The "holiday" allowed a time-out in the rapid decline of the U.S. banking system. The Emergency Banking Act of 1933, passed by Congress on March 9, provided for government inspection of the nation's banks. The Banking Act of 1933, passed a few months later, and the Banking Act of 1935 laid the foundation for reform of the U.S. banking industry. The 1933 Banking Act provided for creation of the Federal Deposit Insurance Corporation (FDIC), which insured depositors against loss of their money in the event of a bank failure. The FDIC restored the public's confidence in the banking system.

All of these measures were part of the New Deal legislation developed under Roosevelt's administration. The New Deal programs were designed to bring relief and recovery to the American people and to industries that were struggling to survive in the Great Depression. The Great Depression was the most severe economic crisis the United State had ever experienced. It began with the crash of the stock market in October 1929 and lasted until the United States entered World War II (1939–45) in 1941.

The structure of the U.S. banking system in the 1920s contributed to the economic problems that led to the Great Depression. There were many small, often rural, single-office banks (unit banks) that by law could not establish branches to broaden their base of depositors. These banks made a careless practice of loaning money for speculation in the stock market (*speculation* means buying stock with the assumption that it can always be sold for a profit). This created a dangerous situation, because people who borrowed money to invest could not repay their loans if stock prices dropped. Many Americans lost money through speculation, and, as a result, they fell behind on their home loan (mortgage) payments.

By 1933, 40 to 50 percent of all home mortgages were in default; that is, the borrowers were behind in payments and faced losing their homes. Home financing was the anchor of the banking system; without loan payments coming in, the banks were in danger of collapse. Roosevelt had to rescue the banking industry, but his administration went a step further by developing housing legislation that would help reform U.S. banking. An emergency measure called the Homeowners' Refinancing Act of 1933, along with the permanent National Housing Act of 1934 (which created the Federal Housing Administration, or FHA), allowed hundreds of thousands of Americans to keep their homes. The legislation put the American dream of owning a home within the reach of all but the nation's poorest.

## Bank failures

In the 1920s an average of six hundred banks failed in the United States every year. This was almost ten times as many annual bank failures as the United States had suffered from 1910 to 1919. The banks that failed were small banks with ties to the struggling farming industry. They were considered local failures and did not cause any loss of public confidence or create nationwide banking panics. The American economy was booming overall, and stock prices were on

BANK

a wild upward ride. Americans generally ignored the 1920s bank failures. Yet these failures were warning signs that the U.S. economy was not healthy.

The economic boom of the 1920s crashed down in October 1929 when stock prices on the New York Stock Exchange plummeted. This crash marked the beginning of the Great Depression. In growing numbers businesses closed

**Thousands of small, rural banks, such as this one in Haverhill, Iowa, closed when the U.S. banking system collapsed in the early 1930s.** *Courtesy of the Library of Congress.*

Confused and angry customers are shown at the closed doors of the Bank of United States on December 11, 1930. *AP/Wide World Photo. Reproduced by permission.*

their doors, individuals lost their jobs or saw their salaries greatly reduced, and many lost their homes or farms. When businesses and individuals failed to make payments on loans or mortgages (home loans), the banks that had made the loans suffered: Unable to collect on these loans, they had great difficulty meeting the demand for withdrawals, especially when depositors who had lost their jobs and income were forced to withdraw their savings to live on. Not surprisingly, banks began to fail at a rapid rate. In 1929 over thirteen hundred banks failed. Closures spread from small rural areas to large geographic areas and into cities.

Between November and December 1930, over 120 banks closed in Tennessee, Arkansas, Kentucky, and North Carolina. In New York City one of the most disastrous failures occurred on December 11, 1930, at the Bank of United States. Although this bank was a private one, the failure sent shock waves across the country, because the bank's name suggested that the whole U.S. banking system was about to fail. Two

## A Cashless Society

What would it be like to wake up one morning and find that the government had shut down all the banks? The only cash available would be what was in your wallet or your piggy bank. Would mobs roam the streets breaking store windows and taking whatever they needed? Would grocers hold off crowds with shotguns? Nothing quite so dramatic happened in early March 1933, when President Roosevelt closed all banks nationwide for seven days.

Many Americans rushed to their bank to see if it was really locked up. But for the most part, the public reacted with relief—relief that President Roosevelt had halted the bank runs, at least for the moment. People laughed and joked about their common predicament. Movies charged a piece of fruit or a vegetable as admission. Salesmen presented the contents of their suitcases in exchange for a train ride home. IOUs were written everywhere. Bus tokens, foreign coins, and postage stamps became part of the odd moneyless society.

However, for some communities that had already endured local bank closures, the amusement of the situation had

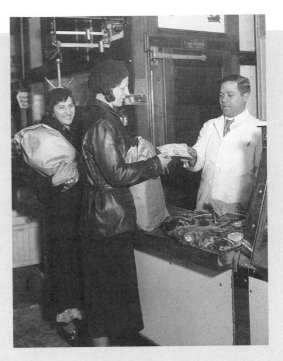

**A housewife in Brooklyn, New York, purchases groceries with an IOU after the banks closed in March 1933.** *Corbis Corporation. Reproduced by permission.*

worn off. In Detroit, Michigan, for example, the nationwide closure stretched residents into a fourth week without cash. It had become difficult just to raise bus fare for school or work. Paychecks could not be cashed, and relief applications poured in when people became hungry. The reopening of the banks on March 13 came none too soon for many.

other large city banks closed in December: the Bankers' Trust of Philadelphia and the Chelsea Bank of New York City.

These failures seriously weakened public confidence in the banking system. The public could not distinguish a strong bank from a weak one, and began to distrust them all. In the 1920s Americans thought of bankers as smart, thrifty businessmen who would look after their customers' money. By 1930 Americans were distrustful and suspicious of the same men. Many thought that bankers had helped cause the Depression by their greed and accumulation of wealth. Americans began hoarding cash, preferring to keep it in mattresses and in cans buried in the backyard rather than in banks.

## Bank runs

During the early years of the Depression the public's lack of confidence in banks took a dramatic form: bank runs. Bank runs began when depositors feared that their bank had weakened; a mere rumor was all it took to start a run. Rather than risk the loss of their savings, depositors lined up to withdraw their money. Since there were almost no pension or retirement systems in the early 1930s, all people had for retirement was personal savings.

No bank keeps enough cash on hand to cover all depositors' accounts at a single time. Banks loan out the money or invest it, keeping only enough cash on hand to cover normal daily needs of depositors. So even a run on a perfectly sound bank could lead to its collapse.

## Bank holidays

During the Depression "bank holidays" were used as a way to halt bank runs. Banks would legally suspend operation and close for business for a period of time. In 1932 and early 1933 bank holidays increased: In November 1932 Nevada declared a statewide holiday while western banks experienced failure after failure. Louisiana declared a statewide holiday in early 1933, and Michigan banks closed for eight days in February 1933. Michigan's bank holiday tied up the cash of nine hundred thousand depositors and froze $1.5 billion in bank deposits.

Bank holidays continued to spread: Indiana, February 23; Maryland, February 25; Arkansas, February 27; and Ohio, February 28. By March 2, 1933, twenty-one states had declared bank holidays. With banks failing across the country, the public turned to Washington, D.C., for bank reform.

## Senator Glass and Representative Steagall

In 1930 President Herbert Hoover (1874–1964; served 1929–33) called for Congress to investigate the entire banking system and to consider revising the banking laws. Two especially interested congressmen were Senator Carter Glass (1858–1946) and Representative Henry B. Steagall. Before en-

John W. Poole, president of the Federal American Bank, addresses a crowd outside the bank after customers started a run on the bank. *Corbis Corporation. Reproduced by permission.*

tering the Senate, Glass had served in the House of Representatives (1902–19), where he was chairman of the House Committee on Banking and Currency. Glass sponsored the Federal Reserve Bank Act of 1913, which established the Federal Reserve System. The twelve Federal Reserve banks across the country served as a central banking system (see sidebar). For years Senator Glass had been observing how banks were investing in the stock market and making loans to others to invest in stocks. Glass feared that this was risky, and his fears proved correct when the stock market crashed and the value of stocks nosedived. Glass demanded that commercial banking be separated from investment banking. (Commercial banking involves accepting deposits from customers and making personal, business, and industrial loans. Investment banking consists of buying stocks and bonds.) Many legislators were convinced that Glass was right. These lawmakers agreed that speculative investing (buying stocks or bonds with the expectation of making large profits) had no place in commercial banking because it placed depositors' savings at a high risk of loss.

Representative Steagall, elected to the House in 1914, became chairman of the House Committee on Banking and Currency, the same committee Glass had once headed. Steagall was a staunch advocate of deposit insurance, a program designed to protect the bank deposits of individuals by guaranteeing that the government would replace funds lost by depositors due to bank financial problems. He had proposed deposit insurance since the early 1920s but had no success enacting it.

## Reconstruction Finance Corporation

In 1930 and 1931 both Glass and Steagall headed hearings on how to reform the banking system. Meanwhile, President Hoover attempted to mobilize the banking community. He urged cooperation between bankers and federal officials to find ways to end the crisis.

By January 1932, the congressional investigations and Hoover's requests for voluntary cooperation had led nowhere. On January 22, Hoover decided to establish the Reconstruction Finance Corporation (RFC) to make low-interest loans to banks. Hoover expected the RFC to restore the confidence of bankers so they would make loans to business. Fear-

## The Federal Reserve System

The Federal Reserve Bank Act, enacted on December 23, 1913, created the Federal Reserve System. Representative Carter Glass (1858–1946) of Virginia sponsored the act. Later, as a senator, Glass would play a key role in the New Deal banking legislation of the 1930s.

Under the Federal Reserve System, the United States is divided into twelve Federal Reserve districts, each with a Reserve bank. Reserve banks carry out day-to-day operations of the nation's central banking system. They move currency (paper money) and coins in and out of circulation, collect and process millions of checks each day, and supervise and examine member banks for soundness. Overseeing the entire system is the seven-member Federal Reserve Board. The Federal Reserve Board controls the economy of the United States in three major ways: It sets reserve requirements—how much out of every $100 in deposits a bank must hold in reserve in its regional Reserve bank; it adjusts the interest rates it charges member banks that borrow money from the Federal Reserve; and it buys and sells federal government bonds.

ing bank runs, banks had been hoarding all their money and had not been making any loans.

The RFC helped somewhat: The number of bank failures dropped from twenty-two hundred in 1931 to fourteen hundred in 1932. Nevertheless, individuals continued to hoard their money, banks did not make loans as Hoover had hoped they would, and bank runs continued.

## Halting the banking crisis

President Hoover's approval rating was as low as the stock market by mid-1932. His assurances that the economy would soon turn around failed to convince most Americans. Hoover's unpopularity virtually assured a victory for anyone running against him in the November 1932 presidential election. Hoover ran for reelection on the Republican ticket; Franklin D. Roosevelt (1882–1945) was the Democratic candidate. With his personable, calm, and optimistic manner, Roosevelt easily won the election, becoming the thirty-second president of the United States. Under the law at that time, he would not be inaugurated until March 4, 1933. That four-month interval stretched like an eternity for Americans desperate for relief. The Hoover administration was still in office, and its members provided no leadership; they said they had done all they could do. The clouds of the banking disaster grew darker and heavier.

As dawn broke on March 4, 1933, the presidential inauguration day, America's banking system was paralyzed. In his inauguration speech to the anxious nation, President Roosevelt declared war against the banking crisis. A few hours later, in a never-before-seen event in U.S. history, Roosevelt's entire cabinet was sworn in during one ceremony. Normally cabinet members are sworn in one at a time as Congress individually confirms them. Cabinet members, advisers, and representatives of the Federal Reserve attended meetings for the rest of the day. They agreed that the only way to halt the banking crisis was to declare a nationwide bank holiday. Working into the night, President Roosevelt did not attend his inaugural ball, sending Mrs. Roosevelt alone to carry on with the celebrating.

The next day, March 5, Roosevelt met with bankers who had gathered at the White House for a hastily called meeting. It became clear to Roosevelt that the bankers had no plan of their own to end the banking crisis. So later that evening Roosevelt decided on a course of action. On Monday, March 6, at 1:00 A.M., convinced that the banks could not stand one more day of operation without total collapse, Roosevelt declared a nationwide bank holiday from March 6 through Thursday, March 9. He later extended it until Monday, March 13. Roosevelt also called Congress back to Washington, D.C., for a special session beginning March 9.

Instead of panicking, the American public greeted the bank holiday with great relief. At least for a few days, the long economic descent would stop, giving them a break from their anxiety. People rallied together in an almost joking mood about their common predicament of not having access to their money.

# Emergency Banking Act of 1933

Although the public felt relieved by the bank holiday, the mood in the halls of government was tense. Long discussions about the banking crisis continued. Four of those involved in the meetings were the new secretary of the treasury, William Woodin; George Harrison of the New York Federal Reserve; and two departing cabinet members from the Hoover administration, Ogden L. Mills and Arthur Ballantine. These four men are credited with putting together the emergency banking bill, which was ready by noon on March 9 when Congress convened its special session. The president sent the bill to the House, where Representative Steagall introduced it. Almost before he could finish reading the bill, House members shouted, "Vote! Vote!" The bill passed unanimously. The Senate passed the bill by a vote of seventy-three to seven, just before 7:30 P.M. By 8:30 P.M. the Emergency Banking Act of 1933 was on the president's desk at the White House, waiting for his signature. The entire process took less than eight hours.

The newly enacted Emergency Banking Act of 1933 legalized Roosevelt's decision to declare a nationwide bank holiday. It created a process for examining, reorganizing, and reopening the thousands of closed banks throughout the country. It also revived the Reconstruction Finance Corporation (RFC) to provide banks with long-term investment funds. Although the act was passed during a crisis, it was a calm, conservative piece of legislation. Bankers had feared radical changes and were greatly relieved; those who had called for a government takeover of banking were disappointed.

With the powers granted by the act, officials undertook the task of determining which banks were sound enough to reopen on Monday, March 13. They feared that when banks did reopen, panicky depositors would line up to withdraw money just as they had before, draining the banks again. To prevent this, President Roosevelt, knowing the power of the new radio technology, broadcast his first fireside chat on Sunday night, March 12. Estimates indicate that over sixty million people listened to Roosevelt's comforting voice as he explained what action government had taken over the last few days and what would happen on Monday morning. His message was that banks were once again safe for Americans' savings. Roosevelt explained the situation so well that lecturer, humorist, and social critic Will Rogers (1879–1935) later commented, as reprinted in Susan Winslow's 1976 book *Brother, Can you Spare a Dime?*: "Our President took such a dry subject as banking ... and made everyone understand it, even the bankers."

On Monday morning, March 13, people once again lined up in front of banks, but this time they were there to deposit their money. The bank runs were over. Confidence in political leadership and in the banking system had been restored. In eight amazing days (March 6–March 13), the banking system and possibly the country itself had been saved from collapse.

## Banking Act of 1933 (Glass-Steagall Act)

With the immediate crisis averted, attention turned to permanent banking reform legislation. Between mid-March and early May 1933, many conferences were held in Washington, D.C., to work out the details of permanent reform. Legislators reflected on how the banking industry had gotten into so much trouble. Speculation in the stock market had certainly contributed, but the most significant factor in the banking crisis turned out to be the small "unit bank." In the late nineteenth century, banking legislation had banned all nationwide and statewide branching of banks. At that time, it was believed that local, single-office banks would be more responsive to each local community. As a result many banks opened for business with very little capital (money invested in a business and used to run the business). If a certain locality fell on hard times, such as a factory closure or farming problems, the bank usually collapsed. If branch banking had been allowed, a larger, more diversified depositor base could have been developed by the 1920s and early 1930s. When one branch was in trouble, a more stable branch could have bailed it out. The Banking Act of 1933 sought to correct earlier legislation and improve the stability of small banks.

On May 10, 1933, Senator Glass introduced a completed banking reform bill to the Senate, and Representative Steagall introduced the bill to the House. The bill passed Congress by mid-June, and President Roosevelt signed the Banking Act of 1933 into law on June 16. Roosevelt congratulated Senator Glass and Representative Steagall on shepherding through Congress the first major banking bill since the Federal Reserve Bank Act of 1913.

The Banking Act of 1933 (commonly known as the Glass-Steagall Act) included the following provisions: (1) As

Senator Glass had urged, commercial banking was entirely separated from investment banking; (2) As Representative Steagall had urged, an insurance on deposits was created. A new agency, the Federal Deposit Insurance Corporation (FDIC), was created within the U.S. Treasury Department to provide up to $2,500 deposit insurance for each depositor account at FDIC-insured banks; (3) The expansion of branch banking was permitted; (4) The Federal Reserve was given more control over loans made to FDIC-insured banks; (5) Interest payments on checking accounts were prohibited to eliminate competition among banks to pay higher and higher rates; (6) Officers of banks could not receive loans from their own banks because of the conflict of interest in granting such a loan.

The Banking Act of 1933 laid the foundation for extensive changes in the U.S. banking industry. Two years later President Roosevelt signed into law another Banking Act. The most important provision of the Banking Act of 1935 restructured the Federal Reserve System so that power rested with the Federal Reserve Board in Washington, D.C., rather than in the twelve regional Federal Reserve banks (see sidebar). The 1935 Banking Act also strengthened the FDIC, authorizing this agency to set standards for member banks, examine banks for compliance with those standards, take action to prevent troubled banks from failing, and pay depositors if insured banks failed.

## Federal Deposit Insurance Corporation

The most enduring legacy of the New Deal banking reform legislation is the Federal Deposit Insurance Corporation (FDIC). The FDIC was an immediate success. It returned depositor confidence, all but eliminated bank runs and bank failures, and protected against wild fluctuations (wide swings down or up) in the nation's money supply. Over fourteen thousand banks had joined the FDIC by 1935. Bank failures dropped to only forty-four in 1934 and thirty-four in 1935.

By 2000 about 98 percent of all commercial banks were FDIC members, and each account was insured up to $100,000. The FDIC insurance fund was built up through yearly fees paid by member banks. If this fund ever proves to be insufficient to meet the needs of depositors, the FDIC is authorized to borrow money directly from the U.S. Treasury.

## Stabilization of the banking system

Like other New Deal legislation, the Emergency Banking Act of 1933, the Banking Act of 1933 (Glass-Steagall Act), and the Banking Act of 1935 were milestones in public policy. Their passage gave the federal government the lead role in coordinating the U.S. banking system; the government—not individual bankers—would control the nation's money supply. After the passage of the 1935 act, the Federal Reserve Board took on the permanent assignment of stabilizing overall economic activity in the United States.

## Housing: The ideal American home

The image of the ideal American home has changed over time. In the early and mid-1800s a comfortable home on a large plot of farmland was the American dream. However, as farming communities grew into towns and towns grew into cities, Americans began to define the ideal home in terms of a house, yard, and neighborhood with connecting roads. By the 1890s and early 1900s thousands of immigrants came to the United States from European cities. They generally settled in the center of cities, where common laborers were needed. Privileged urban dwellers tended to move to the edges of towns, away from the common laborers and the city bustle, to enjoy a home with a yard.

Public transportation in urban communities included rail lines and trolleys. Commuter villages grew up along transportation lines. Cheap land, low home prices, good wages, and efficient transportation allowed working-class families and the emerging middle class to move to the end of the trolley line, where space was plentiful for a house and garden. By the 1920s many thousands of Americans had purchased the amazing automobile. In their Oldsmobiles and Model Ts, Americans explored the edges of their cities and dreamed of owning a single-family home in the suburbs (a community on the outskirts of a city).

Between 1922 and 1929, 883,000 new homes were built each year, more than doubling the home-building rate for any previous seven-year period. New suburbs dotted the outskirts of every major city, and suburban neighborhoods filled with the American bungalow. The humble bungalow, an attractive one-and-a-half-story home, cost between $1,500 and $5,000, easily affordable by the growing middle class. Most wealthy people paid cash for their homes, but the lower middle and middle classes obtained mortgages. Mortgages

are home loans from a banking institution. During the 1920s home buyers typically made a down payment of one-third to one-half the price of their home and mortgaged the rest. For a $3,000 home the down payment would be between $1,000 and $1,500; the rest would be covered by a home mortgage from a banking institution. Over time, the buyer would repay the bank the amount of the home loan plus interest.

**A typical bungalow-style home from the early 1900s.** *National Archives and Records Administration. Reproduced by permission.*

## The inner-city slums

As the suburbs expanded with newly built houses, the dwellings in the inner cities deteriorated. The massive influx of immigrants were forced into already overcrowded living spaces. Too poor to afford either a car or trolley fare, they had to live within close walking distance of their jobs. The once-fashionable inner-city dwellings with large rooms were subdivided into tiny rooms with little light or airflow. More

apartments meant more rent for landlords, so housing structures were hastily built on every available bit of land. The structures reached higher and higher, shutting out light to neighboring buildings. These multistory structures were referred to as tenements. The dwellings gradually grew rundown, and sanitation facilities were overwhelmed. Inner-city areas became known for poverty, crime, and filth; these areas were called slums. With the onset of the Depression, overcrowding and poverty only worsened.

## The Depression strikes a blow to housing

The Depression struck severe blows to home owners, tenement dwellers, and the construction industry. As Americans lost their jobs or saw their incomes decrease, they fell behind in mortgage payments. Failing to make payments (defaulting) on a home mortgage led to foreclosure by the holder of the mortgage, usually a bank. (*Foreclosure* means that the bank seizes and then auctions off the home owner's property to pay off the mortgage loan amount.) In 1932 between 250,000 and 275,000 people lost their homes to foreclosure. By 1933 foreclosures reached one thousand a day, and 40 to 50 percent of all home mortgages in the United States were in default.

The home financing system was collapsing. Housing prices overall had dropped by about 35 percent. A home worth $6,000 before the Depression would suddenly be worth only $3,900. Banks trying to sell foreclosed homes frequently found no buyers; and if a bank did find a buyer, it still might not get enough money from the sale to cover the entire mortgage. Banks that depended largely on mortgage payments failed and had to close their doors. Many middle-class families who lost their homes (or who were threatened with the possibility) experienced fear, uncertainty, and a taste of poverty for the first time in their lives.

**A United States Housing Authority poster encourages the cleanup of inner-city slums.** *Courtesy of the Library of Congress.*

The sale of new homes halted as people merely tried to hang on to their existing homes. With no market for new houses, the construction of residential property fell 95 percent between 1929 and 1933. Repair expenditures also fell dramatically from $50 million to $500,000. Suburban homes and buildings in the inner cities both went without repair. The condition of tenements continued to worsen.

## Ineffective programs

By the end of 1930 President Herbert Hoover (1874–1964; served 1929–33) knew that home owners' difficulties and the sagging construction industry were dragging down the already ailing economy. Almost one-third of the unemployed had been in construction. The Hoover administration tried two approaches to remedy the situation. However, both pieces of resulting legislation were flawed and proved ineffective. The Federal Home Loan Bank Act, signed by President Hoover on July 22, 1932, was designed to establish a reserve of home loan money for banking institutions. However, loan requirements were set too high. In the first two years of the act's operation, forty-one thousand applications for home loans were made. Three were approved.

Hoover's second measure was just as ineffective. The Emergency Relief and Construction Act of 1932 provided loans to corporations formed to construct low-income housing and improve housing in slums. But the act required these corporations to be exempted (excused from paying) from state taxes. Only New York had laws in place for such exemptions; other states had no public support to pass such laws. Only one project, the Knickerbockers Village in New York City, was started under this act.

## New Deal for housing

Franklin D. Roosevelt (1882–1945) became president of the United States on March 4, 1933. He knew he needed to revive the housing market if unemployment was to be conquered and banks were to again serve as mortgage lenders. Several congressmen, including Senator Robert F. Wagner (1877–1953) of New York, suggested developing grand-scale European-style housing projects. But President Roosevelt held the very American notion that the ideal home was a single, privately owned structure on a small plot of land. He had no interest in multilevel, multifamily dwellings. However, Roosevelt was a practical man and knew that urban housing problems would have to be resolved within the urban setting. So Roosevelt decided on a path of stopping foreclosures and making private homes more affordable. In 1933 and 1934 New Deal legislation concentrated on these issues as well as the related goal of stimulating the home construction industry.

On June 13, 1933, Congress passed the Home Owners' Refinancing Act, which created the Home Owners' Loan Corporation (HOLC). Next, on June 28, 1934, Congress passed the National Housing Act, which created the Federal Housing Administration (FHA). President Roosevelt also needed to address inner-city housing problems. The most important resulting legislation was the National Housing Act of 1937, better known as the Wagner-Steagall Housing Act.

## Home Owners' Loan Corporation (HOLC)

The goal of the Home Owners' Loan Corporation (HOLC) was to stop the overwhelming number of home foreclosures, which were undermining the health of banking institutions. The HOLC allocated loan money to refinance tens of thousands of mortgages that were in danger of default and foreclosure. Refinancing means setting up a loan under new repayment terms to make it easier to pay back the loan. The HOLC replaced the unworkable terms of the Federal Home Loan Bank Act, a leftover from Hoover's administration.

The two legacies of the HOLC are the amortizing mortgage and standardized appraisal methods. *Amortize* means to allow a loan to be repaid with monthly payments that are always the same amount. These payments include principal and interest, and the principal balance gradually declines until the loan is paid back in full. (Principal is the original amount of money loaned. Interest is additional money paid to the lender for use of the loan money.) The HOLC charged borrowers only 5 percent interest and allowed repayment over a fifteen-year period. This simple loan repayment plan contrasted with typical 1920s mortgages of 6 to 8

 **Edgeman Terrace**

In 1939 the Wilmington Construction Company built four hundred six-room houses north of Wilmington, Delaware. This development, called Edgeman Terrace, was the forerunner of tract home developments (similarly constructed homes built along a tract, or piece, of land) that would be built throughout the twentieth century. Backed by the Federal Housing Administration (FHA), Edgeman Terrace used standardized model homes and lot sizes, and standardized construction methods. Each home's selling price was $5,150 with a $550 cash down payment. The FHA mortgage guarantee allowed buyers to pay an incredibly low $29.61 monthly payment for twenty-five years. That payment included principal, interest, mortgage insurance, and property taxes. An apartment of the same size in New York City cost $50 a month to rent. The FHA made it cheaper for Americans to buy than to rent. Part of the New Deal legacy, this agency continues to make homes affordable for more Americans in the twenty-first century.

percent interest with only five-year repayment periods. At the end of five years the loan would not be paid back in full, so the home owner would have to borrow the remaining amount or pay the loan off in one large payment. Both of these options were all but impossible in the Depression years, and therefore many people failed to make their payments and lost their homes to bank lenders.

Standardized appraisal methods gave the HOLC a good estimate of what a house was worth so that the agency would know how much to lend the buyer for the purchase. HOLC appraisers visited the house and wrote down its characteristics, such as type of construction, repairs needed, and prices of nearby homes. HOLC appraisers across the country were trained in uniform procedures, so each appraiser's judgment would be similar and prices would be based on a firm set of standards. Amortizing mortgages and standard appraisal methods are cornerstones of the real estate and banking industries at the beginning of the twenty-first century.

The HOLC was set up as an emergency agency only. It stopped accepting loan applications in mid-1935 and issued its last loans in early 1936. By then the HOLC had refinanced up to one-fifth of all mortgaged urban homes in America, approximately 992,531 home loans, and effectively stopped the flood of foreclosures. The HOLC spent the next fifteen years collecting its payments and ended its operations in 1951.

The refinanced loans not only stopped foreclosures but also reduced the number of cases of delinquent (overdue) property taxes. With more property tax money coming in, communities could again meet payrolls for police, schools, and other services. Millions were spent on repair and remodeling of homes, putting thousands back to work in the building trades. Thousands of other jobs were stimulated in manufacturing and transportation of construction materials. Through the HOLC President Roosevelt's goals of halting foreclosures, making homes affordable, and spurring the construction industry were all realized.

# Federal Housing Administration (FHA)

The National Housing Act of 1934 established the Federal Housing Administration (FHA) as a permanent New

Deal program. The act reflected President Roosevelt's goal of stimulating the housing sector without government spending: Rather than make direct home loans, the FHA would insure the mortgage loans made by banks. If a home owner failed to make the mortgage payments, the FHA would pay the lending institution the amount that was owed. In response, bankers made loans easier to get, because they took on less risk with FHA-insured loans. Secondly, following trends set by the HOLC, the FHA required all of its insured mortgages to be amortized. However, the FHA extended the loan repayment period to twenty-five or thirty years, which greatly reduced monthly payments and allowed more people to qualify for a mortgage. These improved terms for borrowers spurred new home construction and sales. The FHA also set minimum construction standards to better ensure the quality of homes.

Unfortunately there was a downside to the FHA achievements. The FHA favored single-family projects in suburban areas. It actually contributed to inner-city decay by pulling much of the middle class out of the city into affordable suburban homes. Statistics gathered for St. Louis, Missouri, between 1935 and 1939 show that 92 percent of new homes insured by the FHA were located in suburban areas. Hence, the housing policies of the 1934 act and its amendments did not extend to the poor living in the inner cities. Soon after passage of the 1934 act, proponents for government housing programs for the needy began to push for housing programs that addressed the needs of those living in poverty in the inner cities. The first national housing bill to do so was the 1937 Wagner-Steagall Housing Act.

## Wagner-Steagall Housing Act

The Wagner-Steagall Housing Act (also known as the National Housing Act of 1937) created the United States Housing Authority (USHA). This act provided loans to local public agencies (called local housing authorities, or LHA) for construction of low-rent housing projects. Once a project was complete, the USHA would determine how much rent low-income families could afford and then would make up the difference between what the families paid and the actual cost of providing the housing. Another important feature of the act was a provision for clearing out slums. For every new dwelling unit built, a slum housing unit had to be torn down. This was called "equivalent elimination."

The problem with this act was that the forming of local housing authorities was purely voluntary. If a community did not want to tarnish its image with low-cost government housing, it could refuse to form a local housing authority. Because of this, the Wagner-Steagall Housing Act had very limited success. Only 188,000 individual family units were under construction or completed by January 1, 1941.

## Powerful impact

New Deal legislation for banking and housing eliminated much of the risk from daily living. The Federal Deposit Insurance Corporation (FDIC) assured everyday Americans that their bank deposits would be protected and paid back to them if their banks failed. The Federal Housing Administration (FHA) insured mortgages so the banks that made the mortgage loans carried little risk. The FHA also set building standards for home construction, ensuring that Americans could buy good-quality homes with the money they borrowed. The Home Owners' Loan Corporation (HOLC) introduced low-interest, long-term amortizing mortgages and standardized appraisal practices, both of which continue to benefit home buyers and lenders in the twenty-first century.

## For More Information

### Books

Benston, George J. *The Separation of Commercial and Investment Banking: The Glass-Steagall Act Revisited and Reconsidered*. New York, NY: Oxford University Press, 1990.

Burns, Helen M. *The American Banking Community and New Deal Banking Reforms, 1933–1935*. Westport, CT: Greenwood Press, 1974.

Duchscherer, Paul. *The Bungalow: America's Arts and Crafts Home*. New York, NY: Penguin Books USA, 1995.

Fitch, Thomas P. *Dictionary of Banking Terms*. New York, NY: Barron's, 1990.

Glaab, Charles N., and A. Theodore Brown. *A History of Urban America*. 3rd ed. New York, NY: Macmillan, 1983.

Jackson, Kenneth T. *Crabgrass Frontier: The Suburbanization of the United States.* New York, NY: Oxford University Press, 1985.

Kennedy, Susan E. *The Banking Crisis of 1933.* Lexington, KY: University Press of Kentucky, 1975.

Lancaster, Clay. *The American Bungalow, 1880–1930.* New York, NY: Dover Publications, 1995.

Wicker, Elmus. *The Banking Panics of the Great Depression.* New York, NY: Cambridge University Press, 1996.

Winslow, Susan. *Brother, Can You Spare a Dime? America from the Wall Street Crash to Pearl Harbor: An Illustrated Documentary.* New York, NY: Paddington Press, 1976.

## Web Sites

*American Bankers Association.* http://www.aba.com (accessed on August 14, 2002).

*Federal Deposit Insurance Corporation.* http://www.fdic.gov (accessed on August 14, 2002).

*Federal Reserve System.* http://federalreserve.gov (accessed on August 14, 2002).

*Housing and Urban Development (HUD).* http://www.hud.gov (accessed on August 14, 2002).

*Lower East Side Tenement Museum.* http://www.tenement.org (accessed on August 14, 2002).

# 4  Farm Relief

Throughout U.S. history farming has been an important way of life for American families and essential for the nation's economic health. During the first two decades of the twentieth century farmers experienced economic growth and prosperity. The period of 1909 through 1914 is often referred to as the golden age of agriculture. By then, the agricultural character of the various regions of the United States had become well established: Dairy and poultry farms dominated in the Northeast, tobacco and cotton farms in the South, corn and hog production in the Midwest, wheat farms in the Great Plains, open-range livestock grazing in the western states, and vegetables, cotton, and orchards in California.

When World War I (1914–18) disrupted food production in Europe, U.S. farmers supplied Europeans with food. However, at the conclusion of World War I, the resumption of European food production brought a rapid decline in demand for U.S. farm products. The decline led to large surpluses (more supply than was needed) and falling prices in the United States, but farmers continued to produce at their World War I levels to try to cover their operating expenses. Although

most parts of the U.S. economy prospered during the 1920s, the decade proved to be a harsh, lean time for farmers. Farmers became angry and frustrated by the lack of action by President Calvin Coolidge (1872–1933; served 1923–29), who refused to address their problems. When Herbert Hoover (1874–1964; served 1929–33) took office in 1929, the economy appeared to be healthy except in agriculture. And times would only get harder for farmers: In October 1929 the New York Stock Exchange crashed, signaling the start of the Great Depression. The Great Depression, which lasted until 1941, was the worst economic crisis in U.S. history.

In an effort to help U.S. farmers and manufacturers, Congress passed the Hawley-Smoot Tariff Act in 1930. A tariff is a tax charged on imported products. The U.S. tariff was intended to make foreign goods cost more than homegrown and American-made products; that way, people in the United States would be more likely to buy the American goods, thus sustaining U.S. farmers and manufacturers. Unfortunately

**Farmers unable to make a living during the Great Depression were often forced to auction off their property in order to pay off bank loans. Here, a farm auction takes place in Hastings, Nebraska.** *Courtesy of the Library of Congress.*

**Striking dairy farmers spill milk from a nonstriker's truck near Harvard, Illinois, where they are operating a blockade.** *Corbis Corporation. Reproduced by permission.*

the act caused other nations to also enact protective tariffs. These tariffs soon decreased world trade by 40 percent. Export of U.S. farming products had supplied 25 percent of all U.S. farm income, but these exports halted when other countries adopted their own tariffs. As a result, farming income, which supported between 25 and 30 percent of Americans, was further devastated.

The U.S. economy continued to spiral downward between late 1929 and 1932. The U.S. banking system was in turmoil as more and more banks failed; manufacturing dramatically decreased; and with at least 25 percent of the workforce unemployed, many Americans were losing their land and homes. By 1932 farmers were the hardest hit by the economic disaster. Their income was one-third of what it had been in 1929, and it had been dropping steadily throughout the 1920s. Between 1929 and 1932 approximately four hundred thousand farms were lost through foreclosure. (Foreclosure happens when an individual falls behind on property loan payments; it means that the bank that made the loan takes the property and sells it to recover the loaned money.) Farmers were dismayed by the federal government's lack of action.

## Revolt: "farmers' holidays"

President Hoover, like Coolidge before him, firmly believed that government should not take an active role in relief or in economic reform. Angered by Hoover's failure to help in raising farm prices, desperate farmers protested: They burned crops, dumped milk on highways rather than sell it at a loss, and organized strikes, refusing to take their produce to market for weeks. They hoped these "farmers' holidays" would reduce the nation's supply of farm produce and raise prices. Occasionally violence erupted as farmers blocked highways in Nebraska and Iowa to prevent food from reaching markets.

## New Deal for farmers

With the entire U.S. economy worsening, Franklin D. Roosevelt (1882–1945) ran as the Democratic presidential candidate in the November 1932 election. Promising a "new deal" for Americans, Roosevelt easily defeated the unpopular Hoover. New Deal legislation was designed to bring relief and then recovery on many economic fronts, but President Roosevelt (served 1933–45) gave special priority to federal government assistance for farmers.

Roosevelt named agricultural expert Henry Wallace (1888–1965) of Iowa as secretary of agriculture; Roosevelt chose Rexford Tugwell (1891–1979), a close adviser, as assistant secretary of agriculture. Everyone recognized that for agricultural assistance to gain acceptance, the programs would have to be operated locally rather than by federal officials in Washington, D.C. On March 16, 1933, only twelve days after Roosevelt's inauguration, Wallace gathered farm leaders from around the country in Washington to draft a revolutionary farm bill. This group described its goal as "agricultural adjustment" of farmers' income: how to decrease farm production but still allow farmers enough income to survive and regroup.

## Agricultural Adjustment Act

On May 12, 1933, Roosevelt signed the Agricultural Adjustment Act into law. The act established the Agricultural Adjustment Administration (AAA). The AAA was Roosevelt's first New Deal economic recovery program directed toward farmers. At their March meeting the farm leaders had made reduction of farm production their main focus, and the AAA reflected this focus: The AAA would pay farmers to limit their crop production. Reducing crops was the only way to get crop prices to rise. The crops in greatest surplus were wheat, cotton, corn, and hogs. Farmers who agreed to limit crop production according to the AAA's plan would receive government payments. The production control program was completely voluntary, but with the poor economic condition of farms, many farmers felt they had no choice but to participate. AAA checks became the chief source of income for some farmers. The income helped them avoid losing their farms to the bank; it also allowed them to buy goods, which helped other industries. To raise the funds needed to pay farmers for reducing production, a tax was placed on processing companies—flour mills, textile mills, and meat packinghouses. The AAA gave county agents from state agricultural extension services and local farmer committees authority to oversee the program at the local level.

Not unexpectedly, some problems in reducing crop surplus immediately arose. The Agricultural Adjustment Act did not pass until May 1933, so many crops had already been planted. The AAA offered to pay farmers to plow under more than ten million acres of cotton. To those farmers the AAA paid out $112 million dollars in the summer of 1933. Hogs were also in great surplus that summer. Six million hogs were slaughtered and discarded in September 1933.

Many criticized the AAA's policy of destruction, because Americans were going hungry. In response to the outcry, Secretary of Agriculture Wallace arranged for the Federal Surplus Relief Corporation, formed in October 1933, to purchase over a hundred million pounds of baby pork (the meat of hogs) and distribute it to people enrolled in relief programs.

## Reducing farm debt

Another key focus for farm relief was farm debt reduction. President Roosevelt created the Farm Credit Administration (FCA) to make loans more available to farmers. Congress provided funding for the agency by passing the Emergency Farm Mortgage Act in May 1933 and the Farm Credit Act in June. The Farm Credit Act also created a system of banking institutions for farmers. The FCA replaced the Federal Farm Board, an agency established by former president Hoover, which had made 7,800 loans to farmers totaling $28 million. In the FCA's first twelve-month period, it approved 541,000 loans for $1.4 billion. The FCA program gave hundreds of thousands of families the means to keep their farms.

On January 31, 1934, Congress passed the Farm Mortgage Refinancing Act, which provided money to refinance farm home loans. (*Refinance* means to set up new, easier repayment terms.) In June 1934 Congress passed the Frazier-Lemke Farm Bankruptcy Act, which limited the ability of banks to take away the farms of those experiencing severe financial hardships.

## The Dust Bowl

By the summer of 1931 a drought (an extended period of little or no rainfall) began to take a toll on the Great Plains region of the United States. The drought would soon solve wheat overproduction problems in the region. However, the extended drought became the worst in U.S. history, not ending until 1939.

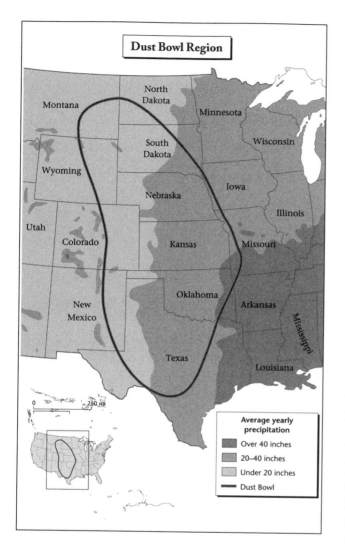

**Dust Bowl Region**

Montana · North Dakota · Minnesota · Wyoming · South Dakota · Wisconsin · Utah · Nebraska · Iowa · Illinois · Colorado · Kansas · Missouri · New Mexico · Oklahoma · Arkansas · Texas · Louisiana · Mississippi

0 ——— 250 mi

**Average yearly precipitation**
- Over 40 inches
- 20–40 inches
- Under 20 inches
- Dust Bowl

The Dust Bowl region covered much of the Great Plains throughout the 1930s.

The drought prevented winter wheat crops (planted in the fall of 1931) from growing enough to protect the soil from yearly windstorms that came from the north. By late January 1932 dust storms began to blow over the southern Great Plains. Winds of sixty miles per hour swept across the Texas Panhandle, and black dust clouds reached ten thousand feet into the air. And the storms steadily worsened. The hardest-hit areas were western Kansas, eastern Colorado, northeastern New Mexico, and the Oklahoma and Texas Panhandles. Collectively, these areas were known as the Dust Bowl. Dust storms had always occurred in these areas, but in the 1930s they were far more severe. In the preceding twenty years farmers had removed millions of acres of natural grass sod to plant wheat, and hundreds of thousands of cattle had been driven north from Texas to Kansas year after year. Native grasses had slowly been destroyed. When the drought arrived in 1931 and wheat failed to grow, the soils were left exposed to the strong winds that blew over the land. Millions of tons of blinding black dirt would boil up into massive clouds and sweep across the plains. The storms brought periods of total darkness during daylight hours and left behind long half-light periods as particles of dust stayed suspended in the air.

The thick clouds of dust would force businesses and schools to close as residents sought shelter. People got dust in their eyes and noses and grit between their teeth. Dust piled up like snow against houses and fences. People would hang wet sheets in windows and doorways to catch the dust. Housecleaning after a storm involved removing buckets of dirt. Baking in the oven was preferable to cooking on the

stovetop, because the oven offered better protection from dust. Meals were eaten immediately after preparation; otherwise dust would cover them. The storms were especially hard on farm animals. Range cattle died in the fields with two inches of dirt lining their stomachs. Chickens were smothered in henhouses.

By the mid-1930s thousands of families had lost crops and livestock, and they began to leave the region. Most had lost their farms to foreclosure. They would pack a car with all their belongings and simply drive away. This migration out of the Dust Bowl was the largest migration in U.S. history. Many headed to the agricultural fields of California, Oregon, and Washington.

## New Deal for drought victims

For those who remained on their land within the Dust Bowl, federal government relief often was their only

## Black Sunday

The worst of all the dust storms descended on Kansas on April 14, 1935. Severe storms had been blowing for weeks, destroying millions of acres of wheat in Kansas and Nebraska. But the sun had broken out in Kansas on Sunday, April 14, and people ventured out for church and other activities. Then with sudden fury a black cloud appeared on the horizon. It descended with terrifying energy—sixty- to seventy-mile-per-hour winds—and total blackness. Though few people died from this or other such dust storms, many suffered serious lung ailments, commonly called dust pneumonia. This storm, and other major dust storms, also caused substantial economic hardship for farmers and rural communities due to the major loss of topsoil and damaged houses and farm property. The April 14 storm literally buried farm equipment and partially covered houses in dust dunes created within hours. The day became known as "Black Sunday."

means of survival. In addition to various debt relief programs, the Agricultural Adjustment Administration (AAA) created the Emergency Cattle Purchase Program in May 1934. The program purchased and destroyed thousands of starving cattle. With the Drought Relief Service coordinating relief activities, the meat from cattle that still had food value was given to the Federal Surplus Relief Corporation for distribution to needy families.

Despite relief efforts, by the mid-1930s thousands of small farmers had lost their farms. People complained that the programs of the AAA favored large landowners and large-scale corporate farming over small family farms. Responding to the small farmers' needs, President Roosevelt signed the Emergency Relief Appropriation Act in April 1935; the act included $525 million for drought relief. On April 30, Roosevelt signed an executive order establishing the Resettlement Administration (RA) to assist small farmers who did not own land but who rented land from large landowners. This group of small farmers included tenant farmers, who used their own tools; sharecroppers, whose tools were provided by the landowners; and migrant workers, who followed the seasonal crop harvest and harvested for their living. Tenant farmers and sharecroppers both had to give part of their harvest to the landowner. The goal of the RA was to resettle these poverty-stricken farmers, moving them from poor land to more-productive land that they might eventually buy. The majority of farm families eligible for resettlement lived in the Dust Bowl region or in the Southeast.

There were many critics of the RA, including some within the Roosevelt administration. They thought efforts to preserve the small family farm were misguided. They believed the only real future for U.S. agriculture was in large commercial farms that could make use of new mechanized farm machines designed for mass production. Critics of the RA feared that establishing areas of small farms would only create isolated pockets of lasting poverty.

Given these concerns, in July 1937 Congress passed the Bankhead-Jones Farm Tenancy Act, which made low-interest loans available to tenant farmers and small landowners so they could purchase equipment and/or expand their own land. A few months later President Roosevelt created the Farm Security Administration (FSA). The RA and all its departments were absorbed by the FSA. Although it did not abandon the resettlement program, the FSA also loaned money to families for necessities (such as food, clothing, seed, feed, and fertilizer) to sustain them where they were.

## Okies

By the mid-1930s hundreds of thousands of refugees from the Dust Bowl—western Kansas, eastern Colorado, northern New Mexico, and the Oklahoma and Texas Panhandles—traveled west in search of jobs in the agricultural fields of California. Others came from sharecropping farms in the Southeast. They piled all their belongings in an old car, loaded up the family, and headed west. A few walked, pulling their belongings in a cart behind them. Rarely did they find better conditions in the West. Most became migrant workers living in severe poverty and unwanted by local residents. Californians called the migrants "Okies" (short for "Oklahomans"), regardless of what state they were actually from. The Resettlement Administration built several camps for the migrants in an attempt to improve sanitation and protect them from hostile local residents.

## Conserving the soil

The dust storms were a social and economic disaster for families in the Dust Bowl; they were also an environmental disaster. Hard, bare ground was left after valuable topsoil blew away. At the time, little was known about how to prevent wind erosion. As early as 1930, Congress had authorized the Department of Agriculture to establish a series of soil erosion experiment stations and set up model plots of land. In 1933, as the dust storms roared across the Great Plains, the Soil Erosion Service (SES) was created under the Department of the Interior to operate the stations and promote farmer cooperation. Hugh Hammond Bennett, soil scientist and the "father of soil conservation," was named to head the SES. The SES soil scientists worked with farmers to encourage new

farming practices that conserved the soil. For example, rather than burning the last stubble of wheat after harvest or allowing livestock to graze on it, farmers left the stubble in the ground; this helped keep soil in place. In addition, trees were planted in rows to provide windbreaks.

On April 27, 1935, Roosevelt signed the Soil Conservation Act, which shifted the SES to the Department of Agriculture, where it was renamed the Soil Conservation Service (SCS). The SCS greatly expanded the SES program and established an extensive conservation (the planned management of natural resources, such as soil and forests) program. The latest soil conservation techniques, such as contour plowing (plowing across a hill rather than up and down), were demonstrated to farmers. To encourage farmers to practice the new soil conservation techniques, the SCS offered to pay farmers about a dollar an acre for areas where they applied the new techniques.

**A young Oklahoma mother and her two children, stranded in Imperial Valley, California.** *Courtesy of the Franklin D. Roosevelt Library.*

On February 27, 1937, Roosevelt introduced a program encouraging states to pass their own conservation laws. Farmers could then establish their own local conservation districts. These districts allowed expansion of the conservation programs beyond the federally operated demonstration areas. The SCS programs and local programs of conservation began to take effect: By 1938 it was estimated that 65 percent less soil was blowing across the plains, despite the continuing drought.

West of the Dust Bowl other conservation concerns prompted more New Deal legislation. Ranchers had grazed livestock on open public rangeland since the mid-nineteenth century without any regulations. (Public land consists of millions of acres of western lands never settled because of lack of water, remoteness, or poor desert soils.) Ranchers allowed cattle and sheep to overgraze the land, and this destroyed the natural grasses of the rangelands. In 1934 Congress passed the Taylor Grazing Act to regulate grazing on public land. Much tighter control of public land became the policy of the federal government from that time on. The work of the Civilian Conservation Corps (CCC) proved invaluable to both the SCS and to rangeland improvement. The CCC built fences, planted trees as windbreaks, and made other range improvements (see Riding the Rails chapter).

## Supreme Court strikes down the Agricultural Adjustment Act

In January 1936 the U.S. Supreme Court struck a blow to New Deal agricultural programs by ruling the Agricultural Adjustment Act unconstitutional in *United States v. Butler*. The Court ruled against food processing companies being taxed to support the Agricultural Adjustment Administration's programs. Congress responded immediately with passage of the Soil Conservation and Domestic Allotment Act. Under the new act farmers were paid for soil conservation and for planting crops that deplete the soil the least. This act proved somewhat ineffective because not enough farmers voluntarily followed its guidelines. Therefore, in 1938 Congress passed a new Agricultural Adjustment Act, which made the features of the Allotment Act permanent and helped regulate farm production.

## Benefits of farm relief

Despite the Supreme Court ruling in 1936, Roosevelt considered farm relief and recovery measures some of the most successful New Deal programs. Producing positive results quickly, the Agricultural Adjustment Administration and other farm programs were among the strongest of New Deal programs. Although no strong recovery resulted, the agricultural decline that had begun in 1920 was halted. Farm income increased approximately 50 percent between 1932 and 1936. Prices of farm products rose 67 percent. Farm debt decreased by a billion dollars. The federal government replaced banks and insurance companies as the key holder of farm mortgage debt.

# Farm Security Administration photographs: A powerful documentary tool

Photographs are some of the best records of the impact of the Great Depression. During the 1930s documentary photography reached a high point in the United States. (Documentary photography produces photographs that capture a subject so well that the pictures tell a story about an individual, a situation, a structure, or a landscape.) The documentary photographs of the living and working conditions Americans endured during the Depression became part of the historical record of the United States.

In the 1930s a handful of photographers employed by the Resettlement Administration (RA), later the Farm Security Administration (FSA), produced tens of thousands of extraordinary images of American life. The RA/FSA photographers turned their cameras to poor sharecroppers and tenant farmers, to black American cotton pickers, coal miners in Appalachia, migrant families harvesting crops in California, and flood victims along the Mississippi and Ohio Rivers. Taken in black and white, the simple, stark, and powerful photos appeared in newspapers, magazines, and special exhibits. The photos helped the American public understand the needs of those in poverty and make sense out of social welfare programs created under Roosevelt's administration. The photographs, commonly known as the FSA photographs, span a six-year period, from 1935 to 1941. For most Americans at the start of the twenty-first century, images of America in the 1930s are based on the FSA photographs.

# Historical Section of the Resettlement Administration

The collection of FSA photographs got its start when Roosevelt appointed Rexford Guy Tugwell (1891–1979) to lead the Resettlement Administration (RA). Tugwell knew that in order to carry out the agency's duties he would have to rally public support. He had published a book in 1925, *American Economic Life and the Means of Its Improvement*, in which he used many photographs to dramatize American life; he understood the power of photographs. So Tugwell established the Historical Section in the RA's Division of Information and charged it with photographing rural poverty and the condition of the land itself. Tugwell named Roy E. Stryker to administer the Historical Section.

## Roy E. Stryker

Roy Stryker (1893–1975) had done the photographic research for Tugwell's book and had become familiar with the work of photographers Jacob Riis (1849–1914) and Lewis Hine (1874–1940), both of whom had an interest in social reform. Although not a photographer himself, Stryker understood how effectively documentary photography could illustrate the conditions that confronted the RA. Stryker also had an encyclopedic knowledge of U.S. geography and the economic factors that affected each area. With a missionary-like eagerness, Stryker set out to make the rest of the nation understand the problems of rural citizens. Stryker's first duty at the Historical Section was to gather a staff of photographers. He looked for idealism and talent rather than photographers with established reputations. The pictures taken by these photographers would tell the story of the rural poor to millions of Americans.

Before Stryker would send photographers into the field, he required them to carefully research their assigned areas. Stryker would then follow up with his own lessons on each area; he loved to teach and did so with great enthusiasm. Then Stryker would outline an assignment using "shooting scripts." The scripts were general notes about what types of pictures were needed, such as where the people met, what a person saw outside his or her kitchen window, what wall decorations were in homes, and the condition of the land around homes. Finally the energetic, persuasive Stryker would review the entire scope of the assignment immediately before a photographer's departure. Both Stryker and his photographers enjoyed these pep talks.

Although Stryker specified what pictures he needed from an area, he also allowed his photographers the freedom to shoot anything of interest that would help tell the story of a region. John Collier, one of Stryker's photographers, once said that his assignment was to photograph the smell of

An FSA photograph taken
by Arthur Rothstein
depicting the eviction of
sharecroppers from a farm
in Missouri, 1939. *Courtesy
of the Library of Congress.*

apple pie and burning leaves in autumn in New England.
With their pictures the FSA photographers interpreted the
lives of migrants, the unemployed, the displaced, and the
rural poor. The photographs were not sensational; they focused on real people and situations. They made it easier for
the American public to understand the upheavals resulting
from economic and weather-related disasters.

## The FSA photographers

Stryker assembled a remarkable pool of photographers
for his Historical Section. In July 1935 Stryker hired Arthur
Rothstein, a former student of his at Columbia University,
and Dorothea Lange (1895–1965), who was eventually the
best known of the RA/FSA photographers. Two of Rothstein's
most famous pictures are "Dust Storm, Cimarron County [Ok-
lahoma], 1936," depicting a father and his sons striding to
shelter during a dust storm, and "The Skull, 1936," pho-

tographed in Pennington County in the South Dakota Badlands. "The Skull," a picture of a cow's skull on parched land, hinted that the desert would soon claim the land that ranchers had overgrazed with livestock. Within weeks of the publication of both pictures, a congressional committee went to the Badlands of South Dakota to investigate.

Dorothea Lange was working on the West Coast, photographing the condition of migrant workers in California, when Stryker hired her on the strength of her photos alone. The two did not meet until nine months later. Lange's photographs are full of compassion. Her most famous picture is "Migrant Mother." Lange encountered the portrayed woman and the woman's three daughters at a pea pickers' migrant camp in California's Nipomo Valley. The *San Francisco News* ran a story accompanied by two of Lange's photos from the camp on March 10, 1936. Relief authorities immediately sent supplies and food to the camp.

One of Arthur Rothstein's more famous photos, "Dust Storm, Cimarron County [Oklahoma], 1936."
*AP/Wide World Photo. Reproduced by permission.*

A talented painter, Ben Shahn (1898–1969), also came to Stryker's attention in mid-1935. Besides his painting skill, Shahn possessed the ability to take photographs that screamed for social justice. Many of Shahn's photographs went into the Historical Section files even though he was only on Stryker's payroll during the summer of 1938.

Walker Evans (1903–1975), the true photographic artist of the group, came to the Historical Section in October 1935. Evans had a nonconformist artistic spirit that often conflicted with Stryker's organized approach to photographic assignments. Evans often disappeared for months on assignment. Such absences riled Stryker, who liked his photographers to keep in touch when they were in the field. Nevertheless, when Evans resurfaced, he did so with flawless, amazing photographs that kept Stryker in awe of his talent. In 1936 Evans took a leave of absence from the Historical Section to work with author James Agee (1909–1955) in Hale County, Alabama. Describing the life of rural poverty there, Evans's photographs and Agee's words appeared in 1941 in the book *Let Us Now Praise Famous Men,* an American classic. In mid-1937 Evans and Stryker parted ways permanently. Along with Shahn, Evans was one of the most artistically influential photographers of Stryker's group.

Carl Mydans also came to Stryker in 1935. He contributed photos of northeastern cities before taking a long assignment in the South. Mydans stayed with the Historical Section less than a year before moving to the new photo magazine *Life* in October 1936. Taking his place was Russell Lee. Lee, trained as a painter, would become a core photographer of the group and stay with Stryker until 1942. Dedicated to publicizing the struggle of Americans affected in one way or another by the Depression, he headed to Michigan, Wisconsin, and Minnesota. Later he would do some of his best-known work in Pie Town, New Mexico.

John Vachon, an unemployed graduate student in Washington, D.C., was thrilled to be hired by Stryker in 1936 as an "assistant messenger." In his later years Vachon laughed at his eagerness to take that humble title, but his college major of Elizabethan poetry had ill prepared him for a job during the Depression; so he was grateful for any work. Vachon advanced to junior file clerk and then, he noted, junior file clerk "with a camera." Vachon's interest and skill in pho-

## Life and Look Magazines

The first important American photo magazines were *Life* and *Look*. Henry Luce (1898–1967), founder of *Time* magazine, decided that pictures as well as print could tell an interesting story. He printed the first issue of *Life* in 1936, and it was an instant success. Americans lined up to buy issues. *Look* was founded in 1938 by Gardner Cowles to compete with *Life*. Both photo magazines were interested in finding drama in everyday life and in covering big events. Coverage included construction of the Grand Coulee and Bonneville Dams in Washington and Oregon, projects of the Tennessee Valley Authority; poverty in the South; the Dust Bowl; and military buildups in Europe leading up to World War II (1939–45).

One of *Life*'s first staff photographers was Margaret Bourke-White (1906–1971). She created some of the first photographic essays ever attempted. For *Life*'s first issue she completed a photographic story on Montana boomtowns. Bourke-White worked with author Erskine Caldwell (1903–1987) to produce a book about the severe conditions in the rural South during the Depression. The book, *You Have Seen Their Faces* (1937), received a great deal of attention in *Life*.

tography steadily grew, and Stryker saw that Vachon had a future in the field. By 1940 Vachon was an official junior photographer with, as Dorothea Lange put it, the ability to find subjects whose desperation made viewers uncomfortable.

The last three photographers to join the Historical Section were Marion Post Wolcott, Jack Delano, and John Collier. Wolcott produced some of the finest photography of children in the Historical Section file. Delano was skilled in presenting the living conditions of miners but also did in-depth work on migrant worker camps on the East Coast. Stryker sent him on assignment in 1941 to the Virgin Islands and Puerto Rico. (Delano ended up staying in Puerto Rico and made it his permanent home.) Collier contributed a wide range of photos, from Portuguese fishermen in Rhode Island to Mexican Americans in New Mexico.

## FSA/OWI photographs online

By December 1941 the FSA's budget was slashed as the United States entered World War II (1939–45). The Historical Section was transferred to the Office of War Information (OWI). Stryker still headed the Historical Section, and a few of the FSA photographers followed him: Russell Lee, John Vachon, and John Collier. Their mission switched to focusing on America's war preparation, showing America's best can-do side. Aircraft factories and women in the labor force were important subjects for the camera lenses. In 1943 Stryker prepared to leave the OWI to take a photography job at Standard Oil of New Jersey. Paul Vanderbilt, a curator of collections, carefully organized and boxed the FSA/OWI prints and negatives, but their ultimate destination was unknown. Poet Archibald MacLeish (1892–1982), an old friend of Stryker and at that time serving as librarian of Congress, gave them a permanent home at the Library of Congress in Washington, D.C. The boxes contained 277,000 negatives and 77,000 prints—the combined work of the RA, FSA, and OWI—and these are collectively known as the FSA/OWI collection. At the beginning of the twenty-first century the entire remarkable collection can be viewed online at http://memory.loc.gov/ammem/fsowhome.html (the Library of Congress's Internet site for the American Memory program).

# For More Information

## Farm relief

### Books

Agee, James, and Walker Evans. *Let Us Now Praise Famous Men: Three Tenant Families.* Reprint. Boston, MA: Houghton Mifflin, 2000.

Hamilton, David E. *From New Day to New Deal: American Farm Policy from Hoover to Roosevelt, 1928–1933.* Chapel Hill, NC: University of North Carolina Press, 1991.

Hurt, Douglas. *American Agriculture: A Brief History.* Ames, IA: Iowa State University Press, 1994.

Perkins, Van L. *Crisis in Agriculture: The Agricultural Adjustment Administration and the New Deal, 1933.* Berkeley, CA: University of California Press, 1969.

### Web Sites

*U.S. Bureau of Land Management.* http://www.blm.gov (accessed on August 12, 2002).

*U.S. Department of Agriculture.* http://www.usda.gov (accessed on August 12, 2002).

# Dust Bowl

## Books

Booth, David. *The Dust Bowl.* Toronto, Ontario, Canada: Kids Can Press, 1997.

Davidson, James A. *Patches on My Britches: Memories of Growing Up in the Dust Bowl.* Bloomington, IN: 1st Books Library, 1998.

Ganzel, Bill. *Dust Bowl Descent.* Lincoln, NE: University of Nebraska Press, 1984.

Meltzer, Milton. *Driven from the Land: The Story of the Dust Bowl.* New York, NY: Benchmark Books, 2000.

Rutland, Robert A. *A Boyhood in the Dust Bowl, 1926–1934.* Niwot, CO: University Press of Colorado, 1997.

Shindo, Charles J. *Dust Bowl Migrants in the American Imagination.* Lawrence, KS: University Press of Kansas, 1997.

Stanley, Jerry. *Children of the Dust Bowl: The True Story of the School at Weedpatch.* New York, NY: Crown Publishing, 1992.

Worster, Donald. *Dust Bowl: The Southern Plains in the 1930s.* New York, NY: Oxford University Press, 1979.

## Web Sites

*National Association of Conservation Districts (NACD).* http://www.nacdnet.org (accessed on August 12, 2002).

*National Resources Conservation Service (NRCS).* http://www.nrcs.usda.gov (accessed on August 12, 2002).

# FSA photographers

## Books

Garver, Thomas H. *Just Before the War: Urban America from 1935 to 1941 As Seen by Photographers of the Farm Security Administration.* New York, NY: October House, 1968.

Hurley, F. Jack. *Portrait of a Decade: Roy Stryker and the Development of Documentary Photography in the Thirties.* Baton Rouge, LA: Louisiana State University Press, 1966.

O'Neal, Hank. *A Vision Shared: A Classic Portrait of America and Its People, 1935–1943.* New York, NY: St. Martin's Press, 1976.

Reid, Robert L., and Larry A. Viskochil, eds. *Chicago and Downstate: Illinois As Seen by the Farm Security Administration Photographers, 1936–1943.* Urbana, IL: University of Illinois Press, 1989.

Rothstein, Arthur. *The Depression Years.* New York, NY: Dover Publications, 1978.

Stryker, Roy E., and Nancy Wood. *In This Proud Land: America 1935–1943 As Seen in the FSA Photographs.* Greenwich, CT: New York Graphic Society, 1973.

Thompson, Kathleen, and Hilary MacAustin, eds. *Children of the Depression.* Bloomington, IN: Indiana University Press, 2001.

## Web Sites

"America from the Great Depression to World War II: Photographs from the FSA-OWI, 1935–1945." *American Memory (Library of Congress).* http://memory.loc.gov/ammem/fsowhome.html (accessed on August 12, 2002).

*Franklin Delano Roosevelt Library.* http://www.fdrlibrary.marist.edu (accessed August 12, 2002).

*Life* Magazine. http://www.life.com (accessed August 12, 2002).

# Works Progress Administration

Harry Hopkins (1890–1946) was President Franklin D. Roosevelt's friend, adviser, key relief coordinator, and head of the Works Progress Administration (WPA). In a 1933 radio address that was later published in June Hopkins's 1999 book, *Harry Hopkins: Sudden Hero, Brash Performer,* Hopkins said: "Who are these fellow-citizens? Are they tramps? Are they hoboes and ne'erdowells? Are they unemployables? Are they people who are no good and who are incompetent? Take a look at them, if you have not, and see who they are. There is hardly a person...who does not know of an intimate friend, people whom you have known all your life, fine hard-working, upstanding men and women who have gone overboard and been caught up in this.... They are carpenters, bricklayers, artisans, architects, engineers, clerks, stenographers, doctors, dentists, farmers, ministers."

It was for these carpenters, bricklayers, engineers, and other workers that President Roosevelt (1882–1945; served 1933–45) created the Works Progress Adminstration. Established in 1935, the WPA was a unique program designed to get the unemployed off relief rolls by providing jobs at mini-

"Laborers Wanted": Men line up to apply for jobs clearing snow in New York City, January 1934. *AP/Wide World Photo. Reproduced by permission.*

mal pay until workers could find jobs in private business. Besides employing regular laborers, the WPA extended its programs to include unemployed artists, musicians, writers, and actors. Innovative and controversial, these programs spurred growth in American art.

The Great Depression, the worst economic downturn in U.S. history, began with the crash of the stock market in late 1929. The economy steadily worsened in the early 1930s, and by 1933 over twelve million Americans—25 percent of the workforce—were unemployed. In the first few months of his presidency, Roosevelt introduced the New Deal, an array of government-sponsored social and economic programs designed to bring relief to the struggling nation. The WPA became a key program in the New Deal.

From May 1935 to July 1943 the WPA provided millions of people with work. However, because of the overwhelming number of unemployed, the program was unable to reach many of those who were eligible. So millions more had to rely on state and local relief organizations, which were often ill prepared and unable to provide adequate help. Nevertheless, the WPA was immensely important to a great many people, putting money in their pockets and giving them hope for the future. It was a bold experiment in hard times.

## Beginning of work relief

Work relief was a concept Franklin Roosevelt had successfully employed while he was governor of New York (1929–33). Instead of providing direct relief, or giving money directly to the needy and expecting nothing in return, work relief programs required recipients to earn the money by performing work for the public benefit. Roosevelt felt that direct relief was damaging to self-respect, and he had become a strong believer in work relief.

The idea of work relief quickly became part of the New Deal. On April 5, 1933, a month after taking office as president, Roosevelt launched the Civilian Conservation Corps (CCC). The CCC was a work relief program designed to employ young men to build hiking trails, fight forest fires, lay telephone lines, and build dams. Later that year, with winter weather approaching and people needing money for shelter and food, Roosevelt established the Civil Works Administration (CWA) to provide temporary jobs to a few million of the unemployed. The CWA became the largest employer in the nation's history, putting four million people to work through the winter on projects such as cleaning neighborhoods and digging drainage ditches.

The most ambitious early New Deal work relief program was the Public Works Administration (PWA), created in

**A WPA poster, by Albert M. Bender, promoting the Civilian Conservation Corps.** *Courtesy of the Library of Congress.*

June 1933. Under the direction of Secretary of the Interior Harold Ickes (1874–1952), the PWA employed workers to construct thousands of new public facilities across the country. The projects included hundreds of municipal water systems, hospitals, schools, and major dams.

## Works Progress Administration is created

By 1935 the Depression continued, and unemployment remained above 20 percent. To rejuvenate relief and recovery efforts, Roosevelt pushed through a new wave of economic programs. Among these was the Works Progress Administration, created in May 1935. In terms of the number of people it employed, the money it expended, and the number of projects it undertook, the WPA was the largest work relief program ever attempted. At its peak, the WPA employed thirty thousand administrators and an average of 2.3 million workers each year between 1935 and 1940.

Earlier New Deal work relief programs had largely been left to the states to administer. However, the WPA was to be completely administered by the federal government. Roosevelt appointed Harry Hopkins (1890–1946), his trusted adviser and head of earlier New Deal programs, to lead the WPA. Hopkins was a social worker with years of experience directing relief and work relief programs; many of those years were spent working for Roosevelt in the New York state government. So as not to compete with private enterprise, Hopkins kept WPA wages significantly below what similar jobs would pay in the private sector, even though those jobs were unavailable. WPA projects were also carefully chosen so that private businesses would not have to compete with the federal government. WPA regulations required that 90 percent of those hired had to come from existing relief rolls and that only one member of a family could be hired.

Seventy-five percent of WPA enrollees worked on engineering and construction projects. Located in almost every county in the nation, WPA workers were highly productive. They built or repaired 1.2 million miles of culverts (drainage pipes under roads), laid 24,000 miles of sidewalks, built almost 600,000 miles in new roads, repaired 32,000 miles of existing roads, built 75,000 bridges and repaired another 42,000, installed 23,000 miles of storm and sanitary sewers, and constructed 880 sewage disposal plants. They built 6,000 athletic fields and playgrounds, 770 new swimming pools, and 1,700 new parks, fairgrounds, and rodeo grounds. They constructed or repaired 110,000 public libraries, auditoriums, stadiums, and other public buildings and built 5,584 new school buildings. They also served 900 million school lunches and repaired 80 million library books. Within a brief period of time the WPA had significantly improved the nation's infrastructure. (Infrastructure is the basic framework or system of public works in a country, such as roads, power plants, and public buildings.)

Located in almost every county in the nation, WPA workers were highly productive. Within a brief period of time the WPA had significantly improved the nation's infrastructure. *AP/Wide World Photo. Reproduced by permission.*

Ellen Sullivan Woodward (1887–1971) headed the Women's Division of the WPA and oversaw more than four hundred thousand women workers. Most of these women worked in the WPA's nine thousand sewing centers around the country. Woodward also started training and employment programs in mattress making, bookbinding, domestic service, canning of relief foods, school lunch preparation, and child care.

## National Youth Administration

For young people the WPA included the National Youth Administration (NYA). The NYA provided education, training, and part-time employment to students and other young people ages eighteen to twenty-five. Young people who were out of school could work seventy hours a month for no more than $25 a month. High school students could work part-time for no more than $6 a month, and college students could make up to $20 a month. NYA workers

## Congress Investigates Un-American Activities

The WPA provided work relief for millions of people during a challenging time in U.S. history, the Great Depression. The agency took the innovative approach of including artists in its employment program. However, not everyone in the United States regarded government-sponsored art programs as a positive development. Conservatives in Congress, those who hold traditional views, saw artists' organizations as a threat to traditional American values and the U.S. government. With the rise of communism in Russia and fascism in Germany and Italy, public fear of the spread of communism (an economic system in which all property and goods are owned in common and a single political party controls all aspects of society) and fascism (a strong, centralized nationalistic government led by a powerful dictator) was great in the United States. The economic hard times of the Great Depression had shaken people's faith in the American system of capitalism (an economic system where goods are owned by private businesses and price, production, and distribution is privately determined based on competition in a free market) and some turned to radical politics to seek basic change in U.S. society.

In 1938 the U.S. House of Representatives created a committee to investigate possible threats to national security posed by U.S. citizens. Named the House Un-American Activities Committee (HUAC), it was more commonly known as the Dies Committee, after Congressman Martin Dies (1900–1972) of Texas, who was the chairman of the group. The committee immediately began to investigate Federal One and, in particular, the Federal Theater Project (FTP). Hearings were held, and passionate defenses were offered by administrators of the WPA programs and their supporters.

The Dies Committee negatively affected the arts in general and the FTP in particular by raising public suspicions of political motives of artists. The FTP was shut down in June 1939. FTP actors publicly expressed indignation through their performances by changing the endings to some plays. In one case New York City stagehands knocked down the set in view of the audience at the conclusion of the performance. Many of the FTP actors and workers found jobs in commercial or community theaters.

spruced up schools, landscaped parks, read to the blind, worked as teachers' aides, constructed recreational facilities and parks, acted as nurses' aides, worked in school cafeterias, and conducted museum tours. The NYA program allowed students to contribute to their family's income while staying in school. Most of the student workers lived at home, but rural youths were moved to residential centers. The students in both settings were trained in masonry, welding, baking, barbering, carpentry, and plumbing.

Of all the New Deal agencies, the NYA had one of the better records in providing assistance to black Americans. That success was largely due to Mary McLeod Bethune (1875–1955), who led the NYA's Division of Negro Affairs. An important advocate for black American rights, Bethune was the highest-ranking black American in the Roosevelt administration. Of the young people who participated in the NYA, between 10 and 12 percent—or about three hundred thousand youths—were black Americans.

# Federal One

American artists were hit hard by the Depression and struggled just to survive. The number of art teachers in schools declined dramatically in the 1930s. And in New York City, 210 out of 253 theaters had closed by 1932. To bring attention to their situation, artists began staging hunger marches and outdoor sales of artwork. In New York City private charities offered relief to artists, classifying them in the same aid category as white-collar workers (workers whose work does not consist of manual labor). Franklin Roosevelt was governor of New York at that time, and under Roosevelt's leadership, Harry Hopkins organized work relief for unemployed artists in the state.

In 1933, after Roosevelt became president, Roosevelt and Hopkins took the concept of work relief with them to Washington, D.C. President Roosevelt created the Public Works of Art Project (PWAP) under the administration of the U.S. Treasury Department, and one million dollars was committed to the project. More than thirty-six hundred artists participating in the PWAP worked on the decoration of public buildings. The creation of the PWAP reflected the Roosevelt administration's belief that, like other workers, singers and dancers and other artists deserved work relief appropriate to their occupation.

On August 2, 1935, Roosevelt extended aid to artists even further by creating Federal One as a branch of the WPA. The largest New Deal program to aid artists, Federal One pro-

Posters such as this were created by WPA artists and published as part of the Federal Art Project between 1936 and 1941. *Courtesy of the Library of Congress.*

vided relief to visual artists, actors, musicians, composers, dancers, and writers. Holger Cahill was appointed national director. Federal One hired a range of people, from professional artists to unskilled workers who served as gallery attendants and other support staff. The program's mission was to popularize American art by producing artwork that would portray the unique character of the United States and its citizens. Administrators believed this would be best accomplished through art that realistically depicted everyday American life. They believed that art should benefit ordinary people, not just the wealthy or educated.

Federal One consisted of several programs, including the Federal Music Project, the Federal Writers Project, the Federal Art Project, and the Federal Theater Project; the variety of programs allowed artists to work in their specialties. Federal One was both praised and criticized and was always controversial. Many people in the United States had a hard time thinking of singing and dancing as work. Some Americans felt that the enrollees were simply avoiding getting a "real" job, that is, a traditional occupation such as business or a trade.

Nevertheless, Federal One made a significant contribution by documenting various aspects of American culture, such as its folklore and its music, that might otherwise have been lost. In addition, most Americans had never before heard a symphony or seen the work of accomplished artists. The cultural programs of Federal One were designed to address these gaps.

### Federal Music Project

The Federal Music Project (FMP) was directed by Nikolai Sokoloff, a former conductor of the Cleveland Symphony. The FMP employed fifteen thousand out-of-work musicians to participate in orchestras, chamber music groups, choral groups, opera performances, military bands, dance bands, and theater productions. The FMP had a goal of establishing regional orchestras across the country and providing free or low-cost concerts and music lessons. At one point musicians were participating in five thousand performances—in front of three million people—each week in theaters and schools across the country. They introduced millions of Americans to different kinds of music.

The FMP also coordinated music education programs in twenty-seven states and documented (wrote down in detail) works by American composers that had never been put in writing before. The FMP collected and preserved American folk music and other types of authentic, traditional American music. The music was documented, generally for the first time, so that it would not be lost forever when the traditional musicians died. The FMP made a significant contribution to American music scholarship and was the least controversial of the Federal One projects.

## Federal Writers Project

The Federal Writers Project (FWP) employed almost seven thousand writers, researchers, and librarians, who worked on projects in forty-eight states during the program's peak year of 1936. By 1942 the FWP had produced 3.5 million copies of eight hundred different publications. Its best-known product was the American Guide Series, illustrated guidebooks for every state and numerous cities. The fifty-one volumes in the series included maps, information on towns, natural features, and tourist attractions, as well as essays on history, folklore, politics, and local culture. FWP authors also wrote materials on American natural and cultural history for young children, older youths, and adults.

The FWP sent thousands of writers out to compile oral histories. (Oral histories are memories of a time or event that are passed along from person to person and generation to generation orally, not from a book.) The writers talked with Native Americans, frontier women, Appalachian miners, and others from various cultural groups across the nation; they then wrote down the details from these interviews, providing insightful portraits of life in the 1930s. One of the most dramatic collections compiled by FWP writers was the *Slave Narratives,* consisting of more than two thousand oral histories from black Americans who had formerly been slaves.

The Historical Records Survey (HRS) section of the FWP cataloged national records. The HRS employed approximately six thousand writers, librarians, archivists, and teachers annually. HRS workers undertook a huge task in compiling and analyzing state and county records and the records of some private organizations; this effort would aid historians, government officials, and researchers in the future. The HRS prepared bibliographies of American history and literature, an atlas of congressional roll-call votes, an index to unnumbered presidential orders, and a list of collections of presidential papers. In addition HRS workers compiled lists of portraits and manuscript collections in public buildings and church archives.

After the surprise attack by Japan on U.S. military installations at Pearl Harbor in December 1941, and the subsequent U.S. declaration of war on Japan, the FWP was absorbed into the Writers' Unit of the War Services Division. Many writers employed by the FWP would go on to fame, including Ralph Ellison (1914–1994), John Cheever (1912–1982), Conrad Aiken (1889–1973), Richard Wright (1908–1960), Saul Bellow (1915–), Studs Terkel (1912–), Dorothy West (1907–1998), and Zora Neale Hurston (1903–1960).

## Federal Art Project

The Federal Art Project (FAP) employed more than six thousand artists. Since few Americans had seen a great work of art, the FAP sought to make art more accessible. The best-known works of art created under the FAP were the murals painted in hospitals, schools, and other public buildings across the nation. (Murals are large paintings applied directly to a wall or ceiling.) The subjects were commonly taken from everyday life: a fishery or steelworkers or the poor. The FAP murals represented a renewed interest in American life by portraying Americans in common situations, such as at work. Such subjects were rarely the focus of artists before the FAP. The Painting Division artists also made smaller paintings, which could be exhibited anywhere, illustrating aspects of American life. They created more than forty thousand paintings and eleven hundred murals.

The Graphic Arts Division funded the creation of prints, replicas of original FAP artwork that were mass-produced on inexpensive paper. The general public could now afford art for display and enjoyment in their own homes and offices. Other divisions produced sculpture, posters, and stained glass. The FAP also employed artists to comprehensively document American folk art and antiques. These artists compiled the *Index of American Design,* which documented American painting, sculpture, and folk art. The Arts Service Division produced posters, handbills, and book illustrations. The Exhibitions Division was responsible for exhibiting the work of WPA artists.

The Art Teaching Division employed teachers at various places, including hospitals, mental health facilities, and community arts centers, to educate the public about art. One hundred art centers with exhibition space and classrooms were established in twenty-two states.

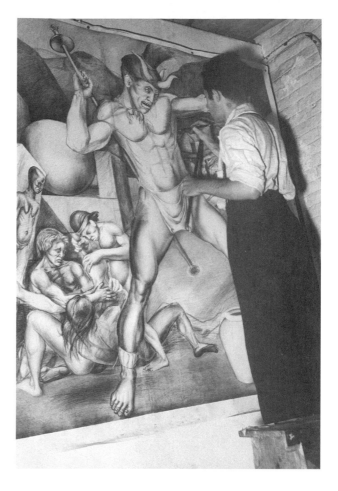

WPA artist Isidore Lipshitz works on a portable mural titled "Primitive and Modern Medicine." *Corbis Corporation. Reproduced by permission.*

Many FAP artists later became famous, including Jackson Pollock (1912–1956), Willem de Kooning (1904–1997), Anton Refregier (1905–1979), and Yasuo Kuniyoshi (1893–1953). However, since there were no standards for quality in the FAP, critics charged that much of the art was bad and that anyone could claim to be an artist. With common portrayals of workers laboring in the factories or fields, many of the FAP subjects were too pro-labor to suit the conservatives in Congress. Conservatives also felt that the art was "leftist," that is, that the artists portrayed the poverty and harsh conditions in the United States—such as black Americans in the rural South or immigrants in slums of northern cities—in a radical way to turn citizens against the government. President Roosevelt responded that, whether good or not, the art reflected Americans' perceptions of their nation and the people in it.

## Federal Theater Project

The most controversial of the Federal One programs, the Federal Theater Project (FTP) was led by Hallie Flanagan. Flanagan had been the head of the Vassar College Experimental Theatre and a college classmate of Harry Hopkins. Flanagan was dedicated to building a truly national theater. The FTP started regional theater groups all over the United States, performing both classic productions and original plays for thousands of Americans. Because it was a relief program, the FTP favored productions with large casts and extensive technical needs—to employ as many people as possible.

The FTP stimulated theater in the United States, producing more than twelve hundred plays and introducing the work of one hundred new playwrights. At the peak of the program's operation, one thousand performances were given before one million people each month. Because admission to productions was often free, many Americans were able to get their first exposure to live theater. The FTP also broadcast "Federal Theater of the Air" to an estimated ten million radio listeners.

FTP actors tackled social issues, educational and cultural works, new plays and musicals, plays never before presented in the United States, standard classics, and children's theater. The FTP also supported vaudeville, variety shows, circuses, marionette and puppet troupes, experimental theater, operas, and dance troupes.

The FTP had regional groups and tour groups that played widely, but the range of productions in New York City alone was remarkable, offering the program's most innovative work. The New York City unit included the Living Newspapers, the Popular Price Theatre, the Experimental Theatre, the Negro Theatre, the Tryout Theatre, a one-act play unit, a dance theater, the Theater for the Blind, a marionette theater, a Yiddish vaudeville unit, a German unit, an Anglo-Jewish theater, and the Radio Division. One of the most popular classic plays was the Negro unit's production of Shakespeare's

*Macbeth,* called *Voodoo Macbeth.* This all-black production was set in Haiti instead of Scotland and included voodoo priestesses as the three witches. The Living Newspapers staged plays in the form of documentaries, providing information and taking a stand on the issues of the day.

Many actors, directors, and producers employed by the FTP would go on to great career success, including Orson Welles (1915–1985), Arthur Miller (1915–), John Huston (1906–1987), Joseph Cotten (1905–1994), E. G. Marshall (1910–1998), Will Geer (1902–1978), Burt Lancaster (1913–1994), and John Houseman (1902–1988). More important, the FTP introduced thousands of Americans to theater during a difficult period in U.S. history. Largely uncensored and a vehicle for free expression, the productions aired the variety of political views at the time. Even though the FTP received strong criticism from Congress for undermining traditionally held American values, FTP productions attracted an estimat-

**One of the most popular Federal Theater Project productions was the Negro unit's production of Shakespeare's** *Macbeth,* **called** *Voodoo Macbeth.* *Courtesy of the Franklin D. Roosevelt Library.*

ed thirty million Americans before the program was disbanded in 1939.

## WPA comes to a close

WPA projects continued into the early 1940s, even as the United States became involved in World War II (1939–45). Many WPA workers transferred to various wartime agencies. The WPA was disbanded entirely in 1943, having served its purpose well. At a time when millions of Americans were without work, the WPA provided not only jobs but also hope for the future.

## For More Information

### Books

Baker, T. Lindsay, and Julie P. Baker, eds. *The WPA Oklahoma Slave Narratives*. Oklahoma City, OK: University of Oklahoma Press, 1996.

Bascom, Lionel C., ed. *A Renaissance in Harlem: Lost Essays of the WPA, by Ralph Ellison, Dorothy West, and Other Voices of a Generation*. New York, NY: HarperCollins, 1999.

Bindas, Kenneth J. *All of This Music Belongs to the Nation: The WPA's Federal Music Project and American Society*. Knoxville, TN: University of Tennessee Press, 1996.

Bold, Christine. *The WPA Guides: Mapping America*. Jackson, MS: University Press of Mississippi, 1999.

Bustard, Bruce I. *A New Deal for the Arts*. Seattle, WA: University of Washington Press, 1997.

Buttitta, Tony, and Barry Witham. *Uncle Sam Presents: A Memoir of the Federal Theatre, 1935–1939*. Philadelphia, PA: University of Philadelphia Press, 1982.

Draden, Rena. *Blueprints for a Black Federal Theatre, 1935–1939*. New York, NY: Cambridge University Press, 1994.

Flanagan, Hallie. *Arena*. New York, NY: Duell, Sloan & Pearce, 1940.

Harris, Jonathon. *Federal Art and National Culture: The Politics of Identity in New Deal America*. New York, NY: Cambridge University Press, 1995.

Hopkins, June. *Harry Hopkins: Sudden Hero, Brash Performer*. New York, NY: St. Martin's Press, 1999.

Housema, Lorraine Brown, ed. *Federal Theatre Project*. New York, NY: Routledge, Chapman & Hall, 1986.

La Vere, David. *Life among the Texas Indians: The WPA Narratives*. College Station, TX: Texas A&M University Press, 1998.

Mangione, Jerre. *The Dream and the Deal: The Federal Writers Project, 1935–1943*. Syracuse, NY: Syracuse University Press, 1996.

Meltzer, Milton. *Violins and Shovels: The WPA Arts Projects*. New York, NY: Delacorte Press, 1976.

## Web Sites

*Federal Theater Project Collection.* http://www.gmu.edu/library/specialcollections/federal.html (accessed on August 17, 2002).

"New Deal for the Arts." *U.S. National Archives and Records Administration.* http://www.archives.gov/exhibit_hall/new_deal_for_the_arts/index.html (accessed on August 17, 2002).

"Selections from the Federal Theatre Project." *Library of Congress American Memory Collection.* http://www.memory.loc.gov/ammem/fedtp/fthome.html (accessed on August 17, 2002).

# Social Security

*"I* see no reason why every child from the day he is born, shouldn't be a member of the social security system. When he begins to grow up, he should know he will have old-age benefits direct from the insurance system to which he will belong all his life. If he is out of work, he gets a benefit. If he is sick, or crippled, he gets a benefit.... Cradle to the grave—from the cradle to the grave they ought to be in a social insurance system." —President Franklin Roosevelt, speaking to Secretary of Labor Frances Perkins.

President Franklin D. Roosevelt (1882–1945; served 1933–45) envisioned a social security program for the people of the United States. He eagerly shared his ideas with his secretary of labor, Frances Perkins (1882–1965), as the process of developing such a program got under way in 1934. The words that open this chapter, relayed by Perkins in her 1946 book, *The Roosevelt I Knew,* became known as Roosevelt's "cradle to grave" statement. The words reveal the deep sense of responsibility Roosevelt felt toward all Americans, who were caught in a desperate struggle to survive the Great Depression of the 1930s.

The Great Depression was the worst economic crisis in U.S. history. The stock market crashed in October 1929; a banking crisis followed. Stores closed, 25 to 30 percent of workers lost their jobs, and people could not pay their bills or buy enough food for their families. Hunger and breadlines became common, and people began to lose their homes because they could not make their regular loan payments. Overcome by the Depression, the nation and its president struggled for solutions.

The Social Security Act of 1935 was one measure in a sweeping series of legislative relief and recovery measures known as the New Deal. Designed to bring prosperity back to the United States, the New Deal programs were created under the guidance of President Roosevelt. The Social Security Act was one of the most important and revolutionary pieces of social legislation ever passed by the U.S. Congress. Social legislation refers to laws that address social issues such as old-age retirement payments, unemployment support, and health care.

The Social Security Act was considered revolutionary because the U.S. government had never before taken on the responsibility of social insurance for its people. Social insurance is a system of government-sponsored social programs that are designed to protect a nation's citizens—especially the aged, the very needy, and the disabled—against economic hardship. Such programs include old-age retirement income, cash payments for the unemployed, and certain health care benefits.

By the early 1930s the Great Depression had driven many unemployed Americans and elderly citizens into desperate poverty. Convinced that the people of the United States needed some form of long-term social insurance, President Roosevelt notified Congress on June 8, 1934, of his intention to develop such a program. Enlisting the help of Secretary of Labor Perkins, he established the Committee on Economic Security on June 29, 1934, to work out the details. Only thirteen and a half months later Roosevelt signed into law the Social Security Act of 1935. Believing the government had created an economic safety net, Americans climbed on the bandwagon of Social Security. They have been fiercely protective of it ever since.

# The move from farms to cities

Certain historical forces in the late nineteenth and early twentieth century made 1934 and 1935 the right time to introduce social insurance in the United States. Social insurance answers a basic human need—the need to face the future with some assurance of economic security. At one time or another all people endure illness, job loss, disability, or old age. Before the twentieth century most Americans lived on family farms and relied on the support of large extended families. In that agricultural society a farmer who owned his own land could at least feed his family in hard times. Fiercely independent Americans never thought of the government as a source of help. However, during the late nineteenth and early twentieth century increasing numbers of Americans left their land and the safety of family to seek jobs in city factories. Only 28 percent of the U.S. population lived in cities in 1890, but by 1930 56 percent lived in the industrialized cities. Their income and livelihood depended entirely on wages from their job. If they lost their job due to injury, illness, or growing old, they and their families found themselves in a desperate situation.

Western Europe had experienced similar population movement as factories sprang up in its towns and cities. As early as the 1880s European governments established social insurance programs to deal with workers injured on the job and to provide for health care. By the time the United States adopted a nationwide social insurance program in 1935, at least thirty-four European nations already operated such programs.

# Self-reliance

Why did the issue of social insurance go unaddressed in America for so long? The answer lies in the uniquely American belief in self-reliance—taking care of oneself. Most Americans steadfastly resisted any suggestion that they needed help, especially from the government. Any help coming from government sources seemed a threat to personal liberty. For the truly needy, help came from charities, volunteer programs, and women's "mutual aid" societies. Nevertheless, ideas of social insurance modeled on European plans began to take root in the minds of a handful of American university professors. In 1907 they formed the American Association for Labor Legislation (AALL). The members of the AALL began calling for unemployment and old-age insurance programs. Some forward-thinking states began to listen.

## States pass social insurance legislation

The AALL promoted practical programs rather than just ideas. They informed Americans about the social insurance programs in Europe. The first results of the AALL's efforts came in 1909, when Wisconsin, Minnesota, and New York passed legislation for workers' compensation (cash payments for those injured on the job). By 1920 forty-three states had passed such laws. States also began to enact old-age insurance legislation. Old-age insurance provides cash payments for elderly people who no longer work. By the early 1930s approximately thirty-five states had old-age insurance plans. However, generally these plans were inadequate and differed widely from state to state. For example, payments in Montana were roughly $7.28 per month, but in Maryland they were $30 per month.

A poster instructing the public to apply for old-age benefits. *Bettmann/CORBIS. Reproduced by permission.*

As the economic misery of the Great Depression deepened in 1930, 1931, and 1932, confidence in traditional sources of security evaporated. Family farms and city jobs were both failing to some degree. Charities and volunteer organizations were overwhelmed by the needs of the elderly and increasing numbers of unemployed people; these organizations could not provide adequate help. Suddenly some form of national unemployment insurance and old-age insurance seemed essential to everyday Americans. Social insurance was an idea whose time had finally come.

# Committee on Economic Security

On June 8, 1934, President Roosevelt notified Congress of his intention to establish a social insurance program. On June 29, 1934, he created the Committee on Economic Security to develop a permanent system of social insurance for the people of the United States. He set December 1934 as the date for the committee to report its recommendations to him.

Roosevelt insisted that Frances Perkins (1882–1965), the secretary of labor, be chairperson of the committee. An effective and trusted adviser of Roosevelt, Perkins appointed the members of the committee mostly from the president's cabinet. Those appointed to the committee were Henry Morgenthau Jr. (1891–1967), Secretary of the Treasury; Homer Cummings (1870–1956), Attorney General; Henry A. Wallace (1888–1965), Secretary of Agriculture; and Harry Hopkins (1890–1946), Director of the Federal Emergency Relief Administration (FERA). The committee turned out to be an excellent mix. Ideas about how to approach the complicated program came from people with different perspectives. For example, Morgenthau and members of the Treasury Department explored and put forth very conservative approaches as well as wide-open ways to finance such a program. Cummings, the attorney general, analyzed legal and constitutional problems that might arise. From his perspective as the head of a relief agency, Hopkins presented the most pressing needs of people caught up in the Depression.

After assembling the Committee on Economic Security, Perkins established the Technical Board as part of the committee. The Technical Board's role was to analyze and put together how the whole social insurance program would be carried out. Unemployment insurance seemed the most urgent social insurance need. The only plan in existence in the United States was the Wisconsin plan adopted in 1932, so Perkins selected a team of individuals from the University of Wisconsin to work on a national plan. The team included Arthur J. Altmeyer (1891–1972), Edwin E. Witte, and a young assistant, Wilbur J. Cohen. All were experts in Wisconsin's social insurance thinking. As months of intense discussions, meetings, and congressional hearings unfolded, it would be Altmeyer and Witte, along with Frances Perkins, who controlled virtually all development of the economic security proposals. Eventually Altmeyer would become known as the "father of Social Security."

## Early ideas for the social insurance plan

The members of the Committee on Economic Security first focused on an unemployment insurance scheme. They began by looking at plans and proposals devised between roughly 1932 and early 1934, including two that had already been introduced to Congress. An unemployment insurance bill, the Wagner-Lewis Bill, had gone to Congress for debate and hearings in February 1934. Senator Robert F. Wagner (1877–1953) of New York had introduced it into the Senate and Representative David J. Lewis of Maryland into the House of Representatives. The bill called for a payroll tax (a tax on wages paid to employees). For example, if an employer or a company had a yearly payroll of $100,000, a certain percentage—perhaps 1 percent, or $1,000—would be due each year. The money would be deposited into an unemployment fund held in the U.S. Treasury in Washington, D.C. Each state would be free to adopt its own law for distribution of the unemployment funds. This plan included a benefit for the employers: They could deduct the federal tax they paid into the fund from their company's federal tax bill. This plan was referred to as a "federal-state" plan, because the federal and state governments would need to work together to carry it out. Another bill, the Dill-Connery Old Age Pension Bill, had also been working its way through Congress in early 1934. This bill attempted to establish a uniform nationwide approach to old-age pension plans (cash payments, usually made monthly, to retired workers)

Congressional hearings on both bills were in full swing in the spring of 1934. An endless stream of interested parties testified, and the hearings began to drag into summer. The weather in Washington, D.C., in the summer grows hot and humid. Air-conditioning did not exist. By June 1934 Congress was exhausted and grumpy. President Roosevelt sent them home, assuring them that by December his Committee on Economic Security would prepare recommendations on the social insurance issue. The members of Congress gladly turned over their findings to the committee and went home.

# A nationwide debate on social insurance

President Roosevelt sent Frances Perkins on a speech-making mission throughout the Depression-weary nation to promote social insurance issues. Perkins suggested that aiding the unemployed and the aged in good times and in bad could help prevent economic depressions in the future. She explained that people receiving social insurance payments would have a little money to spend on goods, thus helping businesses. And for the first time in U.S. history, everyday Americans began to talk and write about social insurance and even seemingly accept the notion that the government could and indeed should help the elderly and the unemployed on a long-term basis.

Francis E. Townsend (1867–1960) and Huey P. Long (1893–1935) began to boldly interject their ideas into the public debate on social insurance. Townsend was a medical doctor who had recently moved from a long-time practice in Idaho to Long Beach, California. Retired and with little income, he became nearly destitute (very poor). He also watched other elderly people in Long Beach struggling to get enough to eat each day. He wrote a letter to the editor of the *Long Beach Telegram*, proposing a 2 percent national sales tax. From the proceeds a $200-a-month payment would be made to every nonemployed citizen over sixty who was not a criminal. Each recipient would be required to spend the entire amount each month to keep the economy going. The amount Townsend proposed in 1934—$200 a month—is roughly equivalent to $3,900 per month in 1998 dollars. Newspapers throughout the country published the letter, and Townsend Clubs sprang up nationwide. President Roosevelt and all those deeply involved in trying to set up a social insurance plan knew Townsend's plan would bankrupt the country. But those who would have been eligible for the benefits saw the plan as an immediate way out of economic misery.

The public popularity of the Townsend plan put some pressure on Roosevelt, but he was even more alarmed by the rising popularity of Huey P. Long (1893–1935). Long, a senator from Louisiana, intended to run for president in 1936. In 1933 he loudly proposed his "Share-the-Wealth" plan in hopes of gathering in many supporters. Long's slogans of "soak the rich," "every man a king," and "a chicken in every

The U.S. Postal Service took on the task of registering citizens and assigning them Social Security numbers. Well before the age of computers, the efficient postal service processed applications and assigned over thirty-five million Social Security numbers in 1936 and 1937. *Courtesy of the Franklin D. Roosevelt Library.*

pot" appealed to many economically disadvantaged Americans. To finance his plan, Long proposed huge taxes on incomes over $1 million and inheritances over $5 million. With the proceeds he would fund old-age pensions for those over sixty, health care programs, free college education, unemployment insurance, and public relief payments to the very poor. Long played on a belief widely held by Americans—that the greed of the wealthy was to blame for the Great Depression. By 1934 Share-the-Wealth societies had enrolled five million members. Pressure from the Townsend plan supporters and the Share-the-Wealth movement no doubt propelled Roosevelt, Perkins, and the Committee on Economic Security to form a workable plan as soon as possible.

## Recommendations readied

President Roosevelt expected recommendations from the committee by December 1, 1934, but the deadline came and went. The committee had worked intensively for nearly six months to resolve conflicting positions on the various programs that fell under social insurance. The old-age pension or retirement plan was at last resolved. Committee members decided on a funding approach in which employees would contribute a percentage of their salary to the pension fund and employers would make an equal contribution for each employee. Employees would gradually accumulate credits to receive cash payments in old age.

Deciding how to fund unemployment insurance (payments to help the unemployed get by from month to month) took more time than anything else. When the December 1 deadline passed, Perkins demanded that the committee meet at her apartment at eight o'clock one evening during the week of Christmas. She disconnected the phone, set out a few bottles of beverages to cheer spirits, and declared that they would work all night if necessary to resolve the problem. At two in the morning all present agreed to the federal-state plan originally introduced in the Wagner-Lewis Bill. President Roosevelt would finally have a social insurance bill to take to Congress.

## The bill goes to Congress

On January 17, 1935, President Roosevelt submitted the work of the Committee on Economic Security to Congress. Arthur Altmeyer (1891–1972), a member of the committee's Technical Board, wrote the bill that went before Congress. Senator Robert F. Wagner (1877–1953) introduced the bill to the Senate, where it went to the Senate Committee on Finance. Senator Pat Harrison of Mississippi skillfully shepherded the bill through the Senate hearings. Representatives David J. Lewis of Maryland and Robert L. Doughton of North Carolina introduced the bill in the House, where it went to the House Ways and Means Committee. The committees listened to vigorous testimony for the first half of 1935. During this period several experts who spoke used the term "social security" rather than "social insurance." This wording quickly took hold, and the legislation became known as the "Social Security Bill."

The recommendations of the Committee on Economic Security held up through the hearings, with one major exception: the old-age pension plans. Secretary of the Treasury

Henry Morgenthau Jr. (1891–1967) testified that it would be all but impossible to collect payroll taxes from scattered farmworkers and domestic workers (such as maids and house cleaners) and from the many small businesses employing less than ten people. The Ways and Means Committee agreed. President Roosevelt, much to his dismay, felt forced to compromise on this key issue. Roosevelt had hoped to have every working person participate in the system. With this compromise only about 50 percent of the workforce would be participating.

The House and the Senate both passed their versions of the bill, then worked out differences by early August 1935. On August 14, surrounded by more than thirty individuals who had worked for the passage of the bill, President Roosevelt signed into law the Social Security Act of 1935. Roosevelt praised Frances Perkins as the one person most influential in the passage of the bill.

Numerous unemployed insured workers register for jobs and file unemployment benefit claims at a state employment office. Unemployment Insurance was perhaps the most important part of the Social Security Act during the Depression. *Courtesy of the Franklin D. Roosevelt Library.*

## The Social Security Act of 1935

The Social Security Act of 1935 launched the American version of social insurance. The act had eleven parts, called titles. Title I dealt with providing monetary assistance to elderly people who had already retired before the act passed. Title II dealt with Old Age Insurance (OAI), or what eventually became known as the Social Security retirement system. Title III, considered the most important provision at the time of passage, was the unemployment insurance plan. Title IV provided support for children whose parents could not adequately care for them. The program was called the Aid to Dependent Children Program. Title V allowed for grants to states for promoting the health of mothers and children, supporting crippled children and neglected children, and retaining persons disabled in industry. Title X offered aid to the needy blind. (Titles V and X were originally the only programs dealing with the disabled.) Title VII set up a three-member Social Security Board to carry out the plan. Titles VI, VIII, IX, and XI took care of funding and administration details.

## Government's quick action

From its proposal stages to final enactment, the social insurance program took less than fourteen months to become a reality. For such a complicated piece of legislation, the Social Security Act moved through Congress with remarkable speed. The United States was in the middle of the most severe economic depression in its history, and the resulting circumstances demanded quick action. The Depression disrupted families and businesses; the states, largely bankrupt, could not support even the smallest social programs. Radical, quick fixes such as the Townsend plan and Huey Long's Share-the-Wealth plan gathered wide support and pressured the government to find a workable program. With a determined calm the Committee on Economic Security, guided by Frances Perkins, Arthur Altmeyer, and Edwin Witte, put together a practical plan that Congress could pass. Perhaps most important, the plan had the unfailing support of an extremely popular president who remained involved through the whole process.

## Start-up

The U.S. Postal Service took on the task of registering citizens and assigning them Social Security numbers. Well before the age of computers, the efficient postal service processed applications and assigned over thirty-five million Social Security numbers in 1936 and 1937. Paycheck withholdings for the old-age insurance started in early 1937, with the first scheduled monthly payments set to begin in 1940. Other parts of the act took effect in 1936 and 1937. The first unemployment benefit was paid in Wisconsin. During the same period, the first public assistance payments for old-age assistance, dependent children, and the blind were paid out.

Did Social Security payments make a difference for those trying to survive the Depression years? The payments in

## Social Security Firsts

- October 14, 1936, the first Social Security field office opens for business in Austin, Texas.

- November 24, 1936, the U.S. Postal Service distributes the first applications for Social Security account numbers. The first Social Security number (SSN) issued, SSN 001-01-0001, went to Grace Dorothy Owen of Concord, New Hampshire.

- March 1937, Ernest Ackerman of Cleveland, Ohio, receives the first old-age Social Security payment. Ackerman, a motorman, retired one day after the Social Security program began in January 1937.

On the one day he participated in the program, a nickel was withheld from his pay. His employer also had to pay one nickel into Social Security. When Ackerman retired, he received a seventeen-cent retirement payment.

- January 31, 1940, sixty-five-year-old Ida May Fuller of Ludlow, Vermont, receives the first-ever old-age monthly benefit check, in the amount of $22.54. A retired legal secretary, Miss Fuller died at age one hundred in January 1975. She received over $22,000 in benefits during her thirty-five years as a Social Security beneficiary.

the first years were too small to provide significant help. Very few benefits (payments) reached Americans in the 1930s, and only slightly more than 222,000 people received small monthly Social Security payments in 1940. The main benefit of the Social Security program during its early years was the peace of mind it offered U.S. citizens: The program demonstrated that the federal government was committed to helping citizens maintain a decent standard of living, no matter what challenges or setbacks they faced. Although few Americans understood the entire social insurance plan, they continued to trust that President Roosevelt was looking out for their general welfare. The launching of the Social Security program marked the beginning of an era in which the federal government would play a role in the everyday life of Americans.

## Changes and long-term impact

The Social Security Act was the most important legislation to come out of Franklin D. Roosevelt's New Deal. It endured and evolved through the twentieth century to become

# MORE SECURITY FOR THE AMERICAN FAMILY

WHEN AN INSURED WORKER DIES, LEAVING DEPENDENT CHILDREN AND A WIDOW, BOTH MOTHER AND CHILDREN RECEIVE MONTHLY BENEFITS UNTIL THE LATTER REACH 18.

FOR INFORMATION WRITE OR CALL AT THE NEAREST FIELD OFFICE OF THE
**SOCIAL SECURITY BOARD**

**The Social Security Act was amended in 1939 to include monthly payments for the dependent spouse and children of an insured worker upon the worker's death.** *Courtesy of the Franklin D. Roosevelt Library.*

essential in the life of modern America. The first major flaw in the act became apparent by 1937. The act provided only retirement benefits, and only to the worker; it made no provisions for payments for dependents (spouses or children). This flaw was corrected by amendments in 1939 when two new categories of benefits were introduced. The first provided payments, known as dependent benefits, to the spouse and minor children (under the age of eighteen) of a retired worker. The second, known as survivors' benefits, provided payments to the surviving spouse and minor children of a worker who died before age sixty-five, the designated age of retirement.

Congress continued to amend the act as times dictated. In the 1940s only 50 percent of Americans were covered by the old-age retirement plan. Congress gradually increased who was eligible until, by 2000, 98 percent of all workers were covered. Major additions to the act included Medicare (1965), a health coverage plan for Social Security recipients age sixty-five and older, and automatic yearly increases tied to cost-of-living increases (1972).

The Social Security retirement plan helped the elderly maintain financial independence. In the 1930s and 1940s, 50 percent of the elderly population lived in poverty. By 2000 only 11 percent of persons sixty-five years of age and older lived in poverty. Social Security was never intended to be the sole source of income for the elderly. However, by 2000 one-third of elderly recipients reported that the Social Security payment was their only income; for another one-third the payment was a major source of income. Approximately forty-five million people received Social Security benefits in 2000. No other U.S. government program has affected the lives of so many Americans.

# For More Information

## Books

Altmeyer, Arthur J. *The Formative Years of Social Security.* Madison, WI: University of Wisconsin Press, 1968.

Brinkley, Alan. *Voices of Protest: Huey Long, Father Coughlin, and the Great Depression.* New York, NY: Knopf, 1982.

Lubov, Roy. *The Struggle for Social Security, 1900–1935.* 2nd ed. Pittsburgh, PA: University of Pittsburgh Press, 1986.

Nash, Gerald D., Noel H. Pugach, and Richard F. Tomasson. *Social Security: The First Half-Century.* Albuquerque, NM: University of New Mexico Press, 1988.

Perkins, Frances. *The Roosevelt I Knew.* New York, NY: Viking Press, 1946.

Roosevelt, Franklin D. *The Public Papers and Addresses of Franklin D. Roosevelt.* New York, NY: Random House, 1938.

Schieber, Sylvester J., and John B. Shoven. *The Real Deal: The History and Future of Social Security.* New Haven, CT: Yale University Press, 1999.

Witte, Edwin. *The Development of the Social Security Act.* Madison, WI: University of Wisconsin Press, 1962.

## Periodicals

Social Security Administration. "A Brief Description of the U.S. Social Security Program." SSA Publication No. 61-009, January 1997.

Social Security Administration. "A Brief History of Social Security." SSA Publication No. 21-059, August 2000.

Social Security Administration. "The Future of Social Security." SSA Publication No. 05-10055, July 1999.

## Web Sites

"Frances Perkins." *United States Department of Labor.* http://www.dol.gov/asp/programs/history/perkins.htm (accessed on August 15, 2002).

Perkins, Frances. "The Roots of Social Security." *Social Security Administration.* http://www.ssa.gov/history/perkins5.html (accessed on August 15, 2002).

*Social Security Administration.* http://www.ssa.gov (accessed on August 15, 2002).

# Education

## 7

The Great Depression, the most severe economic crisis the United States had ever experienced, began in late 1929 with the crash of the stock market. Schools, like every other part of American society, were deeply affected, but the hardships of the Depression were only a temporary setback to upward trends in education that had begun earlier in the decade. For public schools the most difficult years of the Depression were between 1932 and 1936. Cuts in school budgets resulted in shortened school years or school days, lower teacher salaries, teacher layoffs, insufficient funds for books and supplies, cuts in the number and variety of classes offered, and increased class sizes. A significant number of schools, especially rural schools, closed altogether.

Yet through the upheaval several positive and long-lasting changes occurred. Membership in teachers' labor unions greatly increased as teachers organized to work for higher wages, better job opportunities, retirement benefits, and higher standards for teachers. State governments increased their contributions to local education, aiding local communities that were struggling to fund their schools. Many tiny rural schools were combined into larger school districts so that resources could be shared. A school district in the suburbs of Philadelphia, Pennsylvania, became the first to combine white and black schools. President Franklin Roosevelt (1882–1945; served 1933–45) introduced the New Deal, a series of programs designed to bring relief and recovery to America; New Deal legislation created agencies that provided an education for poor and minority youths. By the end of the 1930s U.S. education was poised to resume its upward trend.

## Prosperous times for education

For most schools in the United States, the 1920s were prosperous times. School districts received steady funding. School enrollments boomed: In grades kindergarten through twelve the number of students increased from 23.5 million in 1920 to 28.6 million in 1930; enrollment in colleges and universities approximately doubled in the same time period, to over 1.1 million. New teachers were hired, and their salaries went from an average of $871 a month in 1920 to an average of $1,420 a month in 1930. New schools were constructed, and new classes were added, especially practical vocational classes that included carpentry, auto repair, and cooking.

School districts were run by school boards made up of businessmen and professionals such as lawyers. Schools were managed with businesslike efficiency by their administrators. The businessmen on the school boards as well as those throughout the community generously loaned money for building new schools. They also initiated funding drives and advocated raising taxes to pay for education.

## Inequalities in the school districts

The U.S. Constitution makes no provision for funding of schools by the federal government (the nation's central government headquartered in Washington, D.C.). Instead, funding is the responsibility of the states. And in the 1920s, funding had been left almost entirely to the local school districts, which received their operating money from local property taxes. Under this system many school districts enjoyed steadily increasing support, but other school districts were left behind.

When denied sufficient funding by white school boards, many black communities banded together to build their own schools. *Corbis Corporation. Reproduced by permission.*

There were over 145,000 local school districts in the United States in the 1920s, and some of them struggled with shockingly poor funding. While most of the country's economy boomed, certain sectors were severely depressed through the 1920s—namely, agriculture, coal mining, and the textile industries. The agricultural industry had seen decreases in income since World War I (1914–18). Lower incomes meant school funding, raised through local taxes, was significantly down as well. As a result, rural school districts had run-down buildings, the lowest-paid and most poorly trained teachers, and insufficient books and supplies. The decline in quality of education and the increasing need for children to help on the farm led to a high rate of absenteeism. The poorest school districts were in the black communities.

Elementary schools were adequate in most areas of the country, but there were not enough high schools in rural areas. This shortage was due to fewer students progressing to the higher grade levels, often because of the need to help on the family farm. By the late 1920s there were approximately six thousand high schools with fifty or less students. Some had as few as ten students. These small high schools offered very few programs of study.

## Education for black Americans in the 1920s

In the 1920s schools were racially segregated, which meant that black students and white students attended separate schools. Most black Americans lived in poverty-stricken communities with meager property tax revenues (property tax monies were used to fund local schools; lower property taxes meant less money to spend on the schools, lowering the quality of education). Generally whites made up the school boards and blocked funding for the black schools. In the 1920s the average expenditure per pupil for black students was only 15 to 20 percent of the amount spent for each white student. Especially in the South, it was commonly believed that blacks were incapable of higher learning and therefore had little need for school funding.

When white school boards denied them funding, black communities banded together to build their own schools. Former slaves donated their small savings and profits from farming. Those who had no money donated labor. Together they built schoolhouses, rarely more than shacks, furnished with benches and a wood-burning stove. It is estimated that by 1930 over three thousand of these schools had been built in southern counties; but they reached only 25 percent of black elementary students. Only a handful of black high schools existed in the South. Located in cities, they had generally been built with funds donated by wealthy whites. These schools did not teach traditional academic subjects (such as history, math, science, or languages), but subjects such as carpentry, auto mechanics, bricklaying, laundry work, sewing, and cooking. This vocational education prepared black students for stable but low-paying jobs. With the onset of the Great Depression, even those jobs would be taken from them, by white Americans desperate for any kind of work.

# The Great Depression begins

In October 1929, the New York stock market crashed. The value of stocks nose-dived. Banks and businesses failed, manufacturing slowed, and the agriculture industry continued its downward slide. Many Americans lost their jobs, and almost everyone's income decreased significantly. As businesses and individuals attempted to adjust and survive the worst economic depression in U.S. history, the effect on schools was delayed. Most school districts relied on property taxes for their funding, and most Americans managed to pay their property taxes in 1930 and 1931. However, by 1932 the Depression hit the schools with shocking force.

# Retrenchment

By late 1932, due to job loss or salary decrease, many property owners could no longer pay their taxes. Between 25 and 30 percent of the American workforce was unemployed. It is estimated that 40 to 50 percent of home loans were in default (behind in payments). Tax money that did come in was often used to help the hungry and homeless, instead of for education. As a result cutbacks in education began; this process was known as retrenchment. Retrenchment affected schools across the country. Many schools closed, teacher salaries decreased, class sizes increased, and many classes and programs were eliminated.

Retrenchment was especially hard on rural areas. In Alabama in 1932 and 1933 most children had no school to attend as five out of six schools closed. Georgia closed thirteen hundred schools, and West Virginia closed over a thousand. The states of the Great Plains and parts of Michigan, Ohio, and Montana also faced closures. Overall, attendance in rural schools was down by 60 percent due to school closures and the need for children to help out on the family farms. Many schools that stayed open had to greatly shorten their school year.

Large city schools were, for the most part, better funded. Retrenchment affected each city differently, however, and even varied from area to area within a city. For example, city schools in Detroit, Michigan, saw their revenue (government income through taxes) drop 30 percent in the early

1930s; Grosse Pointe, a wealthy Detroit suburb, was barely affected. Schools in Chicago, Illinois, heavily in debt from building construction, suffered enormously.

Many teachers lost their jobs. Those who remained saw their salaries drop an average of 13.6 percent between the 1929–30 and 1933–34 school years. Some took pay cuts of 25 to 50 percent. By 1934 about three hundred thousand rural teachers earned less than $650 a year; and eighty-five thousand earned less than $450 per year, the equivalent of $5,800 per year in 2000.

From 1930 to 1934 the average class size grew from 20.6 pupils to 24.9; in some cities classes were as large as 40 students. Meanwhile, the number of classes offered declined. Practical subjects, introduced in the 1920s, were eliminated. These so-called fads and frills included physical education, night schools, adult education, vocational classes, home economics, and the arts.

**Rural schools, such as this one in Williams County, North Dakota, suffered greatly during the Depression. Many had to close their doors altogether due to lack of funds.** *Courtesy of the Library of Congress.*

Black schools were the most severely affected by retrenchment. The average black family's income, already low, decreased drastically during the Depression. Teachers' salaries could not be maintained, and books and supplies were nonexistent. As economic conditions worsened, the practical skills taught at black vocational high schools provided no advantage, because the Depression caused elimination of jobs in nearly every industry. In addition, as work became scarce, jobs traditionally held by blacks were given to whites.

During retrenchment schools lost business support. Allies of the schools in the 1920s, businesses had loaned money for school construction and advocated higher taxes to pay for an education for all. Suddenly, in response to the Depression, they reversed their course: Businesses now called for tax cuts to lower their own expenses. Schools needed tax dollars to survive, but businesses needed tax cuts to cover their costs. Businesses also demanded that loans made to the schools for construction be paid back immediately. Even the U.S. Chamber of Commerce, a nationwide businesspeople's group, called for shortening the school day, increasing class size, and cutting teacher salaries. School administrators felt abandoned by their former business allies.

## Educators respond to retrenchment

Teachers began to form professional organizations, calling for higher wages and more control of their workplace. School boards had long considered teachers to be merely employees whose every action could be controlled, but teachers saw themselves as professionals capable of making decisions on their own. Membership in teacher organizations such as the American Federation of Teachers (AFT) and the National Education Association (NEA) increased rapidly. These groups quickly became more outspoken and politically active. The AFT sought higher pay and retirement plans and demanded that teacher hiring standards be maintained at a higher level. In 1932, the NEA established the Joint Commission on the Emergency in Education; the commission's purpose was to counteract the efforts of business leaders who sought school budget cuts and tax cuts, and who demanded immediate loan repayment from the schools. Many educators and the general public believed that the greed of wealthy business leaders was

AVE the CHILDREN—PASS our BILLS
30 CHILDREN TO A CLASS!
+ 200 MILLION DOLLAR BOND ISSUE FOR MORE SCHOOLS
= BETTER CITIZENS
TEACHERS UNION LOCAL · NEW YORK CITY

a major cause of the Depression, so they made a united effort to fight the school budget cuts that business interests favored.

Chicago became the scene of a major conflict between teachers and business leaders. By the end of 1929 the wealthy pressed for decreases in school spending, including holding back teachers' wages while increasing their workloads. Teachers were paid with IOUs, also known as scrip, that simply were pieces of paper recognizing the school district owed money to the teacher. It was hoped the scrip would be paid when sufficient school funds became available once again. By 1932 Chicago owed its teachers $20 million, or $1,400 each. Banks refused to cash the scrip, forcing teachers to deplete their savings, cut back on necessities, and lose their homes. In April 1933 fourteen thousand teachers, supported by students and parents, marched to city hall. When their protests went unheeded, they turned on the banks, vandalizing those that refused to honor their scrip. The Chicago school board, made up of Chicago business leaders, punished

Members of the New York Teachers Union marching to the New York State Capitol, demonstrating for better funding of educational facilities, circa January 1938. *Corbis Corporation. Reproduced by permission.*

## Social Reconstructionism and Loyalty Oaths

The story of education during any period is always accompanied by the educational philosophy (accepted truths and principles) that dominated during that period. Educational philosophy means the latest thinking on education policies and programs; it generally originates among educators at universities. In the 1930s the latest educational philosophy was called "social reconstructionism." This million-dollar wording meant that teachers should endeavor to build a new social order (relations between various population groups and institutions) through their instruction. Social reconstructionists believed the Depression had proved that capitalism (an economic system in which property is privately owed and decisions on production and prices are largely privately determined) was a greedy, cruel, and inhumane economic system. They called for a new social order based on cooperation among residents in a community and collectivism (ownership of goods by a group, not by individuals); they wanted America's abundance to be redistributed to benefit all Americans. Social reconstructionists challenged teachers to bring about these changes.

The philosophy of social reconstructionism was started by a small group of educators at Columbia University Teachers' College. This group, known as the "frontier thinkers," included, among others, George Counts, William K. Kilpatrick, Harold Rugg (1886–1960), John L. Childs,

the teachers by firing fourteen hundred of them, closing some schools, increasing class sizes, and slashing budgets.

Other districts fared better than Chicago. Detroit schools superintendent Frank Cody and Detroit mayor Frank Murphy (1890–1949; served 1930–33) resisted budget cuts. They were encouraged by the support of teachers and by trade unions full of Detroit parents who elected new school board members to fight efforts to cut school budgets. The California Teachers' Association (CTA) blocked budget cuts, as did the Florida League for Better Schools. In Florida a gasoline tax was passed to help with school funding, including teacher salaries.

One of the most important and long-lasting responses to the school funding crisis in the 1930s was an increase in state funding. Although it was technically the responsibility of state governments, school funding had long been left to local communities. Communities used money from property taxa-

and R. Bruce Raup. John Dewey (1859–1952), an already famous and somewhat older educator, aligned himself to a large extent with this philosophy. The group urged teachers to indoctrinate (teach) their students with these new ideas.

Many teachers found the ideas of social reconstructionism compelling; they were interested in trying to build a new economic and social order through classroom instruction. However, most teachers were more concerned with cutbacks in their own school districts than with academic thinking. New social orders and collectivism made little practical sense to these educators. Nevertheless, the ideas of the social reconstructionists frightened many conservatives (those who support traditional ways of doing things), who regarded social reconstructionism as a form of communism (a theory that advocates elimination of private property). They demanded that school boards force teachers to sign loyalty oaths promising to not teach ideas foreign to American capitalism. Newspaper publisher William Randolph Hearst (1863–1951) filled his papers with warnings of the "red" (communist) menace in schools. By 1936 twenty-one states required loyalty oaths. The penalty for breaking the oath was dismissal, and no teacher could afford to be fired during the Depression. The loyalty oath requirement, however, was soon abolished by Congress in 1937.

tion to build and support their schools. Property taxes are based on the value of the property; therefore, school districts in wealthy areas had better schools, because more tax money was received on the high property values in these areas. As property values nose-dived during the Depression, educators looked to state legislatures for funding. Teachers lobbied successfully for increased state government funding for schools. Many states set a minimum funding level, below which no school district would be allowed to fall. Between 1930 and 1940 the portion of school budgets supported by state funding grew to 30 percent, almost double what it had previously been.

## Other lasting changes

Several other lasting positive changes occurred for schools amid the economic turmoil of the Depression. The closure of tiny rural schools and the subsequent consolidation of school districts allowed for more-efficient use of teachers, supplies, and building space. Efforts to consolidate and save expenses led to the first desegregated schools. (*Desegregation,* or *integration,* means black students and white students attend the same school rather than separate schools.) In 1932 the Educational Equality League of Philadelphia (Pennsylvania) formed to promote desegregation as a wise move given the economic hardships of the Depression. In 1934 one suburb of Philadelphia combined black and white schools. Black teachers were hired by the integrated schools, and by 1935 the Philadelphia Board of Public Education had a black member.

## Roosevelt and New Deal education

In the depths of the Depression in late 1932 Americans elected Franklin Delano Roosevelt (1882–1945) as president of the United States, and he was inaugurated in March 1933. President Roosevelt (served 1933–45) immediately introduced a series of programs known as the New Deal to halt America's downward economic spiral. As Roosevelt's New Deal began to help banks, industry, labor, and farmers, educators assumed that Roosevelt would also help education with a program of federal assistance. However, much to educators' dismay, Roosevelt chose to leave public schools without New Deal coverage. New Dealers and professional educators became opponents rather than allies.

Several factors contributed to Roosevelt's decision to let public schools fend for themselves. First, many educators wished to concentrate only on the brightest students; some of them believed that the poorest Americans, the blacks, and other minority groups were incapable of learning beyond the early basics. Roosevelt and New Dealers held an entirely different opinion. They believed the most needy and illiterate (lacking education) could learn if given the chance. Second, a majority of professional educators clung to the idea that education meant traditional classrooms with properly trained teachers instructing. Soon New Dealers would hire nonprofessionals to teach in alternative New Deal education programs. Roosevelt never felt in step with professional educators, whom

The Civilian Conservation
Corps provided training
and jobs to unemployed
young men. *Courtesy of the
Library of Congress.*

he referred to as "the school crowd." He and his commissioner of education, John Studebaker, were constantly at odds. When Roosevelt needed advice on education, he generally turned to his wife, Eleanor, her friends (such as black educator Mary McLeod Bethune), and social workers on his staff.

The third reason why Roosevelt left public education out of the New Deal had to do with spending and the federal debt. Roosevelt believed schools should be funded at the state and local levels. He feared that committing federal aid to all schools would drastically increase the federal debt and that the aid would be almost impossible to pull back as the economy improved. Roosevelt also had a fourth reason for holding back aid: He was at heart a politician, and he needed a broad base of political support. A fragile New Deal coalition (group of supporters) had formed; but if Roosevelt had advocated federal support for schools, he would have created conflict between its members. For example, the labor movement

Young men and women were given alternative education through National Youth Adminstration programs. Here, women are brushing up on their typewriting skills. *Courtesy of the Franklin D. Roosevelt Library.*

(workers organizing to seek better work conditions from employers) was largely Catholic and would likely be angered if equivalent help was not offered to their parochial or private schools. Southerners, another group that gave vital support to New Deal policies, opposed federal funding of public schools because they feared that the federal government would force an end to racial segregation in the schools. For these reasons, therefore, Roosevelt decided to pursue his own alternative education policies rather than support public schools with federal money.

Roosevelt and his administration created educational programs that aided underprivileged youths who might have been written off by the traditional educational system. These programs were created within agencies that were designed to put people to work, mostly on public works projects (projects that benefit the public as a whole). Public works projects included road construction, enhancing the environment, construction of public buildings, and building dams. The agencies involved in these activities included the Civilian Conservation Corps (CCC) and the National Youth Administration (NYA) (see Riding the Rails chapter) as well as the Works Progress Administration (WPA; see Works Progress Administration chapter). Besides providing beneficial public works, these agencies provided income, vocational classes, and on-the-job training to young people. The success of the programs soon proved that given appropriate education, needy youths could learn and compete with their wealthier peers. These programs cost far less than federal funding for all U.S. public schools. Also, as economic conditions improved, Roosevelt could pull back the programs' funding.

Although refusing to fund public schools, the Roosevelt administration did offer some support. The Federal Emergency Relief Administration (FERA), created in 1933, offered financial assistance by paying over four thousand rural school teachers' salaries. Through many public works programs between 1933 and 1939, the Public Works Administration (PWA) and the Works Progress Administration (WPA) were responsible for constructing a majority of new school buildings and upgrading thousands of older school buildings.

## Education at the end of the Depression

As the 1930s came to a close, the lack of funding for schools had not discouraged the gradual upward trend in the number of children attending and graduating from schools. High school enrollment kept schools expanding; with no jobs available, more students opted to stay in school longer. Inequality in funding was an issue that school districts would continue to wrestle with throughout the twentieth century. Nevertheless, through the difficulties of the Depression years, public education had proved to be an institution to which Americans remained committed.

## For More Information

### Books

Anderson, James D. *The Education of Blacks in the South, 1860–1935.* Chapel Hill, NC: University of North Carolina Press, 1988.

Davis, Kingsley. *Youth in the Depression.* Chicago, IL: University of Chicago Press, 1935.

Krug, Edward A. *The Shaping of the American High School.* Vol. 2, 1920–1941. Madison, WI: University of Wisconsin Press, 1972.

Murphy, Marjorie. *Blackboard Unions: The AFT and the NEA, 1900–1980.* Ithaca, NY: Cornell University Press, 1990.

Tyack, David, Robert Lowe, and Elisabeth Hansot. *Public Schools in Hard Times: The Great Depression and Recent Years.* Cambridge, MA: Harvard University Press, 1984.

### Web Sites

*American Federation of Teaching.* http://www.aft.org (accessed on August 14, 2002).

*National Education Association.* http://www.nea.org (accessed on August 14, 2002).

*U.S. Department of Education.* http://www.ed.gov (accessed on August 14, 2002).

# Employment, Industry, and Labor

**8**

"I can remember the first week of the CWA [Civil Works Administration] checks. It was on a Friday. That night everybody had gotten his check. The first check a lot of them had in three years. Everybody was celebrating…. I never saw such a change of attitude. Instead of walking around feeling dreary and looking sorrowful, everybody was joyous. They had money in their pockets for the first time. If Roosevelt had run for President the next day, he'd have gone in by a hundred percent." Hank Oettinger, who was laid off in 1931 and remained unemployed for two years, in Studs Terkel's 1986 book, *Hard Times: An Oral History of the Great Depression.*

The Great Depression (1929–41) was a time of crisis and change for the American worker. The number of unemployed workers rose to a level never before seen in the United States. With few other options for assistance, many turned to the federal government for relief. However, during the early years of the Great Depression, 1929 to 1932, President Herbert Hoover (1874–1964; served 1929–33) appealed to private charities and local government relief agencies to tend to the needy. He also called for voluntary efforts from industry

**A Hooverville in Seattle, Washington, circa 1934.**
*Corbis Corporation. Reproduced by permission.*

to employ as many workers as possible. These appeals proved highly ineffective, and employment opportunities and industry production continued to decline.

In early 1933 newly elected president Franklin Roosevelt (1882–1945; served 1933–45) introduced a new approach involving a massive federal commitment and considerable government spending. Roosevelt's approach included many new federal programs, collectively known as the New Deal, that were designed to help the nation recover from its economic slump. Some of the programs provided funding for jobs. Others provided standard industrial codes for industries to operate by.

During the 1930s many workers organized labor unions for the first time. A union is an organized group of workers joined together for a common purpose, such as negotiating with management for better working conditions. As a group, workers have stronger bargaining power when dealing with company management. Union members hoped for higher pay, shorter hours, and better working conditions. Unions gave millions of workers a greater voice and a sense of unity. However, the road to better pay and improved working conditions was rocky. Strikes became commonplace in 1936 and 1937. Some turned violent.

Although the New Deal programs turned out to be quite effective, employment and industry did not fully recover from the Great Depression until 1941, when the United States entered World War II (1939–45). Then, all at once, millions of jobs became available as almost every part of the economy was called upon to support the war effort.

 **"Hoover" This and That**

During the early years of the Depression, a vocabulary evolved using the name of the president at that time, Herbert Hoover (1874–1964; served 1929–33). Hoover had staunchly opposed granting money to relieve the suffering of people who were struggling in the economic crisis. Many Americans bitterly blamed Hoover for their miserable situation.

In cities all across the United States, including Washington, D.C., clusters of makeshift shelters sprang up on vacant lots. The shelters were made of scraps of metal, lumber, and cardboard and were occupied by the Depression's homeless. Shelter residents did their grocery shopping at restaurant garbage cans and in city dumps. These hapless communities were called "Hoovervilles."

Several other commonly used "Hoover" phrases were coined: "Hoover hogs" were jackrabbits caught for food. "Hoover flags" were empty pocket linings turned inside out. "Hoover blankets" were newspapers. "Hoover wagons" were broken-down cars being pulled by mules. "Hoover tourists" were homeless people catching rides on trains.

# Boom of the 1920s

During the 1920s the U.S. economy, with the exception of farming, boomed. Many industries adopted the assembly-line technique introduced in 1914 by Henry Ford (1863–1947), the automobile manufacturer. As a result, the overall productivity of industry rose rapidly; more consumer goods were available than ever before. Many believed the economic good times in industry were permanent.

Because jobs were plentiful and economic times were good, labor unions did not attract large memberships during the 1920s. Companies would offer retirement pensions or stocks to nonunion employees, hoping to keep them from joining a union. They also freely used force to suppress union strikes. Supporting this antiunion atmosphere were the Republican administrations of Warren G. Harding (1921–23), Calvin Coolidge (1923–29), and Herbert Hoover (1929–33). They refused to adopt any policies recognizing the rights of workers to organize and strike. Still, unemployment was low—less than 5 percent of the workforce through the 1920s—and workers had hope for a bright future.

## The Great Depression begins

For most Americans prosperity came to a sudden end. The initial drop in stock values occurred on October 24, 1929, when the price of stocks and bonds on the stock market began plummeting. The sale of stock in a company provides that company with operating money; however, in late 1929, in only a month's time, the value of stocks had dropped by 40 percent. No one was buying stock because they could no longer expect a return on their investment. Many individuals and businesses went bankrupt (legally declared unable to pay one's debts due to lack of money) and could not repay loans they had taken from the bank. As a result, banks also began going out of business, causing depositors to lose their savings. The average citizen lost confidence in the nation's economy and spent money cautiously, buying necessities only. This led to more companies shutting down and more workers becoming jobless. Increasing unemployment led to a further drop in spending, causing still more cutbacks and layoffs (being let go from a job, usually due to lack of work or lack of funds to pay workers). It was a vicious downward spiral.

Across the United States workers were forced to accept lower wages and fewer work hours; many lost their jobs altogether. Unemployment swept through factories. The economic decline was baffling for most Americans. They did not un-

derstand how the problem had started or what to do about it. In March 1930 President Hoover confidently predicted that the worst of the unemployment would pass by that summer. Yet the unemployment rate climbed from almost 9 percent in 1930 to 16 percent in 1931 and 24 percent in 1932. Without jobs people could not pay for shelter, clothing, or food. Thousands of people stood in breadlines at shelters waiting for free meals of soup and bread. It became increasingly clear that the country was experiencing something much worse than a short-term setback. Nevertheless, Hoover refused to consider federal relief programs (government-sponsored assistance, often in the form of food or money), because he thought they would undermine the people's will to work.

By 1932 relief provided by charities and local governments was falling far short of the need. In January of that year, in an effort to provide some federal assistance for the economy, Hoover had pushed legislation through Congress to create the Reconstruction Finance Corporation (RFC). The

With unemployment on the rise at the start of the Depression, Americans tried to earn a living any way they could. Pictured are street vendors selling apples for five cents apiece, circa 1930. *AP/Wide World Photo. Reproduced by permission.*

RFC provided government funds to struggling banks to keep them in business so that they could provide loans to businesses and thereby boost employment. However, the RFC proved incapable of making any real difference in the economy.

## The economy hits bottom

With a complete loss of confidence in President Hoover, American voters gave Democratic candidate Franklin Roosevelt (1882–1945) a landslide victory in the presidential election of November 1932. However, Roosevelt would not officially take office until March 4, 1933, so the nation had to endure four more months of government inaction. By early 1933 thousands of banks had failed, factory production was down 50 percent, and more than 25 percent of American workers (over twelve million people) were without jobs. Companies, suffering a loss of profits and revenue, began cutting back on their operating expenses. As a result, workers who still had jobs faced long hours, low wages, job insecurity, and poor working conditions. For some, workweeks extended up to sixty or even eighty hours. Industrial accidents were common as workers grew tired and less vigilant of dangers, and companies spent less money on safety measures. Despite these poor conditions, union membership stood at only 2.5 million workers, less than 5 percent of the workforce. (More than 4 million workers had been union members in the 1920s.) Those who belonged to unions were, for the most part, miners, construction workers, or skilled craftsmen. Workers knew that management disliked unions, and many feared that they would lose their jobs if they joined a union. In addition, companies hired spies and armed guards and stockpiled weapons to combat the formation of unions in their factories. Many of the big employers believed the best way to assure that unions did not form among their workers was through threats, if not actual displays of violence. When union workers did strike, companies would give their jobs to strikebreakers (workers who replace those on strike).

## The New Deal arrives

In the first one hundred days of his presidency, Roosevelt pushed through Congress numerous bills that would

create the programs collectively known as the New Deal. New Deal programs were designed to bring economic relief and recovery to the nation. After first reviving the U.S. banking system (see Banking and Housing chapter), Roosevelt began establishing programs to bring relief to the unemployed. The first New Deal program to provide jobs to the unemployed was the Civilian Conservation Corps (CCC), created on April 5, 1933. The CCC would employ 2.5 million young men between eighteen and twenty-five years of age in conservation projects around the nation.

Congress passed the Federal Emergency Relief Act on May 12, 1933, creating the Federal Emergency Relief Administration (FERA). The FERA provided large cash payments directly to city and state relief programs. This marked a dramatic change in the relationship of the federal government to the states, a change Hoover had previously resisted. For every three dollars a state set aside for relief, the FERA would contribute one dollar. This system encouraged states to establish

**About 5,000 unemployed workers lined up outside the New York City Federal Relief Administration offices in November 1933 to register for relief jobs.** *AP/Wide World Photo. Reproduced by permission.*

and operate ongoing relief agencies rather than spending lump-sum federal gift money on short-term projects that would only benefit a few. On May 17 Congress created the Tennessee Valley Authority (TVA), which would eventually employ thousands of workers building dams, power plants, and other facilities in the Southeast.

## The National Industrial Recovery Act

Unlike the previous presidents, Roosevelt and his key advisers, particularly Secretary of Labor Frances Perkins (1882–1965), supported the interests of labor. This major change in the government's attitude toward industry and labor became evident when Congress passed the National Industrial Recovery Act (NIRA) on June 16, 1933. The NIRA represented a key part of the New Deal's attempt at national economic planning. It also formally recognized organized labor, and that gave unions greater credibility in the eyes of workers. As a result, union membership began to grow. During the first year after passage of the NIRA, over a million workers joined labor unions.

The NIRA was a complex law that did several things: First, the law regulated industry and labor through the newly created National Recovery Administration (NRA). Under the NRA each industry would create a code of standards for both management and labor to follow in that industry. Some 546 industrial codes were written. The industries covered included shipbuilding, banking, textiles (clothing), insurance, transportation, and public health. The codes varied greatly from one industry to the next. The textiles industry code was one of the first ones established for the major industries under the act. It banned child labor, raised wages for workers, and reduced production to keep prices for products higher. Businesses that complied with the NRA could publicly display a Blue Eagle emblem to indicate their participation.

Second, the NIRA supported the workers' right to organize into unions, select representatives, and engage in collective bargaining. Collective bargaining is negotiation between representatives of an employer and representatives of labor, with both sides working to reach agreement on wages, job benefits, and working conditions. Under the new law, labor representatives were to be included in the development of industry codes. Wages, hours, and working conditions became key subjects of negotiation, during the development of the codes and during collective bargaining sessions.

Third, under authority of the NIRA, President Roosevelt created the Public Works Administration (PWA). He chose Harold Ickes (1874–1952), the secretary of the interior, to lead the program. Ultimately $3.3 billion was provided through the PWA for massive construction projects such as roads, dams, bridges, and public buildings; these projects would offer jobs for thousands of workers.

A National Recovery Administration poster with trademark Blue Eagle emblem. Businesses that complied with the NRA could publicly display a Blue Eagle emblem to indicate their participation. *Courtesy of the Franklin D. Roosevelt Library.*

## Unemployment rates remain high

By October 1933 it became apparent that recovery was not taking place as quickly as originally hoped. Millions remained unemployed. To address the situation, Roosevelt created the Civil Works Administration (CWA) on November 9, 1933, and appointed Harry Hopkins (1890–1946) to be its director. The CWA provided another $400 million for a work relief program. In just two months, the CWA had hired over four million workers across the country. However, the CWA projects only lasted until the spring of 1934.

It was thought that providing jobs would stimulate the economy by pump priming. Pump priming is a strategy that involves spending government money in ways that quickly put cash into the hands of consumers. Theoretically, if enough people received wages and began buying goods and services again, the economy would eventually come back into balance.However, by late 1934 New Deal programs had not significantly eased unemployment. Unemployment rates remained above 20 percent through 1934 and into 1935.

Critics of the New Deal gained momentum. Some claimed Roosevelt's programs were not benefiting the average worker. Big business, however, was thriving under the NIRA codes. Under these codes, prices for goods were rising faster than workers' wages. In addition noncompliance with the codes was growing, because temptations to violate them were too great and the NRA had few enforcement powers. Also, the NIRA allowed companies to form their own unions, squeezing out the regular unions. Workers were coerced to join these unions rather than independent unions. The company unions, of course, were biased and favored management over workers in most disputes. Many workers soon lost the desire to join unions.

## The New Deal for employment is renewed

In the face of mounting criticism and continuing economic problems, President Roosevelt renewed his effort to ease unemployment. He introduced the Second New Deal in April 1935. On April 8 Congress passed the Emergency Relief Appropriation Act. Under authority of the act, Roosevelt created the Works Progress Administration (WPA) a month later on May 6. The WPA would ultimately provide jobs for over three million people and spend over eleven billion dollars in its relief programs. WPA workers built or improved hospitals, school buildings, streets and roads, power plants, airport buildings and landing strips, public parks, and sidewalks (see Works Progress Administration chapter).

However, another stumbling block soon arose: the U.S. Supreme Court. On May 27, 1935, the Court ruled in *Schecter Poultry Corp. v. United States* that the NIRA was unconstitutional (not in keeping with the U.S. Constitution). Hence the NIRA became invalid. The Court reasoned that the regulation of business was the responsibility of Congress, not the president as designated by the National Recovery Administration. In addition, Congress could only regulate interstate commerce (business occurring across state lines). Because the businesses involved in the lawsuit were not directly involved in interstate commerce, the Court ruled that these businesses could only be regulated by the states, not the federal government. In striking down the NIRA, the Court also erased the workers' legal right to organize and engage in collective bargaining.

## National Labor Relations Act

Only five weeks after the Supreme Court decision that invalidated the NIRA, Congress passed legislation reasserting support for organized labor. The National Labor Relations Act (NLRA), passed on July 5, 1935, is more commonly known as the Wagner Act; its key congressional sponsor was Senator Robert F. Wagner (1877–1953) of New York. The act addressed several aspects of industry and labor relations. It protected the right of workers to join unions. Workers could no longer be fired for joining a union. It prohibited companies from certain unfair business practices, such as interfering in union activities, refusing to bargain with a union, or gaining control over a labor organization. The act also barred unions from forcing workers to join a union. To enforce these provisions the new law created the National Labor Relations Board (NLRB). The NLRB was given considerable leeway to administer the law. If a company was found to be in violation of the Wagner Act, the NLRB could issue "cease and desist" orders to tell an employer to halt questionable activities. If the company persisted in its violation, the NLRB could go to the U.S. Court of Appeals to seek a ruling that would force the company to stop unfair practices. The board could also help employees hold elections to establish unions and select their representatives. After passage of the Wagner Act, union membership rapidly increased.

## Union activity rises

A key moment for the labor movement came in 1935, when eight unions at a meeting of the American Federation of Labor (AFL) decided to form the Committee for Industrial Organization (CIO), a labor organization within the AFL. The CIO focused on mass-production industries such as automobile manufacturers and steel plants. Since

1886 the AFL, a loose federation of independent craft unions, had been the primary unifying force for American labor. The AFL member unions represented highly skilled workers such as electricians and plumbers. The AFL was not eager to represent less skilled industrial workers. Thus a battle with the new CIO developed over whether the AFL should also represent the lesser skilled workers. The CIO was gaining members among rubber workers, laborers in automobile factories, redcaps handling baggage at railroad stations, longshoremen working on the docks, and truck driver (teamster) unions. Unions joining the CIO were not organized by shared skills like the AFL member unions. Instead they were based on a particular type of industry or a shared workplace.

Despite the National Labor Relations Act and the growth of union membership, companies still were unwilling to recognize and bargain with unions. Workers found it necessary to become more confrontational with management. The automobile industry, including related tire manufacturers, had been a leader in U.S. industry since the late 1910s. However, the Depression triggered a major decline in car sales, which led to a drop in the demand for tires. But as the economy somewhat improved and car sales began to rise in late 1935, the Goodyear tire company in Akron, Ohio, announced it was returning to a forty-hour workweek but would pay wages for only thirty hours of work. Rubber workers at plants owned by Goodyear (as well as those at Firestone and Goodrich tire manufacturers) staged a sit-down strike in January 1936. They remained in the factories at their workstations but refused to work until their demand for a thirty-hour workweek was met. By remaining at their workstations, the sit-down strikers stopped employers from replacing them with scab (replacement) laborers and also avoided confrontation on the street with people and police opposing a picket line (striking employees marching outside their place of business holding signs, pickets, explaining their complaints and demands). Finally, in March, Goodyear gave in to a thirty-hour workweek.

Confrontations between labor and industry continued to escalate through 1936 and 1937. In 1936 the United Auto Workers (UAW), a CIO member, became more aggressive in demanding recognition from employers. Despite the col-

lapse of car sales during the Depression, General Motors (GM) had risen to the top of auto sales. GM controlled 43 percent of the market and still showed a profit. Because of its relatively strong financial condition, GM became a first target for the UAW, whose members sought increased wages and benefits. In the fall of 1936 strikes began occurring at some GM plants. The struggle peaked in November as sit-down strikes spread from Atlanta, Georgia, to Kansas City, Missouri, then to Cleveland, Ohio, and on to Detroit and Flint, Michigan. In January 1937 the strike in Flint erupted into a brawl between strikers and the police on the street outside the factory. The police fired tear gas, and strikers retaliated by throwing rocks and bottles. No one was killed, but a number of people were injured on both sides. Michigan governor Frank Murphy (1890–1949), who was supportive of labor, sent in the National Guard to keep order but not to break up the strike. GM finally recognized the UAW and its demands on February 11, 1937. The UAW conflict with GM proved once and for all the power of unionization. The membership of the UAW skyrock-

**United Auto Workers members stage a sit-down strike at the General Motors auto plant in Flint, Michigan, in 1937.**
*UPI/Corbis-Bettmann. Reproduced by permission.*

eted from eighty-eight thousand to four hundred thousand in the next several months after the GM strike.

After the UAW victory, strikes spread to other industries. In March 1937, 170 sit-down strikes involving over 167,000 workers occurred across the nation. Under the increasing threats of strikes and labor unrest, manufacturers, including U.S. Steel Corporation, began more readily entering into agreements with CIO unions. However, some companies still held out against unionization. Republic Steel, for example, refused to recognize its workers' union, represented by the CIO's Steel Workers' Organizing Committee. Finally, about seventy thousand employees walked off the job. At the Republic Steel mill in South Chicago on Memorial Day of 1937 events turned violent when the police blocked marchers from entering the main gate. As demonstrators threw rocks and other objects at police lines, the police opened fire on the workers and their families. Police pursued them across a field, shooting and beating them. Ten demonstrators died and ninety others (including three policemen) were injured. The charge of the police became known as the Memorial Day Massacre. It took until August 1941 for Republic Steel to agree to bargain with labor and another year before it signed a contract with United Steelworkers of America.

## Fair Labor Standards Act

New Deal legislation in 1938 would again strengthen government support of the labor movement. After considerable debate and opposition from conservatives, Congress passed the Fair Labor Standards Act (FLSA) on June 25. This law brought back some elements of the National Industrial Recovery Act, which had been struck down as unconstitutional in 1935.

The FLSA reinstated several of the codes from the old law, including those that established maximum hours and minimum wages and prohibited child labor. It fixed a minimum wage of twenty-five cents an hour and a maximum workweek of forty-four hours. At the time, an estimated twelve million workers were earning less than twenty-five cents an hour. By 1940 wages would rise to forty cents an hour with a workweek of forty hours. Employers who want-

The May 30, 1937, strike at the Republic Steel plant in Chicago, Illinois, took a violent turn as ten people were killed and ninety others were injured. Here, police clash with strikers in what became known as the Memorial Day Massacre. *AP/Wide World Photo. Reproduced by permission.*

ed laborers to exceed the maximum allowable hours had to pay time and a half (one and a half times the employees' hourly wage) for each overtime hour. For the rest of the century the FLSA remained the main legislation protecting workers from long hours and low pay.

## Last labor events

The AFL and the CIO continued their battle to gain the top leadership position among U.S. labor interests; each tried to out-recruit the other for new members. A major split in the nation's union movement occurred in 1938 when the AFL expelled all unions that had formed the CIO. With its new independence the CIO changed its name in November 1938 from the Committee for Industrial Organization to the Congress of Industrial Organizations. The new CIO continued to grow under the dynamic leadership of John L. Lewis (1880–1969).

## John L. Lewis

John L. Lewis (1880–1969) was born in Iowa to a coal-mining family of Welsh descent. Lewis began working in the mines in 1901 and became an original member of the local chapter of the United Mine Workers of America (UMWA). The UMWA was a member of the American Federation of Labor (AFL). After various jobs, Lewis and his family settled in the coalfields of Illinois, where he became increasingly recognized for his union activity. In 1911 he was selected as a field representative for Samuel Gompers (1850–1924), the AFL president. This responsibility speeded Lewis's rise in the UMWA; he became the organization's president in 1920. At that time the union had about four hundred thousand members.

Although Lewis was a firm and determined leader, UMWA membership dropped steadily in the 1920s. Lengthy strikes, lack of state and federal support for unions, and a drop in the demand for coal hurt the union. Lewis was a conservative Republican who believed that government should not be involved in business matters, including labor issues. However, he also recognized an opportunity to further his cause through Roosevelt's New Deal legislation: With passage of the National Industrial Recovery Act in 1933, which provided the first legal protections for union activities, Lewis had almost instant success expanding union membership. As a result of the increased membership and political power, wages of many UMWA members climbed.

Lewis began to pressure the AFL to represent largely unskilled industrial workers in its craft unions (historically, the AFL had represented only highly skilled craftsmen such as electricians and plumbers). In November 1935 Lewis formed the Committee for Industrial Organization (CIO) within the AFL to support industrial unions. The CIO grew rapidly under Lewis's leadership, attracting workers from the automobile, steel, and rubber industries. Lewis was often personally involved in negotiations with industry on behalf of the CIO member unions.

Another setback for labor came in 1939, again from the Supreme Court. The Court outlawed sit-down strikes, the strategy that had served the industrial unions so well earlier in the Depression. Nonetheless, better days for workers and industry were ahead. By 1941, as the United States prepared to enter World War II (1939–45), industries increased production of war materials, and unemployment dropped to less than 10 percent of the workforce. Union membership grew to nine million. By 1945 unemployment was below 2 per-

**John L. Lewis, April 1937.** *AP/Wide World Photo. Reproduced by permission.*

In late 1937 the nation's economy worsened again, and bloody confrontations occurred between strikers and police. The rise in violence led many workers to withdraw from union participation. With the decline in membership, Lewis came under criticism from other CIO leaders for letting the union's influence decline. The critics also charged that Lewis had allowed radicals, including Communists, to become established within the CIO. Based on the increased violence, declining membership, and supposed radical ties, the AFL ousted the CIO from its organization in 1938. It then changed its name to the Congress of Industrial Organizations, and Lewis continued as one of the nation's most visible spokesmen for workers. However, conflicts with other CIO leaders increased as Lewis began supporting Republican candidates while most of labor supported Roosevelt and the Democrats. For example, in 1940 Lewis opposed Roosevelt's reelection. He left the CIO soon after the election and became increasingly distant from the organization. He continued as president of the UMWA, which had withdrawn from the CIO to operate independently. Lewis was a major force in American labor, serving a total of forty years as head of the UMWA.

cent, and fifteen million workers were union members. World War II had, for the moment, brought an end to most industry and labor problems in the United States.

## For More Information

Bernstein, Irving. *Turbulent Years: A History of the American Worker, 1933–1941*. Boston, MA: Houghton Mifflin, 1970.

Bradley, Michael R. *On the Job: Safeguarding Workers' Rights*. Vero Beach, FL: Rourke Corporation, 1992.

Brand, Donald R. *Corporatism and the Rule of Law: A Study of the National Recovery Administration*. Ithaca, NY: Cornell University Press, 1988.

Dubofsky, Melvyn. *Hard Work: The Making of Labor History*. Urbana, IL: University of Illinois Press, 2000.

Dubofsky, Melvyn, and Warren Van Tyne. *John L. Lewis: A Biography*. New York, NY: Quadrangle Books/New York Times, 1977.

Fine, Sidney. *Sit-Down: The General Motors Strike of 1936–1937*. Ann Arbor, MI: University of Michigan Press, 1969.

Galenson, Walter. *The CIO Challenge to the AFL: A History of the American Labor Movement, 1935–1941*. Cambridge, MA: Harvard University Press, 1960.

Gordon, Colin. *New Deals: Business, Labor, and Politics in America, 1920–1935*. New York, NY: Cambridge University Press, 1994.

Schwartz, Alvin. *The Unions: What They Are, How They Came to Be, How They Affect Each of Us*. New York, NY: Viking Press, 1972.

Storrs, Landon R. Y. *Civilizing Capitalism: The National Consumers' League, Women's Activism, and Labor Standards in the New Deal Era*. Chapel Hill, NC: University of North Carolina Press, 2000.

Terkel, Studs. *Hard Times: An Oral History of the Great Depression*. New York, NY: Pantheon Books, 1986.

Vittoz, Stanley. *New Deal Labor Policy and the American Industrial Economy*. Chapel Hill, NC: University of North Carolina Press, 1987.

## Web Sites

*AFL-C10*. http://www.aflcio.org (accessed on August 14, 2002).

*U.S. Department of Labor*. http://www.dol.gov (accessed on August 14, 2002).

# Electrifying Rural America

For many Americans in the 1930s one of the most memorable experiences of a lifetime was the day electric power came to their home. Often with great anticipation homes were readied for "zero hour," the moment the lines were energized. Homes were wired, bulbs were hung, a radio was in place, and, if the family could afford them, appliances such as electric ranges and refrigerators were installed and ready.

The push to bring electricity to all corners of America—including isolated rural farms—began with the presidential campaign of 1932. The Democratic candidate, Franklin D. Roosevelt (1882–1945), promoted the goal of rural electrification, and in November he won the presidency by a landslide. Americans caught in the depths of the Great Depression (1929–41), the worst economic crisis in U.S. history, had pinned all their hopes on the new president.

## Few electrified farms

Electric power began to serve American industry, businesses, and homes in the cities by the 1880s. However, for many years electrification was regarded as a luxury. But by the 1920s electric power was becoming an essential part of modern life. More than half of all urban homes had electric lights, and many of those homes had electric appliances. Despite these advances in cities, few farm families had electricity. By 1930 more than 90 percent of rural homes still used kerosene lamps for lighting; and running water and indoor bathrooms were impossible without powered pumping systems.

President Herbert Hoover (1874–1964; served 1929–33) took a hands-off approach in dealing with such problems. Hoover was solidly in favor of electrification and wanted to improve the lives and productivity of all Americans, including farmers. However, he also believed that private enterprise (a business belonging to an individual or group of people with the expectation of making a profit) should, and eventually would, accomplish this objective of electrifying the nation. But at the time, private utility companies were primarily focused on electric power for industry. They believed that the cost of delivering power to the countryside would be too high and that farmers could not afford to pay at rates that would be profitable for the utility companies.

## Electrification as a campaign issue

The Democratic Party nominated New York governor Franklin D. Roosevelt (1882–1945) for president in July 1932. During a campaign swing through the South in the summer of 1932, Roosevelt was struck by the poverty and related sanitation problems in rural areas. He was convinced that bringing electricity to such areas would be a major step toward modernization. Electricity would make running water possible in homes, and it could power refrigerators to keep food from spoiling. But the power would have to be inexpensive so that people could afford it.

Roosevelt's national electric power priorities sharply contrasted with Hoover's and with the interests of the private utility industry. Private utilities wanted to focus on better serving the 20 percent of Americans who were already consumers of electricity; Roosevelt was concerned with the 80 percent of households that did not have electric power.

To achieve the goal of rural electrification Roosevelt promoted broad governmental planning at the national level; planning decisions would then be carried out in various regions of the nation. During his campaign, Roosevelt promoted large power projects in every region of the country, promising an ample supply of cheap electricity. He pointed to opportunities on the St. Lawrence River in the Northeast, the Tennessee River in the Southeast, the Columbia River in the Northwest, and the Colorado River in the Southwest. The voting public, desperate for a new approach to solving the economic problems of the Great Depression, elected Roosevelt in a landslide victory over President Hoover. Upon taking office in March 1933, Roosevelt launched his plans to end the Depression, introducing special legislation—called the New Deal—that would create relief agencies and programs to help all Americans. Electrifying America was a top priority in the New Deal plan.

## The New Deal electrification programs

New Deal legislators looked primarily to the Bureau of Reclamation (BOR) and the U.S. Army Corps of Engineers (COE) to guide development of the proposed large electrification projects. The BOR, established under the Federal Reclamation Act of 1902, was the primary agency concerned with irrigation in the West. At the start of the New Deal the BOR had twenty-six construction projects under way, involving over $335 million. The COE, established in 1804, was primarily concerned with ship navigation and flood control.

To create jobs for the unemployed, Roosevelt established the Public Works Administration (PWA) on June 16, 1933, under the authority of the National Industrial Recovery Act, which was signed into law that same day. Through the remainder of the Depression, funding for electrification projects would come through the PWA. The projects would provide tens of thousands of jobs.

The New Deal electrification projects were massive efforts. Many were not completed until the 1940s or even later. A few of the more ambitious projects are described in the following paragraphs.

The completed Hoover Dam, then known as Boulder Dam, in January 1935. The name was changed to Hoover Dam in 1947. *Corbis-Bettmann. Reproduced by permission.*

# Southwest: The Colorado River

The first major New Deal hydroelectric power (electricity generated from water power) project was actually one started during Hoover's administration (1929–33). For many years certain interest groups had wanted a dam built on the Colorado River to serve the water and power needs of Los Angeles, California, and surrounding regions. The project finally gained the approval of Congress in 1928. In late 1930 President Hoover authorized the construction of Hoover Dam. The BOR assigned the work to private construction companies. An engineer himself, Hoover saw the massive construction project as a way to create thousands of jobs and strengthen the public's faith in the U.S. economic system.

At the peak of construction in the early 1930s, fifty-two hundred men worked on Hoover Dam around the clock, seven days a week. Because of the size of the job, several large construction companies joined together to form a giant business partnership known as Six Companies. Hoover Dam was the first occasion on which multiple construction companies worked together on a federal government project. These companies would later tackle other large New Deal projects both individually and in various combinations. Some would become the leading construction companies in the world. Marriner Eccles (1890–1977), head of one of the construction companies, became a leading industry spokesman for large public works projects. He would become a key figure in the New Deal, serving as the assistant secretary of the treasury for Roosevelt.

The Hoover Dam workers enjoyed the relative stability of long-term employment during the peak years of the Great Depression. However, the work was hard and dangerous, and pay was not high. Fifty workers died during the construction of the dam. Unskilled workers made fifty cents an hour, and skilled workers such as carpenters made seventy-five cents an hour. Before construction of the dam could begin, the Colorado River had to be diverted through four giant tunnels dug through solid rock formations. Five million tons of dirt and rock would be removed from the future dam site. Finally, by the spring of 1933, as Roosevelt was taking office, construction of the dam itself began. Twelve million tons of sand and gravel were needed for the concrete mix. Roosevelt's secretary of the interior, Harold Ickes (1874–1952), changed the name of the dam to Boulder Dam because Hoover had become quite unpopular with the public. Congress restored the name Hoover Dam in 1947.

The Public Works Administration (PWA) provided $38 million in 1934 for the construction of Hoover Dam; the total construction cost was $114 million. The dam is 726 feet high, similar to a fifty-story building, and 660 feet thick at its base.

It was the world's largest dam at the time. The dam began storing water on February 1, 1935, and in September 1935 President Roosevelt traveled to the project to make a dedication address. The dam began producing electricity in September 1936. Besides irrigating over 2.5 million acres of farmland, it provided Los Angeles, California, with domestic water (through a 260-mile-long aqueduct) and hydroelectric power.

Further upstream, at the source of the Colorado River, was another massive project—the Big Thompson Project. Canals and tunnels, including one tunnel thirteen miles long, would divert Colorado River water from southwest Colorado through the Rocky Mountains to the dry farming region of southeast Colorado. Congress authorized funding for the project in 1937 through the BOR. The PWA provided additional funds to begin construction. The job also included five dams and power plants that would generate hydroelectric power for several regions of Colorado. The entire project would take twenty years to complete.

## Southeast: The Tennessee River valley

The Tennessee River, one of the largest in the United States, flows for 652 miles and drains an area of almost 41,000 square miles. Included in this area are parts of seven states: Tennessee, Virginia, North Carolina, Georgia, Alabama, Mississippi, and Kentucky. During the 1920s the Tennessee River valley was one of the most impoverished regions of the United States. Largely bypassed by the industrial growth taking place in the U.S. in the early twentieth century, it was home to millions of poor subsistence farmers (farmers who only grew enough crops to live on, not sell for profit) who had little opportunity to improve their lives. The region's future looked bleak, yet its rivers, though not well suited to navigation or agriculture, held the potential to produce huge amounts of hydroelectric power.

In 1931 the U.S. Army Corps of Engineers (COE) issued a final report of a comprehensive survey of the Tennessee River and its tributaries. This report made it clear that cheap electric power, flood control, and improved navigation and health conditions could be achieved through a carefully coordinated development of the river system. After assuming

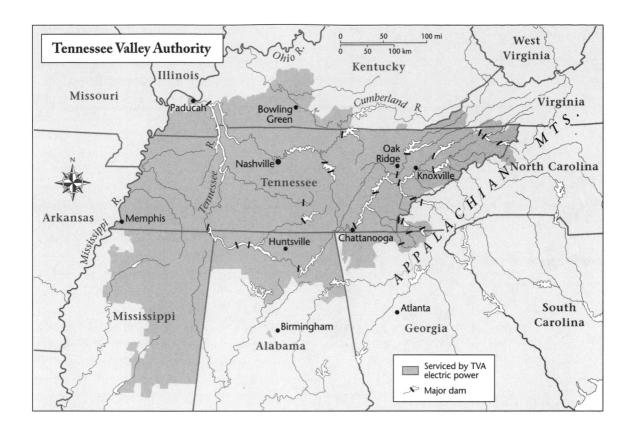

office on March 4, 1933, President Roosevelt followed the COE suggestions, calling for a coordinated program for the entire Tennessee River valley; the program would involve flood control, restoration of land subject to flooding, power development, navigation improvements, and promotion of new industry. Congress enacted the Roosevelt program, and Roosevelt signed the Tennessee Valley Authority (TVA) Act into law on May 17, 1933. The act called for a governing board of three directors, one of whom would be chairman, to guide the program. The TVA would be a government corporation not connected to other federal departments and answerable only to the president. Roosevelt selected Arthur E. Morgan as the TVA chairman.

The TVA act authorized the government to distribute publicly generated power throughout the Tennessee River valley and adjacent areas, primarily to public agencies such as municipal utilities and cooperatives. (A cooperative is a private, nonprofit enterprise, locally owned and managed by

**Map of the Tennessee Valley Authority region.**

**Norris Dam was the first one built under the Tennessee Valley Authority.**
*Courtesy of the Library of Congress.*

those it serves and incorporated under state law.) The act also explicitly stated that the TVA should not compete with existing private power facilities. Because private companies already were in place, the companies and the TVA had to establish boundaries between public and private service territories. In order for the TVA to establish a service area, some areas had to be given up by the private power companies. Naturally the private companies were reluctant to do this, and legal battles ensued between the private power companies in the region and the federal government. Ultimately, after August 1939, the TVA held exclusive electricity markets in most of Tennessee and in large parts of northern Alabama and northeastern Mississippi. The TVA confined itself to this territory for the remainder of the twentieth century.

Dam construction was the most visible TVA program. By June 1935 the TVA employed over sixteen thousand workers, mostly in dam construction. By 1936 five dams were under way. Wilson Dam at Alabama's Muscle Shoals had already been completed in 1925. Once the TVA was established, dams were built in rapid succession on the Tennessee River and its tributaries, according to the COE's recommendations. The first was Norris Dam, begun in October 1933 and named after Senator George Norris (1861–1944; served 1913–43) of Nebraska, who had long argued for development of the Tennessee River valley. The dam was finished in 1936. Construction on Wheeler Dam began one month after the start of Norris Dam. These dams were popular tourist destinations during the Depression: One thousand people visited Wilson, Wheeler, and Norris Dams each day. By the time the system was completed in 1944, the TVA had built sixteen dams.

The TVA also set up an experimental cooperative to distribute electricity. This was the Alcorn County Electric

## Publicizing Electrification

The New Deal utility programs proved to be highly popular with the public. This was due in large part to the extra efforts that were made in publicizing the programs' services and benefits. William L. Sturdevant ran the highly successful Tennessee Valley Authority (TVA) publicity campaign through the TVA Information Office. The office was well funded and employed a full-time staff of twelve. The staff even included a motion picture director.

The TVA Information Office produced articles for professional journals and popular magazines, movies, pamphlets, speeches, traveling exhibits, and photographs. Writers for the publicity office specialized in covering various aspects of the TVA, including power generation, farming improvements, and engineering achievements. TVA employees published numerous articles about the program and gave many speeches. In addition to articles written by the TVA staff, more than two thousand magazine articles about the TVA were produced by other writers during the 1930s. The publicity office responded personally to approximately one hundred thousand letters received from the public between 1933 and 1940. Trained guides led over four million visitors to the dams during that same period. Visitors who were writers or students received special attention and were encouraged to study and write about the TVA's achievements.

TVA photographers busily documented all parts of the projects. Some of their pictures are highly regarded today as works of art. These photographs were used in TVA exhibits at conventions, meetings, schools, and colleges around the country. (The TVA exhibit at the 1939 World's Fair in New York City drew over three million visitors.) The photographs also appeared in fifteen pamphlets published by the TVA Information Office, some of which won awards and became models for school writing classes. The TVA's films included *TVA at Work, Norris Dam,* and *Electricity on the Farm.* These films and others were used in hundreds of schools and seen by nearly one million people by 1940. The special effort to inform the public paid off in immense popular support for the TVA, which protected the agency from political efforts by Congress or others to transfer it to private ownership.

The Bonneville Power Administration (BPA) took a more novel approach for some of its publicity. To spur public support of the Columbia River dams, the BPA hired unemployed songwriter Woody Guthrie (1912–1967) in May 1941 to travel the Northwest for thirty days. He was to write a song a day about the New Deal electrification program in that region, and he would be paid $267. Guthrie ended up writing twenty-six songs, including the American folk classics "Grand Coulee Dam," "Roll On Columbia," "Jackhammer Blues," and "Pastures of Plenty."

Cooperative in northeastern Mississippi, an economically depressed region with many tenant farmers. In addition Congress established the Electric Home and Farm Authority (EHFA) in December 1933. The EHFA was designed to help private manufacturers market electric appliances in the TVA service area. For this economically struggling area the manufacturers made special models to sell at lower prices than normal.

In the 1930s the TVA endured many battles—both internally among its directors and externally with the private power companies—before finally realizing Roosevelt's dream of revitalizing the region. The new series of hydroelectric dams generated massive amounts of new electricity, driving down electric rates and stimulating the modernization of industries and homes in the cities and countryside. Navigation locks (a chamber that can contain a ship and raise or lower water to allow it to pass by a dam) alongside the dams finally established a practical shipping channel into eastern Tennessee, lowering shipping costs and improving the profitability of local businesses.

By 1941 the TVA was the largest producer of electric power in the United States. It was also instrumental in World War II (1939–45), providing electricity for the production of aluminum (for aircraft) and nitrates (for munitions). The TVA continues to serve the Tennessee River valley in the twenty-first century. A government corporation funded by its own revenues from selling electricity rather than regular government appropriations, the TVA produces more electricity than any other utility in the United States. The TVA is part of the social and economic fabric of life in the Tennessee River valley and is one of the crowning achievements of the New Deal.

## Northwest: The Columbia River

The comprehensive nationwide study by the COE that detailed the potential of the Tennessee River valley also included a plan for a system of ten dams on the Columbia River in the Pacific Northwest. Recognized as a vast unharnessed power source, the Columbia River was thought to hold 40 percent of the nation's hydroelectric power potential. President Roosevelt saw the proposed Columbia River projects as a great opportunity to provide work relief (new jobs) on public projects while furthering his goal of electrifying America. The Northwest was a good candidate: In 1933, for example, 70 percent of Oregon farms were not yet electrified.

The Bonneville Dam, located about forty miles east of Portland, Oregon, was the first Columbia River project. The dam would make the Columbia River navigable for oceangoing vessels for an additional forty-eight miles upstream. It would also provide abundant cheap power for the region. The Bonneville Dam presented a major engineering challenge, requiring the obstruction of a river flow ten times that of the Colorado River at Hoover Dam. Work began in October 1933. The total cost of the project was $80 million, with the Public Works Administration (PWA) contributing $42 million.

As work on the Bonneville Dam began, interest increased in a proposed giant project—the Grand Coulee Dam—upstream in northern Washington. Planners hoped to irrigate one million acres in the dry central Washington region to boost the region's agricultural potential. The state of Washington had committed $377,000 to begin the Grand Coulee Dam project in 1933. Roosevelt provided $14 million through the PWA in late 1933 and placed the project under the responsibility of the BOR. Excavation at the dam site began that December.

On August 30, 1935, in the River and Harbor Act, Congress approved funding for the dam. Grand Coulee would become the largest dam in the world. Roosevelt, who visited the construction site in 1937, regarded the dam as the New Deal's model project for showcasing the potential of dams in regional economic development. By 1942 a total of $69 million had been provided and the dam was completed. Construction of the powerhouses and pumping plant was still under way. The Grand Coulee Dam first generated power on March 22, 1941. The project had employed six thousand workers laboring day and night.

In 1937, with power soon to be produced by Bonneville Dam, Roosevelt sought a means to sell the electricity directly to the public. The Bonneville Power Act created the Bonneville Power Administration (BPA). Patterned partly after the Tennessee Valley Authority (TVA), the BPA would sell and distribute to the public electricity generated by Bonneville Dam (and later by other Columbia River public dams, including Grand Coulee). The BPA, using PWA funds and in some cases workers from the Works Progress Administration (WPA), constructed transmission lines and substations around the region. The BPA became the primary provider of electricity in the Pacific Northwest.

## The Rural Electrification Administration (REA)

Noting the TVA's early successes in establishing cooperatives to distribute electricity, Secretary of the Interior Harold Ickes (1874–1952) proposed in February 1934 an ambitious nationwide plan: to involve cooperatives using low-interest, long-term federal loans to construct power lines in areas not already served by private electric companies. To achieve this goal, President Roosevelt created the Rural Electrification Administration (REA) on May 11, 1935. The REA was set up as a lending agency rather than a relief agency; it would provide loans to organizations building rural power projects. The new agency would also provide low-cost federal loans to consumers for wiring houses and buying home appliances (this was similar to the role of the Electric Home and Farm Authority in the TVA region). The goal of such lending was to encourage electricity consumption and thereby bring electric rates down.

Farmers were already well experienced at forming and running cooperatives for marketing their farm products. However, that job did not require the high levels of technical expertise that electrical cooperatives would. To overcome this obstacle the REA offered to provide services that the farmers lacked, including designing appropriate electrical transmission systems to meet their needs. The terms of REA loans were favorable to cooperatives, featuring low-interest rates and a repayment period of twenty years. The cooperatives would buy their power from a private power company, a municipal utility, or the federal government. President Roosevelt signed the Rural Electrification Act of 1936 into law on May 21, making the REA a permanent agency, and appointed Morris Cooke as REA administrator.

To become eligible for an REA loan, cooperatives had to convince the REA that their project would be properly managed and that they would be able to pay back the loan. They

had to hire lawyers, elect officers, recruit members, hire engineers to help design transmission line systems, arrange to buy electric power at wholesale rates, maintain proper records, and work with state power commissions. Few states had laws specifically permitting electric cooperatives, so in 1937 the REA staff drew up a model law that states could follow to describe how co-ops could be legally formed and regulated.

A Rural Electrification Administration (REA) power line brings electricity to this rural North Carolina home. *Courtesy of the Library of Congress.*

Because of the high unemployment rate during the Great Depression, the REA was able to choose its staff from a large pool of people. As a result, the agency hired very skilled and experienced professionals. The REA staff instructed farmers on all the aspects of organizing and operating a successful electric co-op. The REA even showed people how to use electricity. For example, home economists showed women how to operate new electric appliances, and engineers showed farmers how electric motors could help with farmwork. From 1938 until 1942 the REA conducted a traveling show, known as the Demonstration Farm Equipment Tour, to show the proper uses

for electrical household and farm equipment. Thousands of people in twenty states saw this exhibition.

To bring down expenses the REA standardized poles, hardware, power transformers, and electrical wires. Another cost-savings measure was having construction crews use assembly-line methods in building transmission lines, with specialized crews following one another along the route. In this way the REA was able to reduce construction costs: Before the REA program transmission lines cost up to $2,000 per mile. By the end of 1936 the cost was $941 per mile, and by 1939 it was $825 per mile. This cost reduction made rural electrification more affordable for the co-ops. Farmers who had no money were allowed to work on REA crews in exchange for obtaining electric service in their homes.

The dedication of the REA and the rural cooperatives, along with the improved efficiencies in construction, greatly accelerated electrification of rural areas. From 1936 to 1939 the number of rural electricity consumers increased from 700 to 268,000. REA loans climbed from $13.9 million in 1935 to $227.2 million in 1939.

**Two workers assemble power transmission lines in rural San Joaquin, California, in November 1938.** *Courtesy of the Library of Congress.*

## Electrification legacy

A great deal of funding was provided for electrification during the Great Depression years. The Public Works Administration spent over $3 billion for water and power developments, and the Bureau of Reclamation (BOR) provided an average of $52 million a year. (Before the Depression it averaged less than $9 million a year.) The Corps of Engineers added millions more. By 1940 the BOR had twenty-three

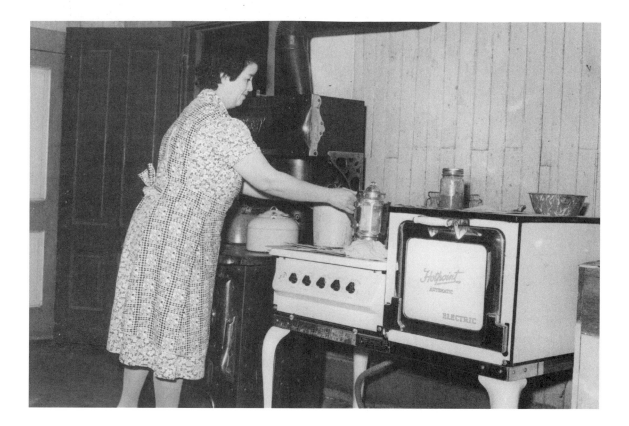

power plants in operation throughout the West and fifteen more still under construction. Though demoralized by the Great Depression, Americans felt some encouragement as they watched the federal government and private business develop these projects.

Though nationwide in scope, the electrification projects of the New Deal would exert particular influence on future economic development of the western United States. The projects would contribute to increased food and pastureland for livestock; extensive crops of vegetables, fruits, and grains; construction of food processing and aluminum plants and other industry; and electricity for cities and farming communities.

The dams fulfilled Roosevelt's vision of cheap electricity and modernization for rural America. Modernization profoundly changed the lives of farmers. Their standard of living rose dramatically, and farm production vastly in-

**A farmer's wife uses her electric stove, which sits next to the wood-burning stove, for the first time.** *Courtesy of the Library of Congress.*

creased. The United States became a world leader in agriculture. The availability of electricity also allowed new industries to spring up in rural areas, providing a wide range of economic enterprises in areas away from the traditional urban industrial centers. In the end the New Deal electrification programs contributed to prosperity in the United States to an extent far beyond Roosevelt's dreams.

## For More Information

### Books

Brown, D. Clayton. *Electricity for Rural America: The Fight for the REA.* Westport, CT: Greenwood Press, 1980.

Cullen, Allan H. *Rivers in Harness: The Story of Dams.* New York, NY: Chilton Books, 1962.

Dunar, Andrew J., and Dennis McBride. *Building Hoover Dam: An Oral History of the Great Depression.* New York, NY: Twayne Publishers, 1993.

Hubbard, Preston J. *Origins of the TVA: The Muscle Shoals Controversy, 1920–1932.* New York, NY: W. W. Norton, 1961.

Lilienthal, David E. *The Journals of David Lilienthal: The TVA Years, 1939–1945.* New York, NY: Harper & Row, 1964.

Lowitt, Richard. *The New Deal and the West.* Norman, OK: University of Oklahoma Press, 1993.

Nye, David E. *Electrifying America: Social Meanings of a New Technology, 1880–1940.* Cambridge, MA: MIT Press, 1990.

Tobey, Ronald C. *Technology as Freedom: The New Deal and the Electrical Modernization of the Home.* Berkeley, CA: University of California Press, 1996.

Wolf, Donald E. *Big Dams and Other Dreams: The Six Companies Story.* Norman, OK: University of Oklahoma Press, 1996.

### Web Sites

*Tennessee Valley Authority.* http://www.tva.gov (accessed on August 15, 2002).

"TVA: Electricity for All." *New Deal Network.* http://newdeal.feri.org/tva/index.htm (accessed on August 15, 2002).

# Women of the New Deal

When Franklin D. Roosevelt (1882–1945) was inaugurated as president in March 1933, the United States was at the depth of the Great Depression, the most severe economic downturn the nation had ever experienced. Almost immediately President Roosevelt and his advisers presented Congress with a series of programs designed to bring relief, recovery, and reform to the nation's ailing economy. Together these programs became known as the New Deal. As the New Deal legislation passed through Congress, many new government agencies were established to carry out the relief programs. In order to accomplish their goals, these agencies needed experienced relief workers. In America the most experienced relief workers were those trained in social work; and most trained social workers were women. Hence the New Deal agencies brought a wealth of new opportunities for these women, who were highly qualified to deal with the problems of the Great Depression. By the end of 1933 thirty-five women had received appointments to prominent government positions. By the end of the decade, fifty-five women held key positions in government.

A few women had played active roles in government before the 1930s. Since 1921 Grace Abbott (1878–1939) had served as chief of the Children's Bureau in the Department of Labor. Mary Anderson had led that same department's Women's Bureau since 1920. Women had won the right to vote in 1920, and several women were elected to the U.S. House of Representatives in the 1920s. However, with the New Deal appointments of women in the 1930s, a new attitude toward women in government began to emerge. This attitude, held by growing numbers of people, was that more women belonged in political circles where they could offer perspectives on social issues not commonly heard before. From Secretary of Labor Frances Perkins, the first woman cabinet member, to Hallie Flanagan, the determined director of the Federal Theater Project, women began to make their mark in the U.S. federal government. The early appointments of women to New Deal agency posts were attributed in part to President Roosevelt's desire to break new ground; in part to the influence of his wife, Eleanor; and in large part to the vigorous work of Molly Dewson, chairperson of the Women's Division of the Democratic National Convention.

## Molly Dewson and the rainbow flyers

In early 1932 Molly Dewson (1874–1962) began a concerted effort to rally women voters behind Franklin Roosevelt's campaign for the presidency. Working with other women Democratic leaders (such as Emily Newell Blair and Sue Shelton White), Dewson's division of the Democratic National Convention strengthened and further organized an already growing network of Democratic women. Each state had a vice-chair and local correspondents who were responsible for distribution of political literature. During the state-by-state struggle for women's suffrage (women's right to vote), a brightly colored, single sheet of facts called a "rainbow flyer" had been delivered door-to-door. A similar flyer went to over six million households across the country during Roosevelt's presidential campaign. The grassroots efforts succeeded in establishing a nationwide women's political network.

After Franklin Roosevelt's election to the presidency, Dewson, Eleanor Roosevelt (1884–1962), and other Democra-

## The Reporter Plan

Molly Dewson, always eager to nurture grassroots support for New Deal programs, established the Reporter Plan in 1934. Still working as the chairperson of the Women's Division of the Democratic National Convention (DNC), Dewson sought to involve more women in the New Deal government programs by educating them on related political issues and on the benefit of New Deal projects. Tapping the existing network of Democratic women, the Reporter Plan called for a select number of women in each county Democratic organization to monitor the progress of a government agency. These women would then report their findings to community clubs and other organizations, in effect serving as local reporters and public information sources.

The Reporter Plan program was based on the belief that by providing women in all walks of life more detailed information on the administration's activities, women voters could play a crucial role in the reelection of Roosevelt in 1936. Five thousand women had signed up to be reporters by the summer of 1934, fifteen thousand by 1936, and thirty thousand by 1940. To engage even more women in New Deal political discussions, the DNC's Women's Division sponsored nationwide conferences on politics, government, and education. Frances Perkins and Ellen Woodward were among the women who spoke at the conferences.

tic leaders such as Nellie Tayloe Ross (1876–1977) and Sue Shelton White met to compile a list of women they believed would serve the government well. Dewson's goal was to recognize at least one woman Democratic leader in each state. Yet Dewson did not want to merely place women in various public offices; she wanted to place the best candidates available into the jobs.

## Frances Perkins, secretary of labor

Considerably before Roosevelt's inauguration in March 1933, Dewson began to lobby Roosevelt to appoint Frances Perkins (1882–1965) as secretary of labor. Roosevelt did not need much persuasion, because he had worked extensively with Perkins when he was serving as governor of New York (1929–33). In New York Perkins had been, among other positions, Roosevelt's industrial commissioner. Thus

Perkins fit the bill: She was not only a woman but also the best-suited person in the country to take over the U.S. Department of Labor, the most recently established department in the president's cabinet. It was actually harder to convince Perkins to take the job than it was to convince Roosevelt to ask her. Dewson met with Perkins to encourage her, but Perkins accepted only after meeting with Roosevelt. During a lengthy discussion with president-elect Roosevelt, Perkins outlined the programs she would fight for, including child labor laws, social insurance programs, minimum wages, and maximum hours. Only when she was convinced that she would have the president's support on these matters did Perkins accept. Hence Perkins became the first woman in the history of the United States to serve as a member of the president's cabinet. In accepting the position she expressed the pride she felt in representing all American women in that historic moment.

Early in her term as secretary of labor, Perkins successfully directed the placement of young men into the Civilian Conservation Corps, a program Roosevelt established in April 1933 to provide work for young men between the ages of eighteen and twenty-five. By early 1934 Perkins was lobbying for social insurance programs such as workers' compensation (monthly cash payments to those injured on the job), unemployment insurance (temporary monthly cash payments to those who have lost their jobs), and an old-age retirement plan. These efforts resulted in the Social Security Act of 1935, signed into law by President Roosevelt in August 1935. He credited Perkins with developing and guiding the legislation through to its passage. In 1938 Perkins paved the way for the passage of the Fair Labor Standards Act. Included in this act were minimum hourly wages and maximum weekly hours.

With the exception of Secretary of the Interior Harold Ickes (1874–1952), Perkins was Roosevelt's longest-serving cabinet member, remaining at her post from 1933 until shortly after Roosevelt's death in 1945. Perkins remained friends with Dewson, and years later she still recalled how Dewson's encouragement helped bring about her acceptance of the cabinet position. Throughout her term as secretary of labor, Perkins was remarkably successful at developing solu-

tions that would protect the rights of workers while promoting economic recovery from the Great Depression.

## Women in government

By 1939, 19 percent of government employees were women, 5 percent more than ten years earlier. The women's rate of federal employment was increasing twice as fast as the men's, but it was doing so only in specific areas of government—in the new federal agencies providing work relief and social security programs. For example, the Works Progress Administration (WPA), created in 1935 to provide jobs for those still out of work, had a woman administrator, Ellen Sullivan Woodward (1887–1971), who served as head of the Women's and Professional Projects Division of the WPA. Woodward oversaw the work of 450,000 women on work relief projects such as sewing, library work, public health programs, educational programs, and research services. Dewson had recom-

**Frances Perkins became the first woman in the history of the United States to serve as a member of the president's cabinet.**
*AP/Wide World Photo. Reproduced by permission.*

**Ellen Sullivan Woodward, center, attends an exhibit of historical craftsmanship sponsored by the Works Progress Administration. Next to Woodward is First Lady Eleanor Roosevelt.**
*AP/Wide World Photo. Reproduced by permission.*

mended Woodward to the WPA's head, Harry Hopkins (1890–1946), and considered the appointment one of her proudest achievements.

Dewson also played a hand in Nellie Tayloe Ross's appointment as the first woman director of the U.S. Mint. Another first for women was Ruth Bryan Owen's (1885–1954) appointment as minister to Denmark, a political position just below that of ambassador. Through her political network Dewson frequently organized letter-writing campaigns to push for certain appointments. As a result of one of these campaigns, Florence Allen (1884–1966) was named to the U.S. circuit court of appeals, the highest position a woman had ever held in the federal judicial (legal) system. Although Dewson always downplayed her personal responsibility for placing these and other women in their New Deal positions, her perseverance and close relationship with the Roosevelts certainly contributed to the number of women in New Deal programs.

Dewson and Eleanor Roosevelt agreed that women's energy and idealism would bring out the humanitarian side of government, its growing concern for the welfare of human beings. The concept of the federal government caring for its citizens' well-being first emerged in the United States in the 1930s, in response to the extreme hardships brought on by the Great Depression.

Mary McLeod Bethune (1875–1955) became the first black American woman to head a federal agency. She was appointed as Negro Affairs director for the National Youth Administration (NYA) in 1936. The NYA was designed to meet the educational and employment needs of America's youths. Bethune successfully oversaw the administration of funds for black schools and educational programs. From 1935 to 1944 she also held the title of Special Advisor on Minority Affairs.

She was the unofficial leader of Roosevelt's "Black Cabinet," various black federal officials who served as an informal advisory group to the president.

Hallie Flanagan (1890–1969) was another prominent woman in the New Deal. She headed the Federal Theater Project (FTP), a project within the Works Progress Administration. The FTP provided work relief for those who had been employed in theater production before the economic crisis of the Great Depression eliminated most of their jobs. The FTP was highly controversial from the start: Many people argued that it was ridiculous to spend public funds to employ actors and artists. Nevertheless, Flanagan developed the program with determination, and the FTP eventually employed more than twelve thousand actors, directors, set artists, stagehands, and others in over twenty-eight states. Collectively they staged productions in more than 105 theaters. Many productions were free to the public, and, because of this, many Americans got their first introduction to live plays and musicals.

Florence E. Allen, the first woman appointed to the U.S. circuit court of appeals. *AP/Wide World Photo. Reproduced by permission.*

## Eleanor Roosevelt

Eleanor Roosevelt (1884–1962), the wife of President Franklin Roosevelt, was a woman of great energy who had wide-ranging interests. During the 1920s Eleanor had joined and participated in many groups, including the League of Women Voters and the Women's Trade Union League (WTUL), as well as the National Consumers' League, where she worked with Molly Dewson. While her husband was governor of New York (1929–33), Eleanor was highly active in the Democratic State Committee; she also continued participating in the WTUL, published articles, and became an accomplished public speaker on social reform. When Franklin Roosevelt ran for president in 1932, Eleanor worked hand in

Eleanor Roosevelt speaks during a radio broadcast on September 16, 1939, in celebration of "Democratic Women's Day." *AP/Wide World Photo. Reproduced by permission.*

hand with Dewson in the Women's Division of the Democratic National Convention. As First Lady, Eleanor, a reformer and women's rights advocate, worked with Dewson to see that many women were placed in government posts, and beginning on March 6, 1933, she started holding weekly women-only press conferences. From 1933 to 1945 she held over five hundred of these conferences for women journalists in the hopes of opening journalism jobs for women and giving women a better understanding of legislative and political life. In 1936 Eleanor began to write a newspaper column, "My Day," commenting on current issues.

Eleanor used her position to advance a number of causes, including the rights of women and improvement of working conditions, and she attended to issues of unemployed women. She championed miners' rights and the rights of black Americans. In 1939 she resigned from the Daughters of the American Revolution after black American singer Marian Anderson (1897–1993) was denied use of their performance hall. She then helped arrange an outdoor concert for Anderson at the Lincoln Memorial in Washington, D.C. Over seventy-five thousand men and women came to listen to the concert.

## Lorena Hickok, investigator of the Depression

One of Eleanor Roosevelt's closest friends was Lorena Hickok (1893–1968), often known as Hick. She was a journalist and one of the first women to work for the Associated Press. A hard-hitting newswoman, she was assigned to cover Eleanor Roosevelt on the 1932 campaign trail. A close friendship developed between the two women, and Hickok soon became a part of the New Deal administration.

Soon after his inauguration in 1933, President Roosevelt established the Federal Emergency Relief Administration (FERA) to get immediate relief to desperate Americans, who were struggling to survive the economic crisis known as the Great Depression. Roosevelt placed Harry Hopkins (1890–1946) in charge of FERA. Hopkins in turn hired Lorena Hickok away from the Associated Press to be his chief investigator. Rather than having Hickok compile more statistics, Hopkins asked her to travel the nation and report to him the conditions she found firsthand. From the summer of 1933 until the end of 1936, Hickok went into the most afflicted areas of the country and reported back to Hopkins. During her tour she met with politicians, civil leaders, and officials from state and local relief programs, to find out how well the New Deal programs were running. She frequently was sent to investigate communities in crisis, whether from labor problems or natural disasters. Likewise, she checked up on localities where Hopkins had reason to suspect New Deal

From 1933 to 1945 Eleanor Roosevelt, center, held her women-only conferences, forcing major newspapers and news-gathering services to have newspaperwomen in Washington, D.C. *Courtesy of the Franklin D. Roosevelt Library.*

programs were being unfairly administered. The information Hickok provided to Hopkins helped him improve coordination between Washington, D.C., and local relief officials.

## Discrimination against women in government

In the eyes of politically active women, one black mark on Roosevelt's New Deal administration was Roosevelt's continuation of Section 213 of the Economy Act, originally signed into law by President Herbert Hoover (1874–1964; served 1929–33) near the end of 1932. The section, which Molly Dewson referred to as "that dumb clause," stipulated that married persons could not be employed by the federal government at the same time. Over sixteen hundred federally employed married couples were affected by this legislation, and although the act did not state that wives should be the first to resign, the majority of people who did resign (or who were fired) were women. In May 1933 women's organizations demanded that Section 213 be voided. However, President Roosevelt was not eager to change the law since it had a lot of public support. Many people believed women working outside the home took jobs away from men who desperately needed work during the Depression. Also, many Americans thought women working outside the home weakened the family unit. When the U.S. attorney general advised Roosevelt that he could not legally void the law, the president found this a politically convenient position to be in since it would not alienate the majority of voters even though the law obviously discriminated against women. The only opposition to the law from the White House came from Eleanor Roosevelt. She believed that the decision for a woman to work outside the home should rest with the family, not Congress. Section 213 was finally repealed in July 1937 with the passage of the Celler bill, which prohibited discrimination based on marital status. The bill bore the name of Congressman Emmanuel Celler of New York who, along with representatives from various woman's organizations, had fought for several years for Section 213's repeal.

There were other instances of discrimination against women, even within the New Deal itself. For example, the

# More Women of the New Deal

**Grace Abbott** (1878–1939): Chief of the Children's Bureau in the Labor Department; active in Women's Trade Union League (WTUL) and National Consumers' League; took position in 1934 at the University of Chicago School of Social Service Administration and contributed heavily to provisions for mothers' and children's programs in the Social Security Act of 1935.

**Clara Mortenson Beyer:** Associate director of the Division of Labor Standards within the Department of Labor from 1934 to 1957.

**Emily Newell Blair:** Prominent woman in the Democratic Party; joined the Consumers' Advisory Board of the National Recovery Administration (NRA) in 1933 and briefly chaired the board in 1935 until the act that established the NRA was declared unconstitutional.

**Jane Margueretta Hoey:** Director of the Bureau of Public Assistance in the Social Security Administration from 1936 to 1953.

**Katherine Fredrica Lenroot:** Succeeded Grace Abbott as chief of the Children's Bureau in the Department of Labor in 1934; coauthored the section of the Social Security Act that created the Aid to Dependent Children Program; suggested a legal strategy to enforce child labor regulations that was incorporated into the Fair Labor Standards Act of 1938.

**Josephine Roche:** First woman appointed as assistant secretary of the treasury (1934), where she was in charge of the Public Health Service; served as chairperson of the Executive Committee of the National Youth Administration (NYA).

**Nellie Tayloe Ross** (1876–1977): First woman appointed as director of the U.S. Mint (1933), where she remained until retirement in 1953 before appointment at the mint, Ross was a national figure in the Democratic Party's women's activities and had served as governor of Wyoming from 1925 to 1927.

**Rose Schneiderman:** The only woman member of the Labor Advisory Board of the National Recovery Administration (NRA); after serving in the NRA post, Schneiderman continued her earlier work for the Women's Trade Union League and served as the New York secretary of labor from 1937 to 1943.

**Sue Shelton White:** Attorney who held a variety of positions, including ones with the Women's Division of the Democratic National Convention, the Consumers' Division of the National Recovery Administration, and the Social Security Board. By 1938 she was special assistant to the Social Security Board's legal staff.

National Recovery Administration (NRA) codes established minimum wages for men and women, but in practice, wages for women workers could remain considerably lower than those for men. This type of inequality greatly angered many women's groups. Relief measures that provided help to mothers received widespread support, yet there was little agreement (even among women's organizations) on how to achieve equal economic opportunities for women.

## Women's progress in government slows

As the 1930s came to a close, the shadow of World War II (1939–45) loomed over Europe and America, and women's progress in U.S. government slowed. Many New Deal programs were being reduced or eliminated as the government switched its focus from domestic issues to the growing conflict in Europe. These programs had provided the greatest opportunities for women, so decreases in funding could only mean decreased opportunity. Molly Dewson had retired, and Eleanor Roosevelt had turned her attention to international concerns. By 1940 women's politics in the United States went into a holding pattern that lasted for the next two decades.

## For More Information

### Books

Black, Allida M., ed. *Courage in a Dangerous World: The Political Writings of Eleanor Roosevelt.* New York, NY: Columbia University Press, 1999.

Costin, Lela B. *Two Sisters for Social Justice: A Biography of Grace and Edith Abbott.* Urbana: University of Illinois Press, 1983.

Evans, Sara M. *Born for Liberty: A History of Women in America.* New York, NY: Free Press, 1989.

Lowitt, Richard, and Maurine Beasley, eds. *One Third of a Nation: Lorena Hickok Reports on the Great Depression.* Urbana: University of Illinois Press, 2000.

McCluskey, Audrey Thomas, and Elaine M. Smith, eds. *Mary McLeod Bethune: Building a Better World, Essays and Selected Documents.* Bloomington: Indiana University Press, 1999.

Mohr, Lillian Holmen. *Frances Perkins: That Woman in FDR's Cabinet.* Croton-on-Hudson, NY: North River Press, 1979.

Roosevelt, Eleanor. *The Autobiography of Eleanor Roosevelt.* New York, NY: Harper & Brothers Publishers, 1958.

Scharf, Lois. *To Work and to Wed: Female Employment, Feminism, and the Great Depression.* Westport, CT: Greenwood Press, 1980.

Ware, Susan. *Beyond Suffrage: Women in the New Deal.* Cambridge, MA: Harvard University Press, 1981.

Ware, Susan. *Holding Their Own: American Women in the 1930s.* Boston: Twayne Publishers, 1982.

Ware, Susan. *Partner and I: Molly Dewson, Feminism, and New Deal Politics.* New Haven, CT: Yale University Press, 1987.


## Periodicals

Sochen, June. "Mildred Pierce and Women in Film." *American Quarterly* 30, no. 1 (1978): 3–20.


## Web Sites

*Franklin D. Roosevelt Library and Digital Archives.* http://www.fdrlibrary. marist.edu/index.html (accessed on August 15, 2002).

*Internet Women's History Sourcebook.* http://www.fordham.edu/halsall/ women/womensbook.html (accessed on August 15, 2002).

*National Women's History Project.* http://www.nwhp.org/index.html (accessed on August 15, 2002).

*Suffragists' Oral History Project.* http://bancroft.berkeley.edu/ROHO/ ohonline/suffragists.html (accessed on August 15, 2002).

# Minority Groups and the Great Depression

As difficult as the economic crisis of the Great Depression was for white Americans, it was even harder on racial minorities, including black Americans, Mexican Americans, American Indians, and Asian Americans. In 1933 the general unemployment rate in the United States was over 25 percent; at the same time, unemployment rates for various American minorities ranged up to 50 percent or more. Given the severe racial discrimination in almost every facet of daily life in America through the 1920s, it was hard for many minorities to distinguish much difference between the Great Depression and "normal" economic times. Nonetheless, for these groups the Great Depression was worse than "normal" economic hardships they had suffered.

During the Depression racial discrimination was widespread, and minority workers were normally the first to lose jobs at a business or on a farm. They were often denied employment in public works programs supposedly available to all needy citizens. They were sometimes threatened at relief centers when applying for work or assistance. Some charities refused to provide food to needy minorities, particularly to blacks in the South. Violence against minorities increased during the Depression, as whites competed for jobs traditionally held by minorities. Minorities were excluded from union membership, and unions influenced Congress to keep antidiscrimination requirements out of New Deal laws. The New Deal was a broad array of federal social and economic programs created under the leadership of President Franklin D. Roosevelt (1882–1945; served 1933–45) to bring relief to the struggling nation. As a result of all these factors, minorities suffered greatly during the Depression. In deep frustration many minority citizens called Roosevelt's programs a "raw deal" instead of a "new deal."

Some improvements did occur by the mid-1930s. For American Indians, John Collier (1884–1968) of the U.S. Office of Indian Affairs introduced the Indian New Deal in June 1934, a program that dramatically changed the course of U.S. Indian policy. Instead of forcing Indians to blend into U.S. society, the new policy provided increased funding for economic development of tribes, promoted continued Indian traditions, and supported tribal governments.

Black Americans began to see some positive changes by 1935. Through the influence of First Lady Eleanor Roosevelt (1884–1962), Secretary of the Interior Harold Ickes (1874–1952), and others, the Roosevelt administration ended racial discrimination in some federal programs, set aside larger amounts of relief aid for blacks, and appointed several blacks to federal positions. As a result, the vast majority of black voters voted for Roosevelt, a Democrat, in the 1936 presidential election, ending a seventy-five-year period of black loyalty to Republican candidates that began with Abraham Lincoln (1809–1865; served 1861–65). Roosevelt created an advisory group (cabinet) of black American government employees to advise him on issues important to them.

Unlike American Indians and black Americans, Mexican Americans and Asian Americans saw almost no advances. For minorities overall, the Depression was a period of great economic suffering, small political gains, and lost social opportunities for gaining greater equality with white Americans.

# Black Americans

Hard times were nothing new for blacks in America. Southern slavery had ended only a few generations earlier. Racism remained woven into every aspect of life in the United States in the 1920s and was freely expressed in public. With the onset of the Depression in late 1929, minorities began losing jobs at a high rate. By 1932 the unemployment rate for blacks was over 50 percent, ranging up to 75 percent in some communities. Previously, minorities had held jobs as elevator operators, farm laborers, street cleaners, garbage collectors, waiters, and bellhops; suddenly those jobs were needed by the larger white population. White women, many seeking work for the first time, took positions as maids, housekeepers, and cooks—positions traditionally held by black women. Only low-paying, dirty jobs that no one else wanted were left for minorities. In Atlanta, Georgia, the degrading slogan "No Jobs for [Blacks] Until Every White Man Has a Job" became popular among whites. Blacks who were able to keep their jobs often had their wages drastically reduced.

Approximately 40 percent of all black American workers in 1930 farmed, but very few owned their own land. Most were sharecroppers and tenant farmers in the South, working on farms of white landowners. Sharecroppers and tenant farmers rented the land they farmed. Landowners supplied sharecroppers with tools to work the land; tenant farmers provided their own tools. As part of the arrangement, both types of farmers owed a portion of each year's crop to the landowner. Families of black sharecroppers and tenant farmers lived in one- or two-bedroom shacks with no electricity, insulation, or running water. Sharecropper and tenant families would move from one farm to another every few years in search of better work and better living conditions. Black sharecroppers formed their own unions seeking better conditions, but they met harsh resistance from white landowners and local law authorities. In addition, although very needy, blacks received little relief aid. This was especially true in the South.

As the economy declined, violence against minorities rose. The lynching of blacks by white mobs increased, primarily in the South. In the United States overall there were eight lynchings in 1932, twenty-eight in 1933, fifteen in 1934, and twenty in 1935. Lynching is mob violence in

which a mob executes (kills), especially by hanging, a person for an alleged crime.

Escaping the poverty and increased racial violence of the South, four hundred thousand blacks journeyed to northern industrial centers during the Great Depression to seek employment. However, jobs were scarce in the North, and blacks had to join the breadlines at relief centers. Organizations such as the Colored Merchants Association in New York City were established to help black businesses survive. Boycotts were organized against stores serving mostly black customers but employing few black workers.

A plantation owner's daughter checks the weight of cotton harvested by a sharecropper. *Courtesy of the Library of Congress.*

## Black Americans and the First New Deal

Franklin Roosevelt had little to offer blacks during his 1932 presidential campaign. The National Association for the Advancement of Colored People (NAACP) had urged him to openly oppose racial discrimination, but Roosevelt, a north-

A group of African American laundry workers stage a strike against low wages and poor working conditions. *Courtesy of the Library of Congress.*

ern Democrat, wanted the votes of southern Democrats in the election. He looked to those same leaders for support of his economic recovery measures after the election. Roosevelt believed his economic legislation would benefit both whites and minorities. However, because racial equality was not made a priority, discrimination became widespread within New Deal programs.

Major New Deal programs established in 1933 offered little opportunity to black Americans: Regional wage rates established by the National Recovery Administration (NRA) did not cover many black occupations, such as farm laborers and domestic helpers. The Agricultural Adjustment Administration (AAA), created to bring economic relief to the nation's farmers, paid farmers to cut back crop production in hopes of increasing market prices. This policy only decreased jobs for black sharecroppers and tenant farmers. The Tennessee Valley Authority (TVA) barred blacks from skilled positions, management, and higher-paying construction jobs. Because of discrimination by local administrators, the Civilian Conservation Corps (CCC) enrolled few young black men to work on conservation projects.

## Black Americans and the Second New Deal

Some hope arrived by the mid-1930s. Eleanor Roosevelt (1884–1962), the president's wife, had long sympathized with the less fortunate in society, and she became committed to changing public attitudes toward racial minorities and improving the economic condition of minorities. She was the first First Lady to take a strong role as a social activist. The president, sensitive to the criticism that his early New Deal programs harmed small farmers and minorities, tried to make changes. Secretary of the Interior Harold Ickes directed local public works administrators to hire black workers on public projects in proportion to their presence in the local workforce. The CCC increased its black enrollees from 6 percent in 1936 to 11 percent by 1939. President Roosevelt created the Resettlement Administration (RA) and appointed as its head Will Alexander, who was highly knowledgeable about black poverty issues. The RA sought to end sharecropping and migratory labor by promoting land ownership. The agency's initial goal was to resettle thousands of poor farm families on productive land.

The Works Progress Administration (WPA), established in 1935, taught almost 250,000 blacks how to read and write. The WPA arts programs established sixteen black theater groups around the country, staged concerts showcasing works of black composers, employed hundreds of black artists, and provided opportunities and training for young black writers and scholars. Roosevelt created the National Youth Administration (NYA) in June 1935 to assist youth. He appointed Mary McLeod Bethune (1875–1955) as director of Negro affairs within the NYA. She was the first black American to head a government agency. The NYA became a model of government assistance for blacks, helping six thousand black youths complete their education.

In response to these government actions under the Roosevelt administration, black voters made a historic

**Asian Americans**

During the second half of the nineteenth century, many workers came to the United States from Asia seeking jobs. They played a highly important role in developing the U.S. economy during this time, particularly in the West, including their participation in mining activities, railroad construction, and agricultural work. By 1882 some 300,000 Chinese had entered the United States for various lengths of time to make money and return back home to assist their families.

It was common, at this time, for Chinese workers to work for less pay than white Americans, causing many to blame the Chinese for lowering the American standard of living by driving down wages. By the late 1870s a strong anti-Chinese sentiment began to surface nationwide driven by fears of massive Chinese immigration. As a result, in 1882 Congress passed the Chinese Exclusion Act, a highly restrictive immigration law that largely stopped the flow of peoples from China into the United States. It marked the first effort by the U.S. government to restrict immigra-

tion. Chinese already in the United States were denied future citizenship as a result of the law, and faced severe discrimination and exclusion from mainstream white American society. In 1907 national policies were also adopted restricting Japanese immigration. In 1924 Congress passed the Immigration Act essentially banning all Asian immigration.

As a result of the immigration laws, Chinese and Japanese populations in the United States had become concentrated in isolated ethnic communities (communities in which the residents largely derive from a single culture) known as Chinatowns. During the Depression years, the work that had drawn Chinese men to the United States during the nineteenth century was no longer available.

By 1965 Congress passed a new Immigration Act largely lifting the bans on immigration from Asian countries. Asian Americans became the fastest growing immigrant group in the United States, rising from 250,000 at the close of the Depression in 1941 to over seven million in 1990.

change in the 1936 presidential election. Optimistic about Roosevelt and his wife, Eleanor, many black voters shifted from voting Republican to voting Democrat. Herbert Hoover (1874–1964), a Republican, won 66 percent of the black vote in 1932 (but still lost the election); Roosevelt, a Democrat, won 76 percent only four years later. After his reelection, President Roosevelt appointed forty-five blacks to various federal positions and created a cabinet of black advisers including Bethune. In 1937 Roosevelt appointed NAACP attorney William Hastie (1904–1976) as the first black federal judge in U.S. history, and in 1939 the Justice Department established its civil rights section.

World War II (1939–45) brought many new jobs for all Americans. However, minorities were often the last to be hired from relief program lists. In 1940 less than 2 percent of workers in the growing aircraft industry were black, and many of those workers were hired into lower-paying janitorial jobs. In June 1941 black labor leader A. Philip Randolph (1889–1979) of the Brotherhood of Sleeping Car Porters pressured President Roosevelt to issue an order prohibiting racial discrimination in defense industries receiving federal contracts. Greater job opportunities came by 1943, as labor shortages in the work force became critical.

## Mexican Americans

Over one million immigrants came from Mexico to the United States between 1900 and 1930, filling the demand for low-wage, unskilled workers in the growing U.S. economy. Most were farmworkers who settled in established Mexican American communities in California and the Southwest; others found work in mines and manufacturing industries. The goal for many of these workers was to save up enough money to go back to Mexico and purchase farmland or establish a business. However, many Mexican immigrants and their children eventually became U.S. citizens.

The demand for minority laborers suddenly ended with the onset of the Great Depression. Competing with whites for whatever low-paying jobs were available, Mexican Americans faced increasing hostility. They were considered part of the economic problem—blamed for taking jobs away from white Americans and absorbing government relief funds. As a result, Mexican Americans became the subject of the largest mass removal effort ever promoted by the U.S. government.

Under the direction of the Hoover administration, federal immigration agents, county sheriffs, and local police approached deportation (the removal of noncitizen immi-

**A family of Mexican migrant sugar beet pickers shares a one-room shack while working on a farm in East Grand Forks, Minnesota.** *Corbis Corporation. Reproduced by permission.*

grants from a country) like a military operation, launching raids and massive roundups of Mexican Americans. Anyone who looked Mexican, including U.S. citizens of Mexican descent, was picked up and taken into custody during street sweeps. Mass arrests were made in public without arrest warrants or any specific reason. Besides conducting street sweeps, agents would go door-to-door demanding proof of legal residency and jailing those who were unable to quickly produce the proper papers.

Racial harassment by government agents was widespread and included beatings and intimidation. Not allowed to post bail for release from jail, the detained were held until the next deportation bus, ship, or train was available. As intended, the raids created chaos and a climate of fear in Mexican American communities across the nation. Many immigrants decided to leave on their own to avoid further threats. In the early 1930s a congressional committee known as the Wickersham Committee investigated the deportation practices and issued a report denouncing the government tactics. However, the Hoover administration denied any wrongdoing and successfully maintained general public support.

## Mexican Americans during the Depression

Between 1929 and 1932, 365,000 people returned to Mexico (75,000 of them departed from the Los Angeles area between 1930 and 1932). An additional 90,000 left for Mexico between 1933 and 1937. Because of the forced migration, stricter immigration policies, and reduced job opportunities, far fewer Mexicans were entering the United States. After one million Mexican immigrants entered the country between 1900 and 1929, between 1930 and 1934 the number of Mexican immigrants entering the United States dropped to half of that number. Those who did come during the Depression were usually joining family members already settled in the United States.

Mexican Americans who remained in the United States during the Depression suffered economically. Unemployment rates in Mexican American communities averaged 50 percent. Farm wages fell from an average daily wage of $2.55 in 1930 to only $1.40 a day in 1933. Some laborers were making only fifteen cents an hour. Faced with racial discrimination, low pay, and poor working and living conditions, Mexican American farm laborers increased their efforts to organize unions, efforts that had begun in the late 1920s. In 1933 the Mexican Farm Labor Union led a widespread strike in southern California; union members demanded a minimum wage of twenty-five cents per hour. Some concessions were gained by the strike. The Confederation of Mexican Farmers and Workers Unions (Confederación de Uniones de Campesinos y Obreros Mexicanos, or CUCOM) became the most active farmworker union in California, with ten thousand members by 1935. Mexican women also organized. Seamstresses in the garment industry formed the International Ladies' Garment Workers' Union (ILGWU). A massive strike in 1933 brought garment production in Los Angeles to a stop and led to a new contract that included increased wages.

A Works Progress
Administration supervisor
instructs a Mexican
American woman in rug
weaving, 1939. *Courtesy of
the Library of Congress.*

New Deal programs had both positive and negative effects on Mexican Americans. The programs offered them limited relief assistance, because many Mexican American families did not have a permanent address, a standard requirement of the programs. The crop reduction program promoted by the Agricultural Adjustment Administration cost many farm laborers their jobs. On the positive side, the Civilian Conservation Corps and the National Youth Administration employed many Mexican American youths. The Resettlement Administration tried to revive small subsistence farming among some Mexican American farmers in the Southwest. In some regions Works Progress Administration (WPA) programs hired workers to document and preserve traditional music, art, folklore, and social customs.

## American Indians

By the 1920s American Indians had lost most of their traditional lands. Most were isolated on reservations or in remote rural communities, trapped in poverty with little education and poor access to health services. Government programs discouraged the practice of Indian traditions. Like other minorities in the United States, American Indians were economically depressed before the Great Depression. A 1928 study by the Brookings Institution, *The Problem of Indian Administration,* documented in detail the plight and the needs of American Indians.

The prospects for change arrived when President Roosevelt (1882–1945; served 1933–45) named Harold Ickes (1874–1952) to serve as secretary of the interior. Ickes was a champion of civil liberties (ability of individuals to exercise their constitutionally guaranteed rights), and he favored a policy of perpetuating traditional native cultures. He appointed John Collier (1884–1968), a leading critic of past federal policies regarding American Indians, to serve as U.S. commissioner of Indian affairs.

## The Indian New Deal

With Ickes and Collier in the lead, the 1930s became a turning point in American Indian history. The policies they instituted became known as the Indian New Deal. Collier used the 1928 Brookings Institution report as a road map to reform the administration of American Indian affairs and rejuvenate Indian cultures and traditions through the U.S. Office of Indian Affairs (later named the Bureau of Indian Affairs, or BIA). The Indian New Deal policy supported the political and cultural existence of tribes and better social services for American Indians. The policy sought to decrease

John Collier stands with the chiefs of the Flathead Indian Tribe as Secretary of Interior Harold Ickes signs into law the Wheeler-Hobard bill on October 28, 1935. The bill provides for Indian self-rule rather than tribes' being under the direction of the Bureau of Indian Affairs. *AP/Wide World Photo. Reproduced by permission.*

government efforts that attempted to force American Indians to blend into the dominant American culture. Collier's goal was to give tribes both legal and organizational capabilities to pursue economic development while maintaining their individual cultures.

To achieve this goal Collier shepherded through Congress the Indian Reorganization Act (IRA), signed into law on June 18, 1934. The act gave tribes the option of adopting written constitutions and establishing democratic forms of government. By creating an IRA government, a tribe would be eligible for federal funds to purchase land, start business ventures, and receive various social services. Of the 252 tribes that voted on the IRA question, 174 tribes voted to accept IRA conditions. However, only 92 tribes actually adopted IRA constitutions. Despite its limited acceptance by tribes, the Indian New Deal stopped the steady loss of American Indian lands and provided a major source of funds for economic recovery among tribes. In these ways the Indian New Deal took a big step toward increasing tribal economic and political independence.

Given the decline of funds available for public schools throughout the nation during the Depression, Congress decided that in some parts of the country it was no longer economically practical to operate health and educational facilities for American Indians separate from those for white Americans, as it had done in the past. Therefore American Indian children living outside reservations would have to begin attending public schools in their area while children living on reservations would generally still have their own schools. However, the addition of more students in already financially strapped public school districts could potentially have led to anger and discrimination against the Indian children. Therefore, Congress passed the Johnson-O'Malley Act in April 1934. Under the provisions of this act, the federal government would pay the public school districts for expenses related to educating American Indian children. With the availability of additional federal funds, many public school districts welcomed Indian children to their schools.

On August 27, 1935, Congress created the Indian Arts and Crafts Board to encourage the production of traditional and contemporary arts and crafts by American Indians and to expand markets for the sale of this artwork. Standards for Indian crafts were adopted, and Indians could trademark their designs. Galleries were established in Washington, D.C., Montana, South Dakota, and Oklahoma, and at the World's Fair in San Francisco in 1939 and 1940. In New Mexico the Works Progress Administration hired artists and musicians to teach crafts and traditions that were in danger of being lost.

John Collier also established the Civilian Conservation Corps–Indian Division (CCC–ID). This special branch of the Civilian Conservation Corps (CCC) sponsored programs on reservations. The CCC, created March 31, 1933, employed young men between eighteen and twenty-four years of age to work on conservation projects. Collier obtained $100 million from Congress for irrigation, soil erosion control, and road construction projects. Between 1933 and 1942 fifteen thousand American Indian young men served in CCC-ID. The agency taught useful skills, provided income for unemployed young men, and restored land that had been highly eroded by overgrazing of livestock.

# For More Information

## Books

Balderrama, Francisco E., and Raymond Rodriguez. *Decade of Betrayal: Mexican Repatriation in the 1930s.* Albuquerque, NM: University of New Mexico Press, 1995.

Brookings Institution. *The Problem of Indian Administration.* Baltimore, MD: The Johns Hopkins Press, 1928.

Daniels, Roger. *Asian America: Chinese and Japanese in the United States since 1850.* Seattle, WA: University of Washington Press, 1988.

Davis, Mary B. *Native America in the Twentieth Century: An Encyclopedia.* New York, NY: Garland Publishing, 1994.

Greenberg, Cheryl Lynn. *"Or Does It Explode?" Harlem in the Great Depression.* New York, NY: Oxford University Press, 1991.

Kelley, Robin D. G., and Earl Lewis. *To Make Our World Anew: A History of African Americans.* New York, NY: Oxford University Press, 2000.

Levinson, David, and Melvin Ember, eds. *American Immigrant Cultures: Builders of a Nation.* New York, NY: Macmillan, 1997.

Philp, Kenneth. *John Collier's Crusade for Indian Reform.* Tucson, AZ: University of Arizona Press, 1977.

## Web Sites

*Ancestors in the Americas.* http://www.pbs.org/ancestorsintheamericas/ (accessed on August 14, 2002).

*Immigration and Naturalization Service (INS).* http://www.ins.gov (accessed on August 14, 2002).

*National Congress of American Indians.* http://www.ncai.org (accessed on August 14, 2002).

# Everyday Living

In the 1930s the economic crisis known as the Great Depression rippled through the United States, affecting almost all American families. The crash of the New York Stock Exchange in October 1929 marked the beginning of the most severe economic downturn in U.S. history. Thousands of banks closed; manufacturing slowed greatly because no one could buy goods; stores closed; 25 to 30 percent of workers lost their jobs. It would be the middle of 1933 before the government took action to halt the downward spiral and offer some relief. President Franklin D. Roosevelt (1882–1945; served 1933–45) began his term of office in March of that year. In the next one hundred days he and his advisers proposed a series of measures that Congress passed into laws. The new legislation created programs for immediate relief as well as programs that would aid in the gradual recovery of America's prosperity. These programs, known as the New Deal, would reach into the lives of almost all Americans.

The harsh economic times affected all but the very wealthy. The working class, middle class, and upper middle class who managed to keep their jobs saw their salaries de-

# Average Yearly Earnings for Full-Time Employees, 1935

| | |
|---|---|
| Lawyer | $4,272 |
| Doctor | $3,695 |
| College teacher | $2,666 |
| Dentist | $2,485 |
| Bituminous coal miner | $957 |
| Construction worker | $1,027 |
| Utility workers | |
|    Gas & electric | $1,589 |
|    Telephone & telegraph | $1,378 |
| Farmers, foresters, fishermen | $288 |
| Railroad workers | $1,645 |
| Insurance agents | $1,632 |
| Medical health service occupation | $829 |
| Domestic maids and chauffeurs | $485 |
| Police and firemen | $1,290 |
| Public school teachers | $1,290 |
| Civilian government employee | $1,759 |

Adapted from Historical Statistics of the United States: Colonial Times to 1970, Part 1, *Washington, DC: U.S. Bureau of Census, 1975, pages 166–176.*

crease. Families figured out ways to "cut corners," "make do," and "keep up appearances." Frequently people who had employment supported family members who had lost their jobs; almost all families had a close relative who suddenly was without an income. Farm families fortunate enough to keep their farms focused on helping their relatives through the very bleak years.

Families shared all they could with the less fortunate. Extending help and kindness toward others was commonplace in the 1930s. An out-of-work family would be invited for Sunday dinner. If a homeless person knocked at the back door, the family would give what food they could.

Although the Great Depression brought forth the many strengths of the American family, it also took its toll. Family structures changed: Marriages were postponed, fewer babies were born, young people lived at home longer or returned to their parents' home when they lost jobs, and households combined to aid struggling relatives. For some,

the strain was too much, and their families broke apart. The hardships of the Depression were most difficult for those who were already poor, those who had barely been making ends meet before the Depression. Included in this group were those in coal-mining areas, the rural poor, black Americans, the elderly, and people living in regions where factories had shut down. These Americans struggled to survive in the midst of poverty, hunger, and illness.

Starting with the middle class, working up the income ladder, and returning to the poorest, this chapter explores the everyday life of American families in the 1930s and how the Depression affected their lifestyles. Approximately 46 percent of American families during the Depression were in the middle class, 12 percent in the upper middle class, 3 to 4 percent in the wealthy category, and a tiny 0.1 percent in the very wealthy group. Thirty-eight percent of American families were considered poor during the Depression, up from 21 percent in 1929. Middle-class and upper-

**In order to "make do" with less, many women sewed their own clothing instead of purchasing clothes from stores.** *Courtesy of the Franklin D. Roosevelt Library.*

middle-class families and even the wealthy tried to carefully plan their expenditures; this was a necessary response to wage reductions and employment changes. For the very wealthy life did not change at all. Their antics and lavish parties continued during the Depression and were reported in the newspaper along with the movie stars' adventures. In stark contrast the poor and very poor simply tried to survive from day to day.

## The middle class

In 1935 and 1936 the median family income was $1,160. Families whose yearly income ranged between $1,000 and $2,500 were considered middle class. Depending on where the family fell within that range, they spent 75 to 100 percent of their income on basic necessities such as food, clothing, and shelter. A typical wage-earning, middle-class family in 1935 consisted of a husband and wife and two children living in a six-room house, either owned or rented, or in a four- to five-room apartment. The maintenance of a comfortable lifestyle often depended on how well the household budget was organized and how well the family adhered to it. Responsibility for the budget frequently fell to the mother of the family. Special budgeting sections appeared in women's magazines, and women would send in personal accounts of how they managed their budgets. Magazines even ran contests for the perfect budget.

### Taking Care of Family Needs

The middle-class mom prided herself on "making do" and stretching the food budget. Mothers and grandmothers found ways to make satisfying meals out of basic foodstuffs found in the pantry, such as flour, cornmeal, and sugar or corn syrup. Meals were simple and filling. Nothing edible was ever thrown out: Leftovers from Sunday's roast became Monday's hot beef sandwiches with gravy, Tuesday's stew with lots of vegetables, Wednesday's meat pie made with leftovers from stew, and Thursday's soup made with the bone and all leftover vegetables. Backyards and vacant lots became vegetable gardens. Women did their own canning, pickling, and preserving to save the expense of buying food at the store. Eggs were common—chickens were raised in both country and city backyards. Even in areas afflicted by drought, where gardens dried up, hens found bugs to eat and kept laying eggs. By taking care of their own necessities rather than purchasing goods and services, families maintained a reasonable standard of living. Mothers and grandmothers also became the family medical adviser as many adults put off visits to the doctor and dentist to avoid medical bills.

Very few clothes were store-bought. Most women were skilled in sewing. Exciting hours were spent picking out fabrics and patterns from catalogs. Foot-operated treadle sewing machines whirred until a garment was completed. The dominant look for women's everyday clothing was a simple printed dress of bright colors. Polka-dot fabrics were cheery and popular. Women used hats, gloves, pocketbooks (purses), and inexpensive jewelry to change the look of their simple outfits.

Fruits and vegetables grown in family gardens were canned and stored for later consumption. *Courtesy of the Franklin D. Roosevelt Library.*

Everything was saved and reused: paper bags, shoe boxes, tinfoil, rubber bands, jars, old clothes, and broken tools. Few labor-saving devices, gadgets, or appliances were in the middle-class house. Although new household devices were the rage in the booming 1920s, few people could afford them by the 1930s. As a result the sale of vacuum cleaners, washing machines, percolators for coffee, and toasters dropped significantly. Refrigerators were the exception. During the 1920s as city homes were electrified, refrigerators appeared in kitchens. Refrigerators greatly added to the flavor and freshness of the American meal. Between 1923 and 1941 the number of homes with refrigerators rose from 20,000 to 3.5 million. Those who could not afford a refrigerator and those who lived in rural areas without electricity had ice boxes to keep food fresh. An iceman brought blocks of ice every other day. During the winter in cold climates, rural families generally took advantage of freezing temperatures outside to devise various ways of preserving food.

## Farm Families

Farm families who owned their house and land and who managed not to lose the farm to debt or drought made it through the Depression by working hard and sticking together. The fortunate farm families not caught in the drought areas of the Dust Bowl (see Farm Relief chapter) could raise a variety of fruits and vegetables for selling, eating, and canning. Cattle were raised for beef and milk; hogs were butchered and either eaten or sold. The men learned to repair their aging farm equipment and make their own tools. Women made their family's clothes. Children scrounged together scraps of building material to make playthings.

## Automobiles

By 1930 even families at the lower end of the middle class were likely to own an automobile. About twenty-six million cars were on the road by 1930. Even during the worst years of the Depression, anyone who owned a car was reluctant to give up driving. By 1933 carmakers began tempting families with streamlined models sporting beautiful curving lines. But holding to strict budgets, people resisted temptation and drove their old cars longer and longer. Male members of the family changed the oil, patched tires, and did whatever they could to keep the car running. Taking care of the more difficult repairs, the auto repair industry actually grew during the Depression.

## Home Ownership

Urban middle-class families in the 1930s tended to own their own home, generally in an area at the edge of town (suburb). A typical house style was the bungalow, which had one and a half stories, two bedrooms, one bath, a living room, and a kitchen. Loss of the family home was perhaps the biggest fear of middle-class Depression-era families. With job losses and decreases in income, many families fell behind on their house payments.

In 1933 and 1934 people who were behind on house payments turned to two agencies established as part of the

New Deal: the Home Owners' Loan Corporation (HOLC) and the Federal Housing Administration (FHA). Through either the HOLC or the FHA, people could refinance their home loans (set up new payment terms that were easier to meet— usually lower payments for a longer period of time). Almost one million home loans had been refinanced by the HOLC alone by 1936, enabling millions of Americans to stay in their homes (see Banking and Housing chapter).

Most upper-class Americans did their best to maintain a refined standard of living. Pictured here are Joseph and Amy Chastek, of Los Angeles, California, with their brand-new 1936 Buick. *Courtesy of Pat Getz. Reproduced by permission.*

## Family Structure

Once-comfortable bungalows often became over-crowded in the 1930s. Young married couples who suddenly found themselves out of work moved back into their parents' home. Elderly parents who did not have sufficient income or savings to support themselves moved in with their grown children. Single people in their late teens and twenties, un-able to find jobs, stayed at home. Everyone had to pool resources to pay for housing, taxes, insurance, car expenses, and food. Crowded conditions strained family relationships. Some families grew closer in the face of hardship, but others broke apart.

Unable to afford their own households, couples postponed marriage. Very long engagements were common. In 1929 the marriage rate was 10.14 marriages per 1,000 persons but dropped to 7.87 per 1,000 persons by 1932. Fewer women between the ages of twenty-five and thirty-five married in the 1930s. Birth rates declined during the Depression. Uncertain about their future, couples had fewer children or no children. Approximately one-quarter of women who were in their twenties during the Depression years did not bear children.

Many families maintained a middle-class income by having several wage earners. Early in the 1930s children between the ages of fourteen and eighteen often provided extra income with paper routes and odd jobs. However, by 1940 the extra wage was more likely to be earned by the wife. Still, only 15 percent of all married women worked outside the home.

## The upper middle class and the wealthy

The income level of an upper-middle-class family in the 1930s began at approximately $2,500 yearly. In the mid-1930s only 12 percent of families achieved this class level; before the 1929 stock market crash, 29 percent had done so. (Between 1929 and 1933 the incomes of affluent doctors and lawyers dropped as much as 40 percent.) The income level of wealthy families generally started at about $5,000 yearly. Approximately 3 to 4 percent of families were wealthy in the 1930s.

The upper middle class and the wealthy watched as some of their friends lost everything in the stock market crash. Severely shaken, they feared they would be next. Nevertheless, most did their best to maintain a refined standard of living or at least keep up the appearance that nothing had changed. Their adjustments to lost income usually amounted to smoking cheaper cigars, riding the subways instead of employing chauffeurs, and giving up servants. Many upper-middle-class women who had never cooked before learned to prepare meals. Secondhand dress shops thrived because most upper-middle-class women had never acquired sewing skills.

## The very rich

As the Depression dragged on through the 1930s, only the most wealthy, the top 0.1 percent, were not affected in some way. While the upper middle class and the wealthy had to make some changes, the very rich made none. Middle-class Americans seem to have had a love/hate view of these privileged families: They looked upon the very rich as celebrities and eagerly followed their every move in newspaper and magazine articles; many of them also blamed the greed of these same people for the Depression. (Generally, the wealth of the very rich was long-standing, tied to industrial and banking giants that emerged in the late 1800s. This wealth remained stable after the 1929 market crash, whereas newly accumulated wealth that was rooted in the wild upward movement of the stock market disappeared.)

Although they were aware that ordinary people were struggling desperately during the Depression, the very rich continued to live their lives as usual. Some adjusted slightly by attempting to make their wealth less visible: Banker John P. Morgan Jr. (1867–1943) sailed his yacht less often, and others cut back on trips to Europe. Meanwhile, the Depression corrected the biggest problem of the wealthy, the "servant problem." During the booming 1920s few individuals were willing to work long irregular hours for low servant wages. But by the time the Depression reached its lowest point, in late 1932, the servant pool had grown dramatically. A gardener in Los Angeles would work for one dollar a week, and housekeepers would work for as little as four dollars a week and meals.

Newspapers and magazines gave extensive coverage to the activities of the very rich, and even the poorest individu-

**Wealthy socialites Brenda Frazier and Edward Hurd Jr., not affected by the dark financial times of the Great Depression, were media favorites in the 1930s.** *AP/Wide World Photo. Reproduced by permission.*

als knew many details of the lives of this privileged class. Lavish parties such as debutante balls, costing between ten thousand and one hundred thousand dollars, introduced young women into high society. New York's wealthiest families—the Vanderbilts, Belmonts, and Harrimans—continued to summer in Newport, Rhode Island, enjoying croquet games on expansive lawns, cocktails, swimming, and sailing. Young Americans of all classes looked to the youthful rich as trendsetters. Known as the Cafe Society, the glamorous youths were seen nightly at posh restaurants. The reigning glamour girl of the Cafe Society in the late 1930s was Brenda Frazier, an heiress due to inherit $4 million at age twenty-one. Young women and girls attempted to copy her makeup and style of clothes.

# The poor

In stark contrast to the very wealthy, the poor struggled each day to merely find enough to eat. The poor made up more than a third of the 1930s U.S. population during the Depression, far more than the 21 percent estimated for 1929 just prior to the Depression. Their income ranged from almost nothing to about one thousand dollars per year. (The federal government estimated that a family of four needed eight hundred dollars a month just to survive in the 1930s.)

Some of the poorest Americans lived in the hills of Kentucky and West Virginia, where the coal mines had closed. Others were agricultural laborers, both black and white Americans, working as hired hands or tenant farmers or sharecroppers in rural areas. In the cities the unemployed and desperately poor lived in tenement slums, and many stood in breadlines for a meal. Some lived in makeshift shacks on vacant lots. All these people had the same main concern: day-to-day survival.

## Coal-Mining Families

Widespread suffering came to the coal-mining families of West Virginia and the Cumberland Plateau of eastern Kentucky. By 1932, when many of the mines closed, thousands were thrown out of work. Many families lived in tents and had no food for days. Days were spent scrambling for something to eat. Men and boys, if they were lucky enough to find work, would spend ten hours in the fields of a farmer, take their pay in food crops (perhaps beans, potatoes, and apples), and then walk three or four miles back home. Women and girls would spend all day picking wild greens on hillsides. Fortunate families had a cow for milk. Hog lard was generally the only meat available. Winters were particularly hard; frozen cabbage was all that came from the garden then.

## The Rural Poor: Tenant Farmers and Sharecroppers

Tenant farming is a system of farming in which families supply their own tools but rent the land they work and live on. Sharecropping is a system of farming in which a landlord supplies the tools and the land. Tenant farmers and sharecroppers were both required to give part of their crops to their landlords. These types of farming were prevalent in southern states, where 75 percent of all black Americans lived. Eighty percent of those blacks were hired hands, sharecroppers, or tenant farmers. All worked from sunrise to sunset in the spring and summer in order to have something to live on in the fall and winter. Frequently landowners advanced families about ten dollars a month in spring. That ten dollars—used for seed and living expenses—was often for a family of eight or more. A hired hand might receive twenty cents for picking one hundred pounds of cotton. In a fourteen-hour day pay usually amounted to no more than sixty cents. By fall, after paying rent, giving portions of the crops to the landlord, and settling grocery bills and doctor bills, nothing was left for the winter.

Most poor rural families, black and white alike, lived in shacks. They had few pieces of furniture and no running water. Malnutrition was common. Most lived on a diet of corn bread, greens from the garden, salt pork, hominy grits (ground corn), and molasses. Children had little access to education. Blacks were terrorized by racist organizations such as the Ku Klux Klan, a secret organization that believed in the domination of whites over blacks by means of terrorism.

## The Urban Poor

Approximately three million black Americans lived in northern cities. In terms of housing they fared little bet-

ter than southern blacks. Blacks along with poor urban whites crowded into tiny apartments. Two hundred families crowded into buildings that once housed sixty families. Landlords managed this by dividing a six-room apartment into six tiny "kitchenettes," each with a single bed, refrigerator, and hot plate. All six families shared the single bathroom. If a family failed to pay their rent, they were evicted (forced to leave the home or apartment). Landlords simply had the family's belongings moved out onto the street. In her book *The Invisible Scar* (1966), Caroline Bird states that eviction was so common that children made a game out of it in day care centers. They would pile up doll furniture in one corner, then move it to another corner. Sometimes people in a neighborhood would march together to an eviction site and move the family's belongings back into the apartment. Usually the family would then stay in their apartment a few more months, with the landlord too intimated to take further action for a while.

Hunger was a nagging everyday problem. Although many vacant lots became vegetable gardens, most inner-city residents had no access to vegetables. They would hunt through garbage from restaurants and city garbage dumps for their food. Children would wait at the back door of butcher shops for bones or chicken feet, which their mothers would use to make a watery soup.

The stealing of food sometimes became a systematic affair, with each family member assigned certain necessary foodstuffs. Fathers reported keeping themselves and older children away from living quarters when younger children were fed, to keep from grabbing food from the youngsters. Sometimes family members took turns eating—some members one day and other members the next day. Public schools in New York City reported one-fifth of their students were malnourished.

Soup kitchens became common in large cities in the early 1930s. Their handouts were simple: stew and bread; soup, bread, and coffee; beans, bread, and coffee. People stood in long "breadlines" each day for the food. The Salvation Army, Red Cross, Catholic charities, volunteer organizations, and various individuals ran the kitchens. In 1931 New York City reported eighty-two breadlines serving eighty-five thousand meals each day.

## "Feed the Hungry"

President Franklin D. Roosevelt (1882–1945; served 1933–45) signed an act on May 12, 1933, creating the Federal Emergency Relief Administration (FERA). This agency was charged with getting food to the hungry. Roosevelt appointed Harry Hopkins (1890–1946) to direct FERA. Hopkins gave one short order to FERA officials: "Feed the hungry, and fast!" By October 1933 the Federal Surplus Relief Corporation (FSRC) was established as a part of FERA. The FSRC took agricultural surpluses that farmers had been unable to sell (such as pork, butter, flour, and syrup) and transported them to state emergency relief officials. These officials distributed the surplus food directly into the hands of the needy. After two successful years the FSRC closed down in November 1935. Agricultural and relief officers arranged to continue food distribution through the Federal Surplus Commodities Corporation (FSCC). The FSCC established the first Food Stamp Plan on May 16, 1939. The FSRC and FSCC activities led to permanent food stamp and school lunch programs later in the twentieth century.

## Leisure time

For Americans who maintained a steady job during the Depression, the workweek was generally five days. The two days off usually included leisure activities. The unemployed also sought ways to fill their "forced leisure" time. Lack of funds forced people to look to life's cheap and easy entertainments. Nine years into the Great Depression the National Recreation Association completed a study of five thousand Americans, asking them to list the leisure activities they participated in most often. The most frequently mentioned at-home activities were card games, board games, and puzzles; listening to the radio; reading newspapers, magazines, and books; visiting, entertaining, conversations on front porches, attending parties and socials; and letter writing. Away-from-home activities included going to the movies, dances, and sporting events; motoring or driving about; picnics; and the newly popular miniature golf. Most activities on the list were available for free or for a low cost. For this reason, the 1930s are often referred to as the "nickel and dime" decade.

Card games were a popular way to enjoy time with family and friends. Bridge was the most popular game among adults and older children. In 1931 five hundred thousand enrolled in bridge classes across the country. Board games such as Monopoly, introduced by Parker Brothers in 1935, gained popularity. In Monopoly people could wheel and deal in real estate even if in real life their house payment was a struggle.

**Four women put together a jigsaw puzzle while on break from work.** *AP/Wide World Photo. Reproduced by permission.*

Jigsaw puzzles became accessible to most people in 1932 and 1933. Before that time, puzzles were expensive because they were made of wood. But in the early 1930s a New England entrepreneur began cutting puzzles out of heavy cardboard. (An entrepreneur is an individual willing to take a risk in developing a new business.) Once the cardboard puzzles could be mass-produced, they could be sold very cheaply. Jigsaw puzzles were also given away in special promotions for products such as toothpaste and non-prescription medicines. By 1934 over 3.5 million jigsaw puzzles were in the hands of Americans. Puzzles could be found at newsstands, drugstores, toy stores, and bookstores. The more affordable "jigs" sold for ten cents; a colossal one-thousand-piece puzzle cost a few dollars. Whether the attraction was working out the puzzle or just not having to worry about more-serious matters, people diligently fit their puzzle pieces together. Solving "jigs" remained a national pastime throughout the 1930s.

**Radio kept Americans informed and entertained throughout the 1930s.**
*Courtesy of the Franklin D. Roosevelt Library.*

## Radio

Listening to the radio became perhaps the most popular form of entertainment in the 1930s. By the middle of the decade two-thirds of American homes had radio sets, and by the end of the decade 80 percent of Americans owned radios. After an initial investment of between fifty and seventy-five dollars, a family could enjoy music, comedy, drama, variety, quiz shows, women's shows, children's shows, and an increasing menu of sports—all in their own living room. Through entertainment programming radios provided a ready escape from economic hard times, but they were also an inexpensive way to keep up with news events of the Great Depression and farming news. The typical family spent hours each evening listening to their favorite programs. Americans stayed glued to their radios when President Roosevelt broadcast a "fireside chat," during which he explained what was being done in Washington, D.C., to ease the nation's economic problems (see News Media and Entertainment chapter).

## Newspapers

While many Americans received some of their news from the radio, the standard news medium was the newspaper. Newspapers provided daily news and were inexpensive. (The *New York Times* cost only two cents in the 1930s.) Papers reported the latest in politics and sports and kept track of Hollywood and high-society celebrities. Newsboys delivered papers directly to homes. Being a news delivery boy was a source of pride because the youngsters knew they were adding needed money to the family income.

## Magazines

Magazines were also popular reading material during the Depression. Magazines addressed a wide range of interests and supported entertainment fields such as movies, sports, and photography. Popular magazines often targeted either women or men. Women audiences purchased romance-oriented magazines such as *Modern Romance* and *True Story*. They also bought movie-oriented publications like *Modern Screen* and *Movie Life*. Men read sports magazines such as *Sports Illustrated*. They also purchased *Esquire,* a magazine featuring a variety of articles about men's lifestyles, and crime and detective magazines like *True Detective Mysteries*. Photography became very popular in the 1930s, and the magazines *Photography* and *Modern Photography* stimulated Americans' interest. Both *Life* and *Look* premiered in the second half of the 1930s. These picture magazines often featured photographs of people damaged by the Depression. The photos served to raise awareness about the extent of the nation's problems.

## Movies

Most Americans lived close to a movie theater, even those who lived in small towns. In 1930 about 110 million Americans attended movies every week. As unemployment

# How Much Did Things Cost in the 1930s?

## Automobiles

| | |
|---|---|
| New Pontiac coupe | $585.00 |
| New Packard | $2,150.00 |
| New Chevy pickup truck | $650.00 |
| Used Ford '29 | $57.50 |
| Auto tire | $6.20 |
| Gasoline (per gallon) | $.18 |

## Clothing: Men

| | |
|---|---|
| Wool suit | $10.50 |
| Trousers | $2.00 |
| Shirt | $.47 |
| Sweater | $1.95 |
| Silk necktie | $.55 |
| Shoes | $3.85 |

## Clothing: Women

| | |
|---|---|
| Wool dress | $1.95 |
| Leather shoes | $1.79 |
| Cloth coat | $6.98 |
| Mink coat | $585.00 |

## Household Items

| | |
|---|---|
| Double bed sheets | $.67 |
| Wool blanket | $1.00 |
| Bath towel | $.24 |
| Wool rug (9 x 12 feet) | $5.85 |
| Electric iron | $2.00 |
| Electric coffee percolator | $1.39 |
| Vacuum cleaner | $18.75 |
| Electric washing machine | $47.95 |
| Console radio | $49.95 |
| 3-piece bedroom set | $49.95 |
| Double bed | $14.95 |
| Wing chair | $39.00 |
| Bridge table | $1.00 |

## Housing

| | |
|---|---|
| Six-room modern house | $2,800 |
| Twelve-room mansion | $17,000 |

## Food

| | |
|---|---|
| Sirloin steak (per lb.) | $.29 |
| Ham (per lb.) | $.31 |
| Chicken (per lb.) | $.22 |
| Milk (per quart) | $.10 |
| Eggs (per doz.) | $.29 |
| Bread | $.05 |
| Coffee (per lb.) | $.26 |
| Sugar (per lb.) | $.05 |
| Potatoes (per lb.) | $.02 |
| Tomatoes (16 oz. can) | $.09 |
| Oranges (per doz.) | $.27 |

*Adapted from "Depression Shopping List, 1932 to 1934" in Loretta Britten and Sarah Brash, eds.,* Our American Century, Hard Times: The '30s, *Alexandria, VA: Time-Life Books, 1998, page 29.*

increased and salaries decreased, attendance dropped to roughly sixty million a week by 1933. The public could not afford to attend the movies as frequently as they used to. The price of admission, only a few cents, was an extravagance for many. However, the millions who faithfully attended represented 60 percent of the population. Americans, it appeared, needed their movies. Because of this need, the movie industry actually prospered in the 1930s. Hollywood produced gangster films, Disney films, comedies, musicals, law and order films, Westerns, drama, and horror thrillers. For a few hours each week Americans could enter their dark, comfort-

Two teenagers dance the jitterbug during the opening of the New York World's Fair in 1939. *Corbis Corporation. Reproduced by permission.*

able movie houses and be transported to another world (see News Media and Entertainment chapter).

## The Dance Craze

Swing, a form of jazz music, created a dance craze in the mid-1930s. After World War I (1914–18) and into the 1920s, black American musicians developed a type of music known as jazz, which had a driving beat and improvised (created on the spot) solos. In the early 1930s most Americans had only heard calm orchestra versions of jazz. But in 1934 at Hollywood's Palomar Ballroom, Benny Goodman (1909–1986), a famous white bandleader, told his band to "swing out." The crowd went wild to the hard-driving jazz beats, and the swing craze was born. Swing could be heard on radio, records, and jukeboxes, and in dance halls around the country. The lindy hop or jitterbug, the Big Apple, the shag, and the Suzy Q were swing dances with basic steps every young person learned. Some steps were physically demanding and involved acrobatic moves. Swing even had its own slang speech, called "jive." If you were hip in the 1930s, you had to speak jive. Here is a sample of jive words:

- **Alligator:** follower of swing
- **Canary:** a female singer
- **Cats:** musicians in a swing band
- **Cuttin' a rug:** dancing to swing
- **Hepcat:** a person who knows all about swing
- **Ickie:** a person who doesn't understand swing
- **In the groove:** feeling swing's beat
- **Jitterbugging:** dancing to swing
- **Kicking out:** dancing fast and free

## Marathons

Endurance marathons were another craze that took Americans' minds off the Depression. Goldfish swallowers, tree sitters, pie eaters, and phone booth crammers emerged across the nation. People were intrigued by how much someone could swallow, or how long they could sit, or how many could fit in a small space. There were also bicycle and roller skate derbies. Another unusual type of marathon was the dance marathon, in which couples would compete to see who could dance the longest. Dance marathons began as a fad but soon became a bizarre way to make money—for participants and for dance hall owners. Couples (male–female pairs only) were required to be on the dance floor and in motion for forty-five minutes of every hour, day and night. Tickets were sold to people who wanted to watch the spectacle. The first contests lasted several days, but later on contests lasted months. Desperate-

A line of boys shoving pie into their mouths during a pie-eating contest in 1939. *Courtesy of the Library of Congress.*

ly needing the prize money, couples became spectacles of exhaustion, sometimes with tragic endings including death.

## Sports

Sporting events and athletes became immensely popular during the Great Depression as Americans looked for ways to divert their attention away from their problems, if only for a little while. People began to personally identify with teams and athletes. Baseball adapted to the nation's depressed economy by allowing games to be broadcast over the radio so people could enjoy the entertainment for free. Players like Babe Ruth (1895–1948) and Lou Gehrig (1903–1941) attracted national attention. Almost every town of any size tied itself to some semiprofessional or professional league. Little League baseball began in 1939. Softball games sprang up everywhere. Business firms, churches, and even neighborhoods formed softball teams. The fun was free and often combined with picnics. Football also gained increased attention. During the Depression, college teams continued battling in bowl games: the Rose, Orange, Sun, Sugar, Cotton, Eastern, and Coal Bowls. The first Heisman Trophy was awarded in 1935 to the top college football player in the nation. Sometimes a sport grew in popularity because of a particular athlete, as was the case with boxing and Joe Louis (1914–1981). The Summer Olympics of 1932 were held in Los Angeles. During the Summer Games American athlete Babe Didrikson (1911–1956) gathered national attention as she excelled in multiple sports. Black American athlete Jesse Owens (1913–1980) dominated numerous track and field events at the 1936 Olympic Games in Berlin, Germany.

On a much smaller scale and closer to home, sports included miniature golf. In 1929 Garnet Carter (1883–1954) of Lookout, Tennessee, built the Tom Thumb Golf Course, where the whole family could play on a series of small courses. That same year he went to Miami and built a course. Miniature golf was an immediate inexpensive hit. By 1930 roadside courses had sprung up in many areas. For people out "motoring" it became quite the rage to stop for a game. For a short while some optimists suggested that the miniature golf industry might lift the United States out of the Depression.

## Vacations

Middle-class and upper-middle-class families could no longer afford European vacations. Instead they hit the road in their automobiles. Gasoline was cheap, and the road offered a momentary escape from hard times. Businesses popped up along highways to serve tourists. Campgrounds and motor courts (motels) appeared for the first time, in California, Texas, and Florida; the motor courts touted private indoor bathrooms. Howard Johnson (c. 1896–1972) opened a string of roadside restaurants. His Big Boy™ restaurants offered hamburgers and fries. Born out of a need for inexpensive Depression-era travel, the roadside culture became a permanent feature of American life.

## What Did Kids Do for Fun?

Besides sharing leisure-time activities with their families and spending hours at the movies on Saturday afternoon,

## Food Entrepreneurs

Entrepreneurs are people who create and market a new item or start a new business. They assume all the risk (such as cash lost) if their venture fails. Although times were difficult in the 1930s, the cleverness of American entrepreneurs still pushed them to try new approaches and take on the management of new enterprises. Several products introduced by food entrepreneurs in the 1930s are still familiar to families at the beginning of the twenty-first century. These products include Fritos®, Kool-Aid®, Spam®, Pepperidge Farm® baked goods, Toll House® chocolate chip cookies, and Skippy® peanut butter.

The tasty little corn chips known as Fritos got their start when Elmer Doolin's mother sold her wedding ring for one hundred dollars and gave the money to Elmer. While traveling through San Antonio, Texas, in 1932, Elmer bought a bag of fried corn chips for a nickel. The chip maker was a Mexican man eager to return home to Mexico. Elmer purchased the chip recipe and the Fritos name (which means "fried" in Spanish) from the man, using the one hundred dollars his mother had given him. One hundred dollars was a lot of money in Depression times. Elmer began selling the inexpensive chips from his car and made about two dollars a day. It was Elmer's good fortune to connect with potato chip king Herman W. Lay. Soon the Frito-Lay chip was being munched coast to coast.

Most of the other products had similar humble beginnings but ended up making their creators wealthy individuals. Edwin E. Perkins introduced Kool-Aid in 1927. By 1930 it was a huge hit. Mothers liked the fact that it was inexpensive yet still a real treat for their children. Perkins was a multimillionaire by 1936. Spam got its start when a Hormel company executive acquired several thousand pounds of pork

many children of the Depression lived in a world of heroes and heroines. Children who lived above poverty level enjoyed following the adventures of various fictional characters; always cheery or exciting, these adventures provided a welcome break from the rather drab days of the Depression. Little Orphan Annie, the redhead of comic strips and radio, was a favorite. With her famous saying "Leapin' Lizards!" she and her dog, Sandy, entertained throughout the Depression. Other superheroes were science fiction characters Flash Gordon and Buck Rogers, hard-nosed detective Dick Tracy, Western hero Tom Mix, and football hero Jack Armstrong. These characters appeared in comics, books, and/or movie house that he needed to use immediately. He added a little spice and put it in cans. In a 1937 naming contest, "Spam" emerged. The inexpensive meat product was a gold mine. Mothers would serve it for Sunday dinner. Pepperidge Farms baked goods resulted when a young Connecticut homemaker, Margaret Rudkin, improved on the plain, additive-filled white bread available in stores. Toll House cookies got their start in the mid-1930s when Ruth Wakefield ran out of nuts for her Butter Drop Dos, or Boston, cookie, a favorite at her Toll House Inn in Whitman, Massachusetts. She quickly chopped up two Nestlé chocolate bars and dumped them into the cookie mix. In 1939 Wakefield signed a forty-year contract with Nestlé to print her recipe on the back of every package of chocolate morsels. In 1933 J. L. Rosefield produced peanut butter that did not separate into oil and peanut meat. He put it in red-white-and-blue tins and called it Skippy peanut butter. Mothers clamored for this affordable nutritious food that their children loved. All of these American food entrepreneurs became millionaires in the Depression.

Irma Louise (von Starkloff) Rombauer was another type of food entrepreneur. In 1930 Rombauer, who had always lived a privileged life, found herself in need of an income when her husband died. She wrote a fun and easy-to-use cookbook, *Joy of Cooking,* and paid a local printer to print three thousand copies. It was an instant hit, especially among upper-middle-class and wealthy wives who had never cooked before the Depression. It gave clear instructions to keep even inexperienced cooks from failing. *Joy of Cooking* was revised and reprinted throughout the remainder of the twentieth century. It became America's most influential cookbook and made yet another Depression-era entrepreneur fabulously wealthy.

cartoons. Two real-life heroines were the English princesses Elizabeth (1926–) and Margaret Rose (1930–2002). Girls played for hours with paper doll cutouts of these royal figures. Little girls also played with dolls patterned after the real-life child movie star Shirley Temple (1928–). All these characters carried the same message—that clean living brings unlimited rewards.

Another favorite pastime for children in after-school hours and during long summer days was designing and building their own toys. A two-by-four piece of lumber, an orange crate, and wheels from a skate made a fine scooter.

Model airplanes of wood and kites of string, paper, and wood were just as much fun for dads and moms as for the children.

Outdoor games of sandlot baseball and "king of the mountain" occupied hours. Jacks, jump rope, and "kick-the-can" were fun—and they were all free. If a swimming hole or pool was available, kids could cool off and play at the same time.

Even though most families saw their income dwindle during the Depression, children did not mope around the house with nothing to do. Many of their activities cost nothing, and they found unlimited entertainment in their favorite adventure stories and simple games.

# For More Information

## Books

Anderson, Jean. *American Century Cookbook: The Most Popular Recipes of the Twentieth Century.* New York, NY: Clarkson Potter, 1997.

Best, Gary Dean. *The Nickel and Dime Decade: American Popular Culture during the 1930s.* Westport CT: Praeger, 1993.

Britten, Loretta, and Sarah Brash, eds. *Hard Times: The '30s.* Alexandria, VA: Time-Life Books, 1998.

Federal Writers Project. *These Are Our Lives.* Chapel Hill, NC: University of North Carolina Press, 1939.

McElvaine, Robert S. *Down and Out in the Great Depression: Letters from the "Forgotten Man."* Chapel Hill, NC: University of North Carolina Press, 1983.

Mendelson, Anne. *Stand Facing the Stove: The Story of the Women Who Gave America "The Joy of Cooking."* New York, NY: Henry Holt, 1996.

Phillips, Cabell. *From the Crash to the Blitz: 1929–1939.* New York, NY: Macmillan, 1969.

Reynolds, Edward B., and Michael Kennedy. *Whistleberries, Stirabout, and Depression Cake.* Helena, MT: Falcon Publishing, 2000.

Rogers, Agnes. *I Remember Distinctly: A Family Album of the American People 1918–1941.* New York, NY: Harper & Brothers Publishers, 1947.

Stowe, David W. *Swing Changes: Big Band Jazz in New Deal America.* Cambridge, MA: Harvard University Press, 1994.

Thacker, Emily. *Recipes and Remembrances of the Great Depression.* Canton, OH: Tresco Publishers, 1993.

Time-Life Books. *This Fabulous Century: 1930–1940.* New York, NY: Time-Life Books, 1969.

Van Amber, Rita. *Stories and Recipes of the Great Depression of the 1930s.* Vols. 1 and 2. Neenah, WI: Van Amber Publishers, 1986–93.

Washburne, Carolyn Kott. *America in the Twentieth Century, 1930–1939.* North Bellmore, NY: Marshall Cavendish, 1995.

Watkins, T. H. *The Hungry Years: A Narrative History of the Great Depression in America.* New York, NY: Henry Holt, 1999.

Winslow, Susan. *Brother, Can You Spare a Dime? America from the Wall Street Crash to Pearl Harbor: An Illustrated Documentary.* New York, NY: Paddington Press, 1976.


## Web Sites

*Betty Crocker Foods.* http://www.bettycrocker.com (accessed on August 15, 2002).

*Food and Drug Administration (FDA).* http://www.fda.gov (accessed on August 15, 2002).

*The Food Stamp Program.* http://www.foodusa.org (accessed on August 15, 2002).

*Kraft Foods.* http://www.kraftfoods.com (accessed on August 15, 2002).

*Radio Sportscasting.* http://www.americansportscasters.com/radio-how.html (accessed on August 15, 2002).

# Riding the Rails

It was 1932 in the United States. Hard times of the Great Depression had hit. Pulling into a rail yard of a small town on an early misty morning was a long freight train. Even before the train came to a complete stop, shadowy figures began jumping from boxcars to the gravel below. Not five or six but sixty or more tumbled from the train with small bundles in hand. Many of their faces were not lined with age; they were the fresh faces of America's youth. Many were teenagers— teenagers "on the bum." They were part of an army of youthful transients, numbering roughly 250,000, who were riding the rails through America.

Along the rails homeless boys and a scattering of girls experienced adventure, awesome glimpses of the American countryside, and a thrilling sense of freedom. But they also experienced hunger, danger, boredom, despair, and hostile railroad security guards known as the "bulls." Three out of four of America's wandering young people said the hard times of the Great Depression caused them to "hit the road."

The crash of the U.S. stock market in October 1929 signaled the start of the most severe economic crisis in U.S.

history. By 1932 and early 1933 many banks had closed, manufacturing had slowed greatly, and millions of people had lost their jobs, money, and homes. Twenty-five percent of American workers were unemployed. Almost everyone suffered some decrease in income. For some Americans—both young and older—the answer was to take to the road in hopes of securing work in another part of the nation. By 1933 the size of the transient population was estimated to be between two and three million, including hundreds of thousands riding the rails.

Beginning in 1933 President Franklin D. Roosevelt (1882–1945; served 1933–45) made an effort to provide help and support for the nation's wandering population. The Roosevelt administration created special emergency legislation—called the New Deal— to address the nation's economic problems, including the transient population. The New Deal programs established by this legislation offered various forms of relief and care services, jobs on public works projects (such as road building and forest maintenance), a network of transient shelters, and education opportunities. Ultimately, because of the size of the transient population, these programs could reach only a small percentage of the wanderers. The army of transients would continue to roam through the 1930s, the length of the Great Depression.

## Increasing numbers on the rails

During the 1920s people who rode the rails were either seasonal workers or permanent transients called hoboes (or tramps or bums). The hoboes were not in search of jobs; instead they sought a detachment from mainstream American society. They were content to live a life of aimless wandering. Seasonal workers traveled from state to state, working on farms as various crops were ready for harvest. Through the 1920s, the railroad police reported that on any given transcontinental freight train about six to eight men would be hitching a ride. By the early 1930s, railroad police reported swarms of transients, up to two or three hundred per train—many of them young boys.

Because transients were constantly on the move, no accurate estimate of their number was ever available. But by

**A young man hops aboard a boxcar and looks down the railroad tracks toward a new destination.**
*National Archives and Records Administration.*

1932 it was estimated that 250,000 youths between the ages of fifteen and twenty-five were riding the rails. Roughly one in twenty American youths had left home. Why had so many young Americans, some no more than twelve years of age, opted for life on the rails?

## Reasons for leaving home

In the 1930s American youths were not in revolt against the government, nor were they revolting against their parents. Most of them left home because they felt they were a burden to their family. Many came from well-to-do families. Others were from families that had always struggled with poverty. As unemployment struck family after family during the Depression, young people of almost every economic class watched as their fathers unsuccessfully searched for work. The boys themselves had often looked for work in their hometown for months, even several years, before leaving. With their families stretching to make ends meet, the boys decided they were just one more mouth to feed. They decided to hit the road in search of work. If lucky enough to find work, they would send money home.

The economic hardships brought on by the Great Depression significantly affected schools. The loss of jobs and income by residents of an area meant fewer taxes were being paid to local governments. A decrease in taxes paid meant smaller budgets for schools. As a result many schools had to shorten their school year or close altogether because they could not afford to pay teachers. A substantial percentage of teenage youths were not attending high school. Under normal conditions most young people would have been in school or working, but the 1930s were not normal times. Some boys hit the road with their parents' blessings to search for a job and a better life.

Another reason for leaving home was to seek adventure. With no work available and summertime school breaks dragging on, Depression-era days in an ordinary town could be boring for teens. Life on the road, riding the rails, seemed to offer great adventure. Many teens from eastern states could not resist the temptation to head west, where incredible sights and cities awaited; the Rocky Mountains, the Grand Canyon, San Francisco, and Los Angeles all beckoned. Western teens looked east and set the Statue of Liberty as their goal. Two popular destinations were the 1933 Chicago World's Fair and the 1936 Texas Centennial Fair. The adventure seekers often had practiced riding the rails for months before they left. With their buddies they would hop a freight train to a nearby town and back. This would build up their courage and give them experience for making a longer trip. Town newspapers frequently reported on their local "boes" (short for "hoboes") who took off to see the country. Even the dangers and hardships they reported sounded thrilling to young people forced to be idle by the circumstances of the Depression. Of course, the adventure-seeking "boes" had a home to return to, and generally they did return after six weeks or so. This could not be said for the majority of young transients, who had left home with the serious purpose of finding work and who felt that returning would only burden their families.

By 1932 youths riding the rails had become a wandering army of thousands. Hopping on a moving freight train as it started up for distant places gave them a thrilling sense of freedom. Yet few were prepared for the dangers, hunger, and hardships that awaited them.

## Food and a place to rest

Along the Southern Pacific Railroad route, small towns in Texas, New Mexico, and Arizona reported several hundred transients arriving daily. Los Angeles became a magnet, with eight thousand passing through monthly. The number of daily arrivals stretched available resources of food and shelter. City relief agencies did not want to spend scarce local revenues on nonresidents. It was hard enough caring for their own citizens who were out of work and hungry.

Hence finding food and a place to rest when they left the train became a daily concern for transient teenagers.

Gradually the youths learned where a meal and a bed could be had. In larger towns the Salvation Army, missions, and city shelters provided meals and beds. Privately sponsored breadlines provided simple meals such as beans, bread, and coffee. The beds at the Salvation Army were clean, but most other accommodations were dirty. Sheets might not have been washed for weeks and were sometimes full of lice or fleas. Beds might be pieces of linoleum on springs or even the tables that had just been used for meals.

On the outskirts of towns and in rural areas, camps called "jungles" were found in brush or trees along the railroad tracks. Flimsy shacks and piles of cans, glass, and other garbage marked camp locations. The camps were often located by a stream or pond used for washing and obtaining drinking water. The water was frequently contaminated and caused illnesses. Broken mirrors hung from trees to use for shaving. The ground was generally the only bed available, and it was not uncommon for rats to run over a sleeping transient. Hunting for twigs or other wood to keep campfires burning during cold weather was a constant task. Sometimes great crowds of boys huddled and slept close by the fires.

If food was not available from overburdened relief houses, finding enough to eat consumed waking hours. Hunger spells sometimes lasted for several days. Various strategies for survival had to be learned. Usually an experienced hobo who had been riding the rails for years served as a teacher for the young transients. For example, experienced hoboes taught that when going to private homes to ask for food, the best approach was knocking at the back door rather than at the front. Often the transient would offer to work for food or money (the work usually involved duties like chopping wood, but little else; inexperienced youths rarely earned enough money to send home). Sometimes families would take pity on a hungry youth and offer a meal and a place to sleep. Then, with the piece of chalk that was always kept in his pocket, the young transient would make a special mark: Somewhere outside the family's house he would write "18"—which was meant to read "I ate." This was a signal to other hoboes that the house was a good place

## Hobo Language

Transients developed their own colorful language to describe the hobo life. Along the rails the following words described the activities and people in this wandering world:

**Catching out:** Hopping on a freight train.

**Dingbat:** A longtime, experienced hobo.

**Dumped:** Physically attacked or assaulted.

**Gaycat:** An individual new to hoboing.

**Grab iron:** The vertical railing on a train car, which a hobo could catch hold of.

**Hitting the Stem:** Going to Main Street.

**Hobo tobacco:** Dried leaves crushed and rolled in a cigarette.

**Hoosiers:** People who are not transients; the general public.

**Hoover tourist:** A transient; as the term implies, people blamed President Herbert Hoover (1874–1964; served 1929–33) for the economic problems that led to increased numbers of transients.

**Jungle buzzards:** Hoboes who lived at a camp for weeks or months at a time.

**Jungles:** Transient camps along the rails where hoboes could stop to rest, wash, and cook.

**Knee shaker:** A plate of food given to a hobo—to be eaten while sitting on the back porch of a house with the plate resting on his knees.

**Lump:** A handout of a sack of food.

**Mulligan stew:** A soup composed of whatever food scraps can be obtained, boiled over a campfire.

**On the fly:** Catching hold of a moving train.

**Railroad bulls:** Railroad police hired to get transients off railroad property.

**Reefer:** Refrigerator car with an ice compartment that provided a place to ride; reefers also provided drinking water from the water dripping below the car.

**Sally:** The Salvation Army, an organization that provided temporary food and shelter.

**Sit-down:** An invitation to come inside a house and eat with the family.

**Yeggs:** Transients with a criminal nature.

to stop. Transients had developed a language of chalk markings or symbols known only to other transients. Their symbols marked where one could find a meal, where to go if sick, safe camps, clean water, and dangerous towns. If a youth obtained only scraps of leftovers from his ventures into town, he would return to the camp, where the other hoboes might have a mulligan stew boiling. Mulligan stew was made with any scrap of food available.

# Dangers on the rails

The hazards of riding the rails were many and could be fatal. The Interstate Commerce Commission reported that approximately twenty-five thousand transients were killed and twenty-seven thousand injured on trains or in railroad yards between 1929 and 1939. Most of the hundreds of thousands of young people "catching out" (hopping on a freight train) were new at "hoboing." New, inexperienced hoboes, called "gaycats," had to learn how to ride the different train cars if they hoped to ever become "dingbats," real hoboes.

Relatively safe places to ride were in empty boxcars, at the ends of hopper cars (freight cars that can quickly discharge their loads through their bottom), and straddling the coupling between two cars while hanging on to the brake rod, a pole running vertically up the end of the car. However, if a transient accidentally stepped on the cutting lever (the device that can uncouple or detach rail cars from each other) between the cars, the train would automatically brake, throwing him off, injuring the train crew and others on the train, and damaging merchandise in the cars. The ice compartment of a reefer (refrigerator car) was a fine place to ride as long as the compartment door was carefully propped open. Otherwise the door would shut, trapping the transient behind the thick insulated walls. However, even with the door propped open, there was still danger that a trainman might fill the compartment with ice and crush the transient. Very dangerous places to ride were on the rods under cars and on top of a loose load in an open boxcar (the load could shift at any time and crush the rider). Riding on top of a closed freight car also had several disadvantages. The hobo could roll off or be suffocated as the smoke-belching train passed through a long, narrow train tunnel. Also, the railroad "bulls" (police) could easily spot someone atop a car. Knowing that transients would always choose boxcars first, railroad companies often added extra empty boxcars to the train to avoid injuries, loss of life, and damage to merchandise.

Transients hopping trains faced arrest if caught by the "bulls." Bulls never threw transients off moving trains, for fear of lawsuits, but they arrested them as soon as trains came to a stop in the yard. Transients could even be arrested for hanging around the rail yard. Sometimes bulls beat the

wanderers. Railroad bulls and town police were at odds over what to do about the situation. Railroad bulls would pull transients off trains, but town police would put them back on, demanding they move to the next town. This experience was known among hoboes as "passing on." Sometimes boys caught in the freight yards or wandering in town would be arrested and thrown in jail. While in jail they were forced to do hard labor on chain gangs.

**Men riding on an open-air flat car near Fresno, California, circa 1937.**
*National Archives and Records Administration.*

**Riding the Rails**

Other common hazards of the rails posed extreme danger for the inexperienced rider. Train wrecks and getting thrown off by sudden turns and stops killed many. Assaults by other transients seeking food or money—or simply out of frustration—occurred frequently. Younger boys were easy prey for older, seasoned transients. Transients also suffered from exposure and undernourishment (transients often went two or three days without food). Medical care in towns was only offered to the seriously ill or injured, to discourage transients from stopping there for help.

Girls, young women, and black Americans were particularly susceptible to the dangers of hobo life on the rails. Females rode the rails in far fewer numbers than boys and men. For safety reasons, such as fear of sexual assault, they often disguised themselves as males and traveled with others. In January 1933 of the estimated 256,000 transients riding the rails, only 11,000 were female; 35 to 40 percent of them were under the age of twenty-one. Black Americans, and other minorities, riding the rails faced the same racism that was prevalent throughout the nation in the 1930s. Especially great danger existed in the South, where lynchings (to execute, especially by hanging, without due process of law) were on the rise during the Depression. This threat of danger discouraged many blacks and other minorities from riding the rails. Almost no statistics are available on blacks riding the rails. However, officials in Buffalo, New York, did a study in 1935 of the 20,000 transients that traveled through their city. Of these, only 660 were black Americans.

Besides enduring physical hardships, those who stayed on the rails for months or years paid a heavy psychological price. Grace Abbott (1878–1939), chief of the Children's Bureau for the U.S. Department of Labor, spoke in 1932 of the lost high spirits of the youths. She described how their excitement gradually gave way to hunger, despair, and hopelessness. Abbott called on president-elect Franklin Roosevelt to develop training and work centers and to provide support for youths who were trying to stay in school. Abbott said the social cost of not developing such programs was the destruction of the morale of hundreds of thousands of youths. Roosevelt listened carefully and moved to create a New Deal for young transients. The Federal Emergency Relief Act, the Civilian Conservation Corps Act, and later the National Youth Administration all established programs to aid young Americans.

## Federal Emergency Relief Act

Upon taking office in March 1933, President Roosevelt immediately addressed the transient problem, or as it was frequently called, the "youth problem." One of the first acts Congress passed as part of Roosevelt's New Deal program was the Federal Emergency Relief Act, signed into law on May 12, 1933. For the purpose of aiding those in need, including transients and the homeless, the act provided cash to the states to establish relief programs. To help students return to college, the act established an agency to fund a work-study program. Students worked part-time for a monthly payment. For students still in school a student aid program was offered. The average $13-a-month payment was just enough to help students stay in school.

## Federal Transient Relief Service

To aid transients of all ages, the Federal Transient Relief Service was established in September 1933. The service set up centers for transients in 250 communities and in 350 work camps in rural areas. These centers provided a meal, a bed, recreation, and study facilities. For those who stayed awhile, the camps provided jobs in road and park maintenance. Besides room and board, camp residents received three dollars a month for spending money. The Transient Relief Service also sent men and women to vocational classes on a wide variety of subjects, such as machinery repair and sewing. By 1935, two hundred thousand transients, one-third of them under twenty-five years of age, were being assisted by the Transient Relief Service. The service was hailed as a tremendous success by social workers, but many Americans argued that it made life too easy for transients, that it encouraged the hoboes' wandering ways. Although the program was just reaching its full effectiveness in late 1935, Congress pulled its funds and the Transient Relief Service closed, except for a few camps that operated until 1937. Transient care between January 1933 and March 1937 cost the federal gov-

The Civilian Conservation Corps gave jobs to thousands of transient young men, who otherwise were wandering the country in search of work. *Courtesy of the Library of Congress.*

ernment over $106 million, including $5 million a month at the service's peak in early 1935.

## Civilian Conservation Corps

One of President Roosevelt's favorite programs was the Civilian Conservation Corps (CCC), officially established on April 5, 1933, only days after the Civilian Conservation Corps Reforestation Act was signed into law. Roosevelt appointed Robert Fechner as CCC director. Fechner proved to be an honest and capable administrator, and he remained at the CCC until his death in 1940. Along with Fechner, an advisory council of representatives from the War, Labor, Agriculture, and Interior Departments oversaw the program.

The purpose of the CCC was to provide jobs for unemployed young men, to provide them food and shelter, to offer instruction in basic work skills, and to make improvements and build facilities on public lands. To join the CCC, enrollees had to be between the ages of eighteen and twenty-five and be single, healthy, and unemployed. They signed up for six months at a time and were expected to go to whatever location and job they were assigned. In return they received a room, food, clothing, and thirty dollars a month, twenty-five of which had to be sent back home to their families, who made good use of the added income. CCC workers kept their other five dollars to buy necessities. Enrollment in the CCC offered a chance to see new parts of the United States. The CCC also gave young people a chance to break free from a poverty-stricken existence at home.

Youths riding the rails rushed to sign up. Many of those signing up were in the East, South, and Midwest; most

of the projects and camps were to be located in the West. The U.S. Army was the only organization capable of moving thousands of enrollees from sign-up centers to work camps in the West. Therefore, the army was involved with the CCC from the start. Within only a few months 240,000 youths had settled into approximately twelve hundred camps. The army created a military type of organization with officers and enrollees. Officers from the army, Coast Guard, Marine Corps, and navy worked together to temporarily command camps. During the day most enrollees worked with the National Park Service, Forest Service, Soil Conservation Service, or Grazing Service. Projects included reforestation (planting trees), road construction, construction of structures on federal lands, prevention of soil erosion, and flood control projects. After work the CCC men lived under army regulations in camps with tents or simple wooden barracks; they ate in mess halls (a place where meals are served to a group). Many CCC facilities looked like army barracks.

**Three teenagers receive auto mechanic training at a residential center run by the Negro Affairs branch of the National Youth Administration.** *Courtesy of the Library of Congress.*

As the CCC developed, education programs became available at most of the camps. Attending classes at night, many young men received high school diplomas. On-the-job training helped the men master many skills, such as engine repair and construction of roads, bridges, fences, and structures (including barracks, ranger stations, barns, and fire lookouts). Acquiring skills in carpentry, wiring, plumbing, and stone masonry prepared the workers for lifetime careers.

The CCC program was also extended to American Indians, whose economic hardships had been largely ignored in the past. In addition to the typical conservation projects, American Indians were assigned to work on projects that aided in protecting their heritage. For example, members of the Haida and Tlingit tribes of southeast Alaska restored totem poles and built new ones in the Tongass National Forest. Before the CCC was terminated in 1941, more than fifteen thousand American Indians had enrolled in the CCC-ID (Indian Division).

The CCC also drew a substantial response from black Americans. The CCC developed eighty-three all-black camps in twelve Southern states and 151 integrated camps elsewhere in the country. By 1940 more than three hundred thousand black Americans had enrolled in the camps.

At the height of its existence, the CCC employed five hundred thousand men in twenty-six hundred camps. One of the most successful programs launched by the federal government in response to the Great Depression, the CCC lasted from 1933 to 1941, when the United States became involved with World War II (1939–45).

## National Youth Administration

When funding for the Transient Service ended in 1935, President Roosevelt established the Works Progress Administration (WPA) to provide massive work relief programs. Within the WPA, Roosevelt created the National Youth Administration (NYA); he appointed Aubrey Williams (1890–1965) as director. To keep youths in school and off the rails the agency provided aid to high school and college students. The NYA provided six dollars a month for needy high school students, twenty dollars a month for college students, and forty dollars a month for col-

lege graduate students. In return the students worked part-time, generally at school-related jobs such as custodial work. For young people who had already left school, the NYA offered opportunities to participate in building community and recreation centers. The NYA served young women as well as men. The agency set up fifty camps specifically designed for young women and provided them with technical and professional job training such as sewing and school lunch preparation. Other work projects sponsored by the NYA were in schools and hospitals. Over 581,000 youths had received cash aid from the NYA by 1936, including 19,000 black American youths under the Negro Affairs branch. Although it was one of the most responsive New Deal programs for minorities, the NYA barely touched the more than 400,000 black Americans between the ages of fourteen and sixteen who were in need of work.

Private organizations also sought to aid young people and support the government's New Deal programs. In 1936 advocates for youth asked Congress to pass the American

**A National Youth Administration camp for unemployed young women, circa 1934.** *Courtesy of the Franklin D. Roosevelt Library.*

Youth Act, which had been developed to replace the NYA. In response to the numerous public schools that had closed in the early 1930s as a result of the Great Depression, the act would have guaranteed the availability of free public education for students and would have given living expenses of at least fifteen dollars a month to needy students. Because of budget cuts, the American Youth Act never made it to the floor of Congress for a vote. Distressed by the lack of action on this legislation, supporters held a pro-youth march in Washington, D.C., in February 1937. In the end this march saved the NYA from congressional budget cutting.

Despite the efforts of the NYA, the CCC, and other New Deal programs, thousands of youths still rode the rails. The programs reached only a small percentage of the wandering population. As a result, for many Americans work would not become available until late 1941, when the United States prepared to enter World War II (1939–45).

# For More Information

### Books

Anderson, Nels. *On Hobos and Homelessness*. Chicago, IL: University of Chicago Press, 1998.

Cole, Olen, Jr. *The African American Experience in the Civilian Conservation Corps*. Gainesville, FL: University Press of Florida, 1999.

Davis, Kingsley. *Youth in the Depression*. Chicago, IL: University of Chicago Press, 1935.

Davis, Maxine. *The Lost Generation: A Portrait of American Youth Today*. New York, NY: Macmillan, 1936.

Douglas, George H. *All Aboard! The Railroad in American Life*. New York, NY: Paragon House, 1992.

Guthrie, Woody. *Bound for Glory*. New York, NY: E. P. Dutton, 1943.

McEntee, James J. *Now They Are Men: The Story of the CCC*. Washington, DC: National Home Library Foundation, 1940.

Meltzer, Milton. *Brother, Can You Spare a Dime? The Great Depression, 1929–1933*. New York, NY: Alfred A. Knopf, 1969.

Merrill, Perry H. *Roosevelt's Forest Army: A History of the Civilian Conservation Corps, 1933–1942*. Montpelier, VT: Perry H. Merrill, 1981.

Minehan, Thomas. *Boy and Girl Tramps of America*. Seattle, WA: University of Washington Press, 1976 (originally published in 1934).

Reitman, Ben L. *Sister of the Road: The Autobiography of Box-Car Bertha*. New York, NY: Sheridan House, 1937.

Uys, Errol L. *Riding the Rails: Teenagers on the Move during the Great Depression.* New York, NY: TV Books, 2000.

## Periodicals

Fawcett, John E. "A Hobo Memoir, 1936." *Indiana Magazine of History* 90, no. 4 (1994): pp. 351–365.

## Web Sites

*Civilian Conservation Corps Alumni.* http://www.cccalumni.org (accessed on August 15, 2002).

*Hobo News.* http://www.hobo.com (accessed on August 15, 2002).

*Riding the Rails.* http://www.pbs.org/wgbh/amex/rails/ (accessed on August 15, 2002).

# News Media
# and Entertainment

The American population became increasingly concentrated in cities in the early twentieth century. Because cities had more public schools than rural areas did, the population's shift to the cities meant that more children had access to education. The literacy (ability to read and write) rate increased accordingly and spawned a thirst for knowledge. To satisfy their need for information, the American public looked to newspapers. Newspaper circulation increased in large cities and small communities. By the 1920s, newspapers could take advantage of improved printing techniques, expanded communication systems, more-efficient news gathering, and increased advertising revenues. Newspaper organizations became big corporate businesses and enjoyed huge profits.

By the early 1920s radio stations started making regularly scheduled broadcasts; two early leaders were KDKA of Pittsburgh and WWJ of Detroit. Radio programming grew steadily in the 1920s. Hollywood movies, which had previously been only novelties, also became big business in the 1920s. On October 6, 1927, the first talkie (a movie with sound), *The Jazz Singer,* premiered. Many people predicted that sound was a passing fad, but theaters wired up and the American public was hooked.

The Great Depression began in October 1929 with the crash of the stock market. It was the worst economic crisis in U.S. history, lasting until the United States mobilized for World War II (1939–45) in 1941. At its worst, unemployment ranged from 25 to 30 percent. The Great Depression affected the newspaper, radio, and movie industries in unique ways: Weaker newspapers merged with healthier papers. Reporters worked long, hard hours; they specialized in certain issues, such as labor, and began to interpret news as well as report facts. Radio became increasingly popular and a regular part of Americans' lives when other types of entertainment became too expensive. (Social workers reported that families would rather part with their ice box than their radio.) Although movie attendance declined in the early 1930s, 60 percent of Americans still regularly paid the few cents charged for admission. In 1939 *The Wizard of Oz* premiered. Its theme song, "Somewhere Over the Rainbow," was testimony that hope was again alive by the end of the decade.

## Newspaper journalism

The onset of the Great Depression in 1929 had major adverse effects on the newspaper industry. A decline of up to 40 percent in advertising revenue between 1929 and 1933 meant less money for wages and production. Most newspapers reduced operating expenses by firing reporters and editors and lowering the wages of others. Those who kept their jobs faced increased workloads and were poorly paid. Workweeks were six days long, ten to twelve hours per day. Job insecurity was a constant. By the late 1930s reporters had unionized (formed trade unions to negotiate better work conditions from employers) and were able to stabilize their economic situation, but the early 1930s were very difficult.

For newspapers that survived the early years of the Great Depression, the 1930s brought major changes. Many newspapers merged with larger papers, forming newspaper chains. Newspaper chains are networks of newspapers located in various cities under a common ownership. Coverage of government activities expanded as the New Deal (policies of

**Dorothy Thompson was one of the most important journalists of the 1930s.**
*Corbis Corporation. Reproduced by permission.*

relief, recovery, and reform introduced by President Roosevelt) thrust government into the everyday lives of U.S. citizens. Rather than having a few reporters covering all facets of the government, newspapers developed full reporting staffs. Different reporters specialized in covering different topics, such as agriculture, labor, economic policies, and social work. Also, in an effort to help the public better understand the complex issues of the 1930s, reporting began to include interpretation of news in addition to the facts. "Who did what and when" was still important, but the "why" behind each story received increasing coverage.

Syndicated columns, written by experienced journalists located close at hand to events occurring in such places as Washington, D.C., or New York City, arose in response to the need for interpretation of national and world news. (Syndication means selling a piece or column written by one journalist to many newspapers across the country for simultaneous publication.) These columns were often printed on the editorial pages, the section of a newspaper where writers could express their own views. At the beginning of the 1930s some of the best-known syndicated columnists writing on economic and political affairs were Frank Kent of the *Baltimore Sun*; David Lawrence (1888–1973), who wrote for several Washington, D.C., publications; and Mark Sullivan (1874–1952) of the *New York Herald Tribune*. Joining that trio by 1931 was Walter Lippmann (1889–1974) of the *New York Herald Tribune*. By 1940 Lippmann was the highest-paid syndicated columnist in the United States; his column appeared in about 165 of the nation's largest newspapers. Heywood Broun (1888–1939) began writing his column "It Seems to Me" for the *New York World* in the 1920s. By the 1930s his friendly, casual writing style had gathered a large reading audience. In 1933 Broun founded the American Newspaper Guild in an effort to organize journalists to fight for better, more stable working conditions. Dorothy Thompson (1894–1961) became one of the most important journalists of the 1930s with her column "On the Record," written for the *New York Herald Tribune.* In the later 1930s she and First Lady Eleanor Roosevelt (1884–1962) were considered the two most influential women in America.

A group of very conservative publishers known as the "press lords" used their papers to strongly oppose President Franklin Roosevelt (1882–1945; served 1933–45) and his policies. The "press lords" included William Randolph Hearst (1863–1951), Robert R. McCormick (1880–1955), and Roy W. Howard (1883–1964). Hearst, for example, supported Roosevelt in the 1932 presidential election, but by 1935 Hearst called the New Deal a "Raw Deal." He believed the government was wrongfully intruding into business and American lives. He denounced the new Social Security Act (1935; see Social Security chapter) and his extremely conservative antigovernment views were reflected in his newspapers. The Hearst publishing empire in 1935 included newspapers in nineteen large U.S. cities. By 1936 more than 80 percent of the press opposed Roosevelt, but he won reelection to the presidency by a landslide. The press came under a great deal of criticism from the American public, who thought the press was out of touch with the views of everyday Americans.

## New Deal press conferences

Regardless of particular journalists' political points of view, President Roosevelt was always considered a "newspaperman's" president. As soon as Roosevelt assumed the presidency in March 1933, it was obvious to all reporters that he would pursue a "new deal" relationship with the press. Unlike previous presidents, Roosevelt undertook press conferences with no prior written questions. He genuinely enjoyed the give-and-take of a news conference. Roosevelt delighted in revealing a news story for the first time. He was informal, lively, reassuring, funny, or sincere—whatever the news of the moment required. The informality and honest information exchange of his press conferences remained constant throughout his years in office. He met with the press an average of eighty-three times a year, a total of 998 presidential

## Roosevelt's Fireside Chats

In the 1930s radio became the primary vehicle for communicating information and news. President Franklin D. Roosevelt instituted his "fireside chats" only eight days after his inauguration. On March 12, 1933, Roosevelt delivered his first chat over radio in a calm and reassuring manner. He explained the crisis in U.S. banking and what he had done about it. Roosevelt had the uncanny knack of seeming to sit right in a person's living room as he explained major events and issues of the day. He always began with "Good evening, Mr. and Mrs. America." The fireside chats allowed Americans to feel an intimacy with their president—to feel as if he understood their situation and their concerns. Whether they agreed or disagreed with what Roosevelt had to say, politicians and journalists were in awe of his skill in making use of the mass media. The radio chats built Americans' trust in Roosevelt as he saw them through the Great Depression and into World War II (1939–45). Roosevelt delivered twenty-eight fireside chats to the nation during his presidency.

news conferences. This was almost four times the combined number of news conferences held by Presidents Dwight Eisenhower (1890–1969; served 1953–61), John F. Kennedy (1917–1963; served 1961–63), and Lyndon B. Johnson (1908–1973; served 1963–69).

Just as the president had, Eleanor Roosevelt developed outstanding relationships with the press. A reformer and women's rights advocate, the First Lady scheduled press conferences for women journalists on Monday mornings at 11:00 A.M. She held her first press conference on March 6, 1933, only two days after the inauguration. From 1933 to 1945 the First Lady opened her "new deal" conferences to women only, forcing major newspapers and news-gathering services to have newspaperwomen in Washington, D.C.

## Radio journalism

Still in its infancy in 1930, radio increasingly invaded the field of news reporting, which had previously been left entirely to newspapers. Advertisers quickly realized they could reach more people over the radio waves. Wealthy businessmen not heavily affected by the Great Depression bought up local radio stations, creating radio network chains. Even at the depth of the Depression in 1932, early major radio networks such as the National Broadcasting Company (NBC) and Columbia Broadcasting System (CBS) were profitable.

To regulate the expanding telecommunications industry, Congress passed the Communications Act of 1934. Part of Roosevelt's New Deal, the act provided for the establishment of the Federal Communications Commission (FCC). The act survives largely intact at the beginning of the twenty-first century: The FCC continues to regulate communication services in all regions of the United States; it also regulates rates and licensing of radio stations. Part of its responsibility is assigning radio frequencies and call letters to radio stations. The FCC also requires that candidates for public office be treated equally and their sponsors identified.

Two of the most famous radio commentators to emerge in the 1930s were Lowell Thomas (1892–1981) and Hans von Kaltenborn (1878–1965). They reported daily events and added their own commentary as radio journalism grew and prospered. In Europe, a political and military crisis that would lead to World War II (1939–45) was unfolding. Radio commentators were in demand to relay events in Europe to the American people. Edward R. Murrow (1908–1965) vaulted to fame in 1938 as a European correspondent and later a war reporter. Newspaper and radio journalism had matured to the point of keeping Americans informed with news from around the world.

## Radio entertainment

Despite the Depression, increasing numbers of American families found a way to buy a radio. They did not want to miss out on major world news or President Roosevelt's "fireside chats." Begun in March 1933, these radio broadcasts allowed Roosevelt to explain his actions and New Deal programs. Americans also wanted to hear popular new entertainment programs. Radio was an inexpensive form of ready entertainment. It offered new avenues to escape the realities of unemployment, homelessness, and hunger, and it quickly became the country's primary entertainment source.

**George Burns and Gracie Allen, a husband-and-wife comedy team, were popular radio stars in the 1930s.** *Corbis Corporation. Reproduced by permission.*

By the mid-1930s two-thirds of American homes had radio sets. By 1939 many rural homes had been electrified through a special New Deal program, and about 80 percent of American homes had radios. After the initial expense, radios proved to be a good investment: The entire family could enjoy drama, comedy, quiz shows, and musical entertainment for free in the comfort of their home. Often the whole family would gather around to listen to programs together.

The 1930s are known as the "Golden Age of Radio." Radio programs multiplied, in number and in type, at an astonishingly quick pace. (This time of rapid, exciting growth was somewhat like the 1990s growth and expansion of the Internet.) Music programming led the way, and, despite growth in news, dramas, and comedies, music still provided 50 percent of radio programming by 1940. At first music was performed live, and studios were built large enough to accommodate full orchestras. Only later was recorded music broadcast. The orchestra of Guy Lombardo (1902–1977) and his Royal Canadians was a favorite as was jazz musician Count Basie (1904–1984). Singers Bing Crosby (1904–1977) and Kate Smith (1909–1986) entertained audiences for decades.

Comedy was a key part of the "Golden Age." Everyone in America knew the comedian Jack Benny (1894–1974) and the tight hold he kept on his money; this characteristic appealed to and amused audiences whose own finances were tight. Popular comedian Bob Hope (1903–) went on to a career in film and television. The husband-and-wife teams of George Burns (1896–1996) and Gracie Allen (1906–1964) and Ozzie Nelson (1906–1975) and Harriet Hilliard (1914–1994) became radio phenomenons in the 1930s. Both couples humorously portrayed an idealized everyday existence in American culture.

Perhaps the most popular radio program of all, *Amos 'n' Andy* was created by Freeman F. Gosden (1899–1982) and Charles J. Correll (1890–1972). These two white men developed a complex world for their characters—two black American men who had moved from the South in search of jobs in a northern city. Considered a comedy, the program captivated listeners, who waited impatiently each evening for another episode about the adventures and mishaps of the twosome.

Radio drama was also popular during the Depression. The great radio theater drama productions of the 1930s included classic scripts and major stars. The most popular were Orson Welles's *Mercury Theatre on the Air,* the *Lux Radio Theater, Screen Guide Theater,* and *Studio One,* later known as Ford Theater. Productions generally were broadcast in "prime" evening hours so families could enjoy the shows together.

Comic strips had long provided entertainment in the newspapers, and some became popular radio programs. *Little Orphan Annie, Buck Rogers, Flash Gordon,* and *Dick Tracy* were children's favorites. Parents, constantly worried over Depression budgets at home, appreciated the conservative message of Annie, who reminded the audience that you have to earn what you get.

## Hollywood

By the 1920s a golden community located in Southern California beneath the San Gabriel Mountains was established as the movie capital of the world. That community, known as Hollywood, captivated the whole nation with its silent films. Talkies (movies with sound) premiered in 1927, as thousands of Americans flocked to the movie houses or "movie palaces." Movie theaters were often the most elaborate and showy buildings in town. Although the stock market crash of October 1929 marked the beginning of a grave economic crisis in the United States—the Great Depression— approximately 110 million Americans a week went to the movies in 1930. The introduction of sound was an exciting development that audiences could not resist, and, as a result, Hollywood's profits continued. However, as economic conditions worsened nationwide, Hollywood began to worry. By the early 1930s attendance had dropped to near sixty million

**Depression-era Literature**

During every period in the history of American literature, talented writers have appeared. The Great Depression years were no different. While some authors wrote without much regard to the situations surrounding them, others produced books that revealed a great deal about an America caught in economic devastation. Prompted by the economic struggles of the Depression, many 1930s writers authored socially conscious books known as proletarian (working-class) literature. Feeling betrayed by the competitive U.S. capitalist society, these writers watched as an elite group of business leaders became extremely wealthy at the expense of the majority of people, who continued to fall further behind economically. Supporting working-class individuals and advancing philosophies of cooperation rather than competition, Michael Gold edited two proletarian magazines, *Masses* and *New Masses*. Grace Lumpkins's *To Make My Bread* (1932) is considered one of the best proletarian novels about the horrible working conditions of textile workers.

Many authors who produced proletarian literature went on to fame, including John Dos Passos, James T. Farrell, Erskine Caldwell, John Steinbeck, Langston Hughes, and Richard Wright. John Dos Passos (1896–1970) believed that the promise of a good life in the United States was being destroyed by a small class of wealthy and powerful people. For him the Depression pointed out the stark distinctions between the economic classes in America. Dos Passos created a historical saga that follows the growth of American materialism in the 1890s to the Depression of the early 1930s; this saga appeared as a trilogy (three novels): *The 42nd Parallel* (1930), *1919* (1932), and *The Big Money* (1936). Standing as tall as Dos Passos in literary artistry was James T. Farrell (1904–1979). Like Dos Passos, Farrell produced a trilogy: *Young Lonigan* (1932), *The Young Manhood of Studs Lonigan* (1934), and *Judgment Day* (1935). The trilogy tells the story of a young Irish American attempting to rise from the bleak existence of the Chicago working class as the Depression closes in.

Erskine Caldwell (1903–1987) wrote powerfully of poor white Americans in rural areas and the brutal treatment of black Americans. His novel *Tobacco Road* (1932) is a study of a poverty-stricken tenant farming family in the South at the onset of the Depression. The book was adapted for the stage and ran on Broadway in New York City for years. Caldwell also published *God's Little Acre* (1933), another novel about a poor family. He teamed up in the mid-1930s with photographer Margaret Bourke-White (1906–1971) for *You Have Seen Their Faces* (1937), a book that documents southern rural poverty.

John Steinbeck (1902–1968) also wrote several decidedly proletarian novels: *Pastures of Heaven* (1932) is about a farm community near Salinas, California; *Tortilla Flat* (1935) tells a story of migrant workers and poor farmers; *In Dubious Battle* (1936) portrays labor problems in California; and *The Grapes of Wrath* (1939), by far the most famous Depression-era novel, tells the story of the Joads, an Oklahoma family that loses its farm to drought and migrates west to the promised land of California. *The Grapes of Wrath* won a 1940 Pulitzer Prize and was made into a movie.

Richard Wright (1908–1960) was a black author recognized for literary excellence in the late 1930s. He took on the issue of racial prejudice and the problems of black Americans in a collection of four short stories, *Uncle Tom's Children* (1938). He completed his first novel, *Native Son,* in 1940 and his second, *Twelve Million Black Voices,* in 1941. Langston Hughes (1902–1967), another black American, was a prolific writer from 1926 until his death in 1967. Considered the poet laureate of black America, Hughes's writings spoke for the poor and homeless black Americans suffering through the Depression.

Documentary literature, another type of writing that emerged during the Depression, came from a few journalists who decided to leave their solitary desks and travel about the country to better understand their fellow Americans and the impact of the Depression on ordinary people. Sherwood Anderson (1876–1941) collected his stories over a two-month period in 1933 and published them in a 1935 book entitled *Puzzled America.* Another well-known book of this type is *My America* (1938), written by Louis Adamic (1899–1951). *Let Us Now Praise Famous Men* (1941) stands out above others in this category. Created by author James Agee (1909–1955) and photographer Walker Evans (1903–1975), the book examines the life of an Alabama sharecropper's family.

Writers' efforts to look at the real America—at the lives of unexceptional people—were encouraged by the Federal Writers Project (FWP). Beginning in 1935 between six and seven thousand unemployed writers received support from the FWP, a branch of the Works Progress Administration (WPA), which was one of the agencies established by New Deal legislation. Before this, federal support for writers had been nonexistent. Two of the most famous writers to receive FWP help were John Steinbeck and Richard Wright. Of the 278 pamphlets and books published by the FWP between 1935 and 1939, "These Are Our Lives" was one of the most critically acclaimed. The stories it contains were recorded with pen and paper by members of the FWP in North Carolina, Tennessee, and Georgia.

Though attendance dropped significantly during the Depression years, millions of Americans still turned to the movies for entertainment. *Courtesy of the Library of Congress.*

per week; the few cents needed to get into a movie seemed an extravagance for many. Yet those millions who faithfully attended represented 60 percent of the population. (In comparison, in the 1970s only 10 percent of Americans attended movies.) It seems that by the 1930s movies had become a cultural institution. Movies were the place to take friends or the family. Movies could be talked about for days, and they set standards for taste, styles, songs, and morals. Although all movie companies suffered major economic setbacks in the early 1930s, the public's need for movies would ultimately save the industry.

## Holding Movie Audiences

To keep audiences coming back, movie theaters tried many tactics. Lowering the price of a movie was not enough, so the double feature was introduced. (Double features consisted of two full-length films.) Walt Disney (1901–1966) introduced his first animated cartoons in the early 1930s, and newsreels were also a new feature. On Saturdays, a day that children filled the theaters, serial-type movies were shown. These to-be-continued stories left the hero or heroine in such a perilous state that viewers had to come back the next week to see what happened.

Gimmicks such as "Bank Night" or "Dish Night" were popular during the Depression. On Bank Nights, usually held on the lowest-attendance night, tickets became part of a lottery for prize money. Bank Nights drew audiences throughout the country—people everywhere were hopeful they might win the money. One movie official commented that he did not even need to show a movie on Bank Night—just have the lottery and many would come. Dish Night was another way to get people to come and keep coming back. Each moviegoer would receive a piece of china; moviegoers could accumulate a whole set of dishes if they attended often enough.

## Gangster Movies

Through the Prohibition days of the 1920s, when the manufacture, sale, and possession of liquor was banned, city gangs provided Americans with illegal alcoholic beverages. The organized gangs became enormously wealthy and powerful and paid off law enforcement officials to ignore the illegal activity. Accounts of gangster exploits were carried in local newspapers, and the American public became fascinated. Hollywood churned out gangster films by the late 1920s and into the early 1930s, and the films were top box-office attractions. Three of the most popular gangster films were *Little Caesar* (1930), *The Public Enemy* (1931), and *Scarface* (1932). The gangsters were portrayed as smart, dynamic, successful, and flamboyant. The films showed the gangsters rising from humble beginnings in big-city slums to wealth and power. Of course, the gangsters' activities ran so far outside the law that in the endings they met early, violent deaths. Law enforcement agencies were portrayed as bungling, paralyzed, and inefficient. This depiction of law enforcement authorities and politicians accurately reflected the public's opinion of law and politics in the early 1930s. The public knew that corruption ran deep. And even if the law and politicians were not corrupt, in the public's mind they were

JAMES CAGNEY IN PUBLIC ENEMY A WARNER BROS. RE-RELEASE

**James Cagney in a scene from the 1931 gangster movie, *Public Enemy*.** *Archive Photos. Reproduced by permission.*

highly ineffective given the poor economic condition of the nation and the government's apparent inability to improve the situation.

Historians and scholars of Depression-era gangster movies have different theories about why Americans faithfully went to gangster movies in the early 1930s. In his book *We're in the Money: Depression America and Its Films* (1971), Andrew Bergman explains that gangster films are stories of individual achievement. For example, Rico, the lead character in *Little Caesar,* follows the model of an American's climb from the bottom rungs of his business upward to the highest level. (Rico is a thinly disguised movie version of Alphonse Capone, 1899–1947, the organized crime boss of Chicago.) And in *Public Enemy* Tommy Powers, played by James Cagney (1904–1986), is an industrious, classy, wise guy and a ladies' man. In the discouraging days of the Depression, Americans connected with these successful characters, who gave them hope in the American idea of rising to a better life. A different viewpoint comes from Robert S. McElvaine in *The Great Depression: America, 1929–1941* (1993). McElvaine sees *Little Caesar*'s Rico as a representation of the greedy businessman who is willing to step on anyone to get to the top. Many Americans believed the greed of businessmen was a prime cause of the Depression. In 1929 American businesses had come crashing down along with the stock market; likewise, Rico comes to a sudden and deserved end. The punishment of the greedy was an appealing movie theme for everyday Americans in the 1930s.

Unconcerned with the reasons behind the films' success, Hollywood knew gangster movies were moneymakers, and Hollywood desperately needed money. Approximately fifty gangster films premiered in 1931 alone. However, even as they packed the theaters, increasing numbers of Americans were becoming uneasy about reveling in the gangsters' stories. Civic groups, religious leaders, and parent-teacher associations denounced Hollywood's glorification of the gangster and its disrespectful depiction of law enforcement. *Scarface* came out in 1932, but by then the anti-gangster crusade had taken hold, and the number of gangster films decreased.

## The Three Little Pigs

Producer Walt Disney (1901–1966) released his cartoon creation *The Three Little Pigs* in 1933. "Who's Afraid of the Big Bad Wolf," the theme song of this short animated film, became a national hit. The "big bad wolf" was widely recognized to be a symbol for the economic depression of the 1930s. Hearing the song helped many people defend against their fear of what lay ahead. Some Americans felt that *The Three Little Pigs* had as much to do with raising the nation's spirits as the New Deal legislation did.

## Shyster Movies

Shyster movies were as popular as the gangster films of the early 1930s. *Lawyer Man* (1932) and *Mouthpiece* (1932) are two classic shyster movies. Shysters are lawyers, politicians, or newspapermen who are dishonest in the practice of their work. In the movies, shysters are slick and charming individuals who con and weasel their way through life. Like gangster films, shyster movies present a laughingstock image of law officials. Shrewder than the law officers, shysters could always control a gangster or crooked politician; no one could get the better of a shyster. For Depression-era audiences who

Charlie Chaplin wrestles with giant mechanical gears in the 1936 movie *Modern Times.* ©*Bettmann-Corbis. Reproduced by permission.*

felt their lives to be so out of their control, this was a welcome Hollywood fantasy. Frequently the shyster characters eventually turned away from their shyster ways to live upright lives. They then proceeded to protect people from other dishonest characters. This theme was very popular in the Depression days.

## Comedy

A popular comedian of the 1930s was Charlie Chaplin (1889–1977). Chaplin performed in films that featured characters full of innocence and decency. Chaplin was a leader in silent films in the 1920s; besides performing, he often directed, produced, composed music, and edited his films. By the 1930s he was billed as one of the top entertainers in film. Considered by many his greatest work, *City Lights* (1931) tells the story of a blind girl and Chaplin's character, "the tramp," and the efforts of a millionaire to show them life is worth living. Many Americans needed to be convinced of this message during the Depression. Also, since the end of the Civil War (1861–65), industrialization of America had progressed at a rapid pace with mass production factories full of machines taking the place of skilled craftsmen. The hero of Chaplin's film *Modern Times* (1936) is a man overwhelmed by machines that are replacing humans in industry. This film reflected the real-life situations of many industrial workers in the 1930s.

## Comedy and Screen Anarchists

Anarchists dislike the activities of government and carry out rebellious acts against it. The Marx Brothers—Chico, Groucho, Harpo, and Zeppo—and W. C. Fields (1880–1946) were prominent "screen anarchists" of the early 1930s. Between 1930 and 1933, at the depth of the Depression, the Marx Brothers and W. C. Fields entertained a despairing population that had come to expect the worst of everyone. These comedians were zany and slapstick, and their antics had Americans laughing with irreverence at topics not traditionally considered funny, such as government and the family. Five popular Marx Brothers films, all produced by Paramount, were *The Cocoanuts* (1929), *Animal Crackers* (1930), *Monkey Business* (1931), *Horsefeathers* (1932), and *Duck Soup* (1933). W. C. Fields's *The Fatal Glass of Beer* and three of his other short films—*The Pharmacist, The Dentist,* and *The Barbershop*—all appeared in 1933.

Even though comedians ridiculed much of American society and many Americans laughed right along with them, increasing numbers of people were seriously concerned about the gangster and anarchist films. They worried that a moral depression was enveloping the United States by way of the movies.

## The Moral Decay Problem

In 1922 Will Hays (1879–1954), the postmaster general under President Warren Harding (1865–1923; served 1921–23), decided to move west to Hollywood and accept a post as head of the Motion Picture Producers and Distributors of America (MPPDA). The MPPDA was a motion picture industry group attempting to clean up the film industry and establish production codes. The West Coast Association of MPPDA agreed to ten "don'ts" in 1927. Those "don'ts" mostly dealt with sex and nudity. After the first silent gangster films of the late 1920s, the MPPDA established in 1930 a longer "don'ts" list, which included a ban on showing sympathy to crime and criminals, making fun of law enforcement, and showing methods to carry out crime. However, the 1930 codes were not enforced. Then in 1933, tired of gangsters being portrayed as heroes while law officers were shown as bumbling and incompetent, several groups joined forces. Catholic Church leaders in America established the Catholic Churches Committee on Motion Pictures. The powerful Protestant Council of Churches and the Central Conference of Jewish Rabbis joined forces with the Catholic Church and forced Hays and the MPPDA to begin enforcing the 1930 code by 1934. Movies cleaned up: Nakedness (including naked babies), double beds, and long kisses were among the many forbidden movie screen images. This cleanup ushered

**Child star Shirley Temple was a top box-office star during the 1930s.**
*Popperfoto/Archive Photos. Reproduced by permission.*

in big musicals, law and order films, screwball comedies, and movies with a positive message.

## Musicals

President Roosevelt's New Deal programs brought new hope for many Americans. Together with the moral codes for movies, this hope for renewed prosperity inspired the squeaky-clean big musicals of the 1930s. The "new deal" in movies began in 1933 with the "big three" Warner Brothers musicals: *Forty-Second Street, Gold Diggers of 1933*, and *Footlight Parade*. Busby Berkeley (1895–1976) produced the dance sequences with beautiful girls, glitter, plumes, and colossal sets. Still, Depression themes run through each film: The main character in *Forty-Second Street* is broke, everyone in *Gold Diggers* is broke, and the star of *Footlight Parade* thinks he may end up in a breadline. The song "We're in the Money" was first sung in *Gold Diggers*; in *Footlight Parade* a sign with a grinning President Roosevelt and another with the Blue Eagle symbol are held up by long-legged dancers. The Blue Eagle was the symbol of the National Recovery Administration (NRA), a New Deal agency.

There were also purely fun musicals, such as *Flying Down to Rio* (1933), *Top Hat* (1935), and *Follow the Fleet* (1936). The lavishness of these musicals lifted spirits, and for Depression-era audiences that was enough to make the films a success.

## Shirley Temple Movies

Shirley Temple (1928–), a curly-headed, multitalented young girl, was introduced to movie audiences in 1933 and became the most popular child film star of all time. Her movies fit perfectly with the new decency codes for films. Temple appeared in six films in 1934 and four in 1935 and

1936. By 1938 she was the top box-office attraction. Some of her most notable films are *Stand Up and Cheer* (1934), *The Little Colonel* (1935), *Curly Top* (1935), *The Poor Little Rich Girl* (1936), *Dimples* (1936), and *The Little Princess* (1939).

Mothers curled their daughters' hair and dressed them to look like the child star. Shirley Temple look-alike contests were popular nationwide. An entire industry grew up around Shirley Temple—dolls, clothes, coloring books, paper doll cutout books, and more.

## The G-Men

Soundly ridiculed in the gangster and shyster movies, law and order returned to movies in 1935. When Roosevelt assumed the presidency in 1933, he appointed Homer S. Cummings (1870–1956) to head the Department of Justice. J. Edgar Hoover (1895–1972) and his Bureau of Investigation were part of the Justice Department. Hoover had a well-organized and highly trained group of special agents itching for real law enforcement action. Cummings charged Hoover and his men with cleaning up a group of outlaws that had been robbing banks in the midwestern states. In two short years, 1934 and 1935, Hoover and his men gunned down or captured the outlaws, including John Dillinger (1903–1934), Bonnie and Clyde, Charles "Pretty Boy" Floyd (1901–1934), and George "Machine Gun" Kelly (1895–1954). Hollywood immortalized Hoover and his men in the sensational Warner Brothers hit *G-Men* (1935). With this film Hollywood helped reestablish the government as the protector of the people. G-men—the "G" is thought to stand for "government"—soon became known to the public as FBI (Federal Bureau of Investigation) agents.

## Screwball Comedy

Screwball comedy in the 1930s was friendly and funny feel-good fare. Talented actors and actresses delivered fast-paced lines as they got into and out of hilarious situations. Screwball comedy story lines attempted to heal and unify the economic classes of America. For example, one of the most popular screwball comedies was *It Happened One Night* (1934). Directed by Frank Capra

(1897–1991) and featuring Clark Gable (1901–1960) and Claudette Colbert (1903–1996), the film unites a lower-middle-class reporter with an heiress. Gable, the reporter, discovers that the heiress's dad works just as many hours as a regular laborer. For the 1930s film audience, the reporter's discovery helped dismantle the Depression myth that all wealthy people are idle. A later Capra film, *Mr. Smith Goes to Washington* (1939) stars the always good-humored James Stewart (1908–1997) as a junior U.S. senator who proves that troubles can be overcome by an old-fashioned faith in democracy.

## Socially Conscious Movies

Socially conscious films (those that raised the public's awareness of political or social issues) were being produced as early as 1932. With the exception of one, *The Grapes of Wrath* (1940), these films were not major box-office hits. They dealt with despair, outcasts, lynchings, hobo children, and economic hardships. *I Am a Fugitive from a Chain Gang* deals with unemployment, unjustified imprisonment, escape, and in the end hopelessness. The film is an expression of the national mood in 1932. *Wild Boys of the Road* (1933) tells the story of high schoolers riding the railroads after their parents lose their jobs. *Fury* (1936) and *They Won't Forget* (1937) are both antilynching films.

Even though Depression themes run through these movies, few of the films realistically portray the day-to-day hardships of the Depression. One exception is the film adaptation of John Steinbeck's novel *The Grapes of Wrath*. Directed by John Ford (1895–1973) and starring Henry Fonda (1905–1982), the movie was released in 1940. It tells the story of refugees from the Dust Bowl migrating to California to find work and a better life. The last socially conscious movie of the Depression era was another Ford film, *How Green Was My Valley* (1941), adapted from a novel by Richard Llewellyn (1906–1983). It tells a story of working-class people in America. Both movies were a clear call for their original audiences to cooperate with one another and stick together in difficult times. With World War II (1939–45) looming, these were lessons not only for pulling through the Depression but for enduring the war to come.

# For More Information

## Books

Allen, Frederick L. *Since Yesterday: The Nineteen-Thirties in America.* New York, NY: Harper & Brothers Publishers, 1940.

Bergman, Andrew. *We're in the Money: Depression America and Its Films.* New York, NY: New York University Press, 1971.

Best, Gary Dean. *The Nickel and Dime Decade: American Popular Culture during the 1930s.* Westport, CT, and London: Praeger, 1993.

Black, Shirley Temple. *Child Star.* New York, NY: Warner Books, 1989.

Britten, Loretta, and Sarah Brash, eds. *Hard Times: The '30s.* Alexandria, VA: Time-Life Books, 1998.

Brown, Robert J. *Manipulating the Ether: The Power of Broadcast Radio in Thirties America.* Jefferson, NC: McFarland, 1998.

Cameron, Kenneth M. *America on Film: Hollywood and American History.* New York, NY: Continuum, 1997.

Douglas, Susan J. *Listening In: Radio and the American Imagination: From Amos 'n' Andy and Edward R. Murrow to Wolfman Jack and Howard Stern.* New York, NY: Crown Publishing, 2000.

Ely, Melvin Patrick. *The Adventures of Amos 'n' Andy: A Social History of an American Phenomenon.* New York, NY: Free Press, 1991.

Emery, Michael, and Edwin Emery. *The Press and America: An Interpretive History of the Mass Media.* Boston, MA: Allyn & Bacon, 1996.

Hilmes, Michele. *Radio Voices: American Broadcasting, 1922–1952.* Minneapolis, MN: University of Minnesota Press, 1997.

Lackmann, Ronald. *This Was Radio.* New York, NY: Great American Audio Corporation, 2000.

McElvaine, Robert S. *The Great Depression: America, 1929–1941.* New York, NY: Times Books, 1993.

Milton, Joyce. *Tramp: The Life of Charlie Chaplin.* New York, NY: Harper-Collins, 1996.

Schilpp, Madelon Golden, and Sharon M. Murphy. *Great Women of the Press.* Carbondale, IL: Southern Illinois University Press, 1983.

Stott, William. *Documentary Expression and Thirties America.* Chicago, IL: University of Chicago Press, 1986.

Streitmatter, Rodger. *Raising Her Voice: African-American Women Journalists Who Changed History.* Lexington, KY: University of Kentucky Press, 1994.

Swados, Harvey, ed. *The American Writer and the Great Depression.* New York, NY: Bobbs-Merrill, 1966.

Toplin, Robert Brent. *History by Hollywood: The Use and Abuse of the American Past.* Urbana, IL: University of Illinois Press, 1996.

Wolseley, Roland E. *The Black Press, U.S.A.* Ames, IA: Iowa State University Press, 1971.

## Web Sites

*American Press Institute.* http://www.americanpressinstitute.org (accessed on August 15, 2002).

*American Society of Journalists (ASJA).* http://asja.org (accessed on August 15, 2002).

*American Society of Newspaper Editors.* http://www.asne.org (accessed on August 15, 2002).

# Prohibition and Crime

In October 1929 the crash of the stock market triggered a crisis in the U.S. economy. By 1930 Americans were starting to realize how severe the economic depression would be. Every day more banks failed, businesses folded, factories closed their doors, and increasing numbers of Americans lost their jobs. This depression was to become the Great Depression that lasted for more than a decade. Those who managed to keep their jobs saw their income greatly decrease. Americans' hope for prosperity faded as they struggled to hold on to a minimal standard of living. To most people the U.S. government seemed distant and ineffective, providing no solutions to the difficulties and no relief.

In addition to the nation's economic troubles, for many Americans there was another source of distress: Prohibition. Prohibition began in 1920 when the Eighteenth Amendment (the Prohibition amendment) to the U.S. Constitution took effect. Prohibition banned the manufacture, sale, and (with the Volstead Act) possession of alcoholic beverages, including beer and wine. The new law did nothing to lessen Americans' desire to drink; people wanted their favorite beverages at meals, at parties, and at their neighborhood bar or saloon. Responding to the public's desire, gangs in the cities organized and delivered the liquor. As a result, by the late 1920s organized crime was established and prospering. Gangsters such as Alphonse Capone (1899–1947) dominated entire cities and became heroes of mythical proportions. Then, beginning in 1933, midwestern outlaws began roaring through America's heartland, robbing banks and outsmarting the hapless local police. For a while these outlaws seemed like modern Robin Hoods to people who had lost all their savings in bank closures. It seemed that Americans had accepted a certain amount of lawlessness in the nation.

After Franklin D. Roosevelt (1882–1945) was inaugurated as president in March 1933, he introduced a New Deal for Americans. The New Deal was a series of programs designed to bring relief, recovery, and reform to the United States. By that time, the Prohibition amendment was recognized as a failure. A new amendment, the Twenty-First, was in the process of being ratified (approved) by the states. It would in effect repeal the Eighteenth Amendment and again legalize liquor. As soon as liquor became legal, the gangsters who had been supplying it on the sly would no longer be needed. This came as a relief to many Americans who had begun to view crime differently. To them it seemed that something more important than the economy was in shambles—they feared America's morals were in a state of decay. They looked to the new federal government to fight crime and restore respect to law enforcement. They were hoping for a "new deal" on crime as well as improvement in the country's economic condition.

In response to the general public opinion, Congress passed anticrime legislation drawn up by President Roosevelt's attorney general, Homer S. Cummings (1870–1956). Carrying out the war on crime would be J. Edgar Hoover (1895–1972) and his agents, or G-men, all from the Bureau of Investigation. In 1935 the bureau changed its name to the Federal Bureau of Investigation (FBI), and the G-men were called FBI agents. Thus the New Deal expanded the federal government's role not only in business and economic matters but in law enforcement as well.

# Prohibition: Stopping the "demon rum"

America's earliest colonists considered liquor a good gift of nature, a necessity of life. Rum was generally present at all community gatherings. However, it was considered a sin to drink too much. But gradually more and more people did misuse rum, and movements sprang up to stop this misuse. These campaigns to promote wise liquor use or curtail use altogether were called temperance movements. By the early 1870s women's groups had formed to fight the "demon rum." The Women's Christian Temperance Union (WCTU) campaigned against liquor and in support of Prohibition. A new major force in the Prohibition movement appeared in 1893, the Anti-Saloon League (ASL). The ASL grew rapidly nationwide and spent millions on anti-alcohol literature and lobbying the federal and state governments for legislation banning alcohol. As a result of ASL's well-orchestrated efforts, individual states began passing Prohibition laws in 1907. Eleven states had passed such laws by the end of 1914. With the powerful ASL influencing congressional elections in 1916, ALS-supported candidates won many seats and, in 1917, Congress agreed to draft a constitutional amendment to establish Prohibition nationwide. The resulting state ratification (formal approval) process went relatively smoothly and the required number of states, thirty-six, had ratified the amendment by January 1919.

Ultimately, at the fateful hour of 12:01 A.M. on January 17, 1920, the Eighteenth Amendment to the U.S. Constitution, the Prohibition amendment banning the manufacture or sale of alcohol, took effect nationwide. Americans in favor of Prohibition expected the amendment to make the United States a perfect, wholesome place to live. To ensure adequate enforcement, Congress had passed the Volstead Act in October 1919, prohibiting the manufacture, sale, barter (trading for), transport, import, export, delivery, or illegal possession of any intoxicating beverage. "Intoxicating" was defined as one-half of 1 percent alcohol by volume. Since beer was normally 3 to 7 percent alcohol and wine was up to 15 percent alcohol, both were included in the ban. Special permits were allowed for the production of alcohol for medicinal, religious, and industrial use.

Prohibitionists believed the enforcement of the Volstead Act would be easy and inexpensive. They believed "wets" (anti-Prohibitionists) would obey the law and gracefully accept the inevitability of Prohibition. Their outlook proved quite wrong.

## Beating Prohibition: A national pastime

During the first year of Prohibition, problems with enforcement quickly multiplied. It became apparent that many Americans did not feel obligated to stop drinking when Prohibition became part of the U.S. Constitution. Although the rate of compliance with the law was difficult to determine, polls indicated that only about one-third of the adult population was willing to abstain. (*Abstain* means to refrain from drinking alcoholic beverages.) Those who wanted to drink were not stopped by Prohibition.

Where did the illegal liquor come from? Most of it came from illegal stills in homes across the country. Americans could learn all they needed to know at any library, where books and magazines described methods of distilling alcohol in ordinary kitchens. Stores sprang up selling all the needed supplies. Ready-to-use stills of one- to five-gallon capacity were also sold. Most stills were family operations set in basements, in tenement buildings, or behind stores. After only a few years, organized gangs began taking over these operations. Of course, most home stills were too small for gangs to bother with, but the larger operations became part of gang networks. To protect their deliveries of alcohol to customers, many still owners had to pay off the gangsters. Gangs also operated their own large distilleries and paid enforcement agents, police, and politicians to look the other way. By the late 1920s organized crime was established and immensely wealthy. Prohibition, intended to bring abstinence (the voluntary decision not to drink alcoholic beverages) and therefore harmony to the lives of Americans, had instead unleashed a crime wave.

A large amount of illegal liquor came from outside the United States; it was smuggled in from the seas off both the east and west coasts and brought overland from both Canada and Mexico. The boom of bootlegging (smuggling) liquor into the United States overwhelmed Prohibition agents. Organized crime was heavily involved in bootlegging, and daily reports of bribery and corruption eroded the public's respect for the law.

Americans did not stop drinking alcohol, but Prohibition did change their drinking habits. Before Prohibition nearly all heavy drinking was done in saloons, restaurants, cafés, and cabarets (restaurants featuring singing and dancing shows). Prior to Prohibition, saloons were generally the domain of men as drinking by women was socially unacceptable. Prohibition changed that custom. During Prohibition at-home drinking became commonplace and, as a result, women as well as men were able to drink their favorite alcoholic beverages.

## The Origin of "Bootlegger"

In certain regions of colonial America, colonists had made it illegal for Native Americans to possess liquor. Therefore, some Indian traders would strap bottles to their legs and conceal them with their boots—hence the term "bootlegger." In time, any person who illegally transported liquor was referred to as a bootlegger.

When people wanted to step outside their home for a drink, they went to a speakeasy. After Prohibition took effect, saloons and bars had merely gone behind closed doors to operate secretly as speakeasies. The "speaks" catered to women as well as men. To enter, all a person had to do was "speak" an "easy" code word or phrase such as "Joe sent me," and the door would be opened. New York City's saloons grew from sixteen thousand before Prohibition to at least thirty-three thousand "speaks" by the early 1920s. Of course, the cost of a drink was many times more than what it had been before Prohibition. Supplied by gangsters, several hundred thousand speakeasies across the nation served drink after drink. If agents raided a "speak" and arrested its bartender, another bartender took over and generally reopened the speakeasy the same night.

In defiance of highly unpopular laws banning alcohol, in the 1920s drinking became a symbol of independence and sophistication. People associated drinking with romance and adventure. Breaking the law had become a national pastime, perhaps even more popular than baseball. Otherwise law-abiding citizens delighted in finding ways to break the law of Prohibition—to them drinking seemed only slightly illegal.

Understaffed government agencies had the impossible task of trying to dry up America and keep it dry. Attempts to do so proved futile. Also, the federal government lost millions of dollars in revenue taxes, which before Prohibition were col-

**Federal agents pour whiskey down the sewer after raiding an illegal speakeasy.** *Corbis Corporation. Reproduced by permission.*

lected on the sale and manufacture of all alcohol. At the same time, enforcement efforts cost more than a billion dollars.

## Organized crime and Al Capone

Prohibitionists never anticipated that a legal ban on drinking would foster public lawlessness and organized crime, but that was exactly what happened with Prohibition. Before 1920 criminal gangs had limited their activities to thievery, gambling, and murders. After Prohibition took effect, these same gangs transformed into organized groups of bootleggers intent on supplying America with illegal alcohol. Gangsters became millionaires. Bribery and corruption of law enforcement officers became widespread. Newspapers profiled gangsters' lives and activities on the same pages that featured the Hollywood stars. Low-life thugs, previously looked upon as menaces to society, became public heroes.

Above all other gangsters, one stood out: Alphonse Capone (1899–1947). Only half a year before the stock market crash of 1929, Alphonse Capone had captivated Americans. They marveled at his wealth and power. He had reached across ethnic boundaries to form racketeering ties with Jews, Italians, Polish groups, and black Americans. His empire—built on prostitution, gambling, and above all, bootlegging—reached from New York to Chicago. Capone's Chicago gang cooperated with gangs in New York and with the infamous Jewish Purple Gang of Detroit. Capone maintained several bases in Chicago, the hub of the organized crime world. He dominated not only business but the politics of Chicago as well. Although Capone seemed invincible, his fame caught the attention of the federal government. Only days after taking office in March 1929, President Herbert Hoover (1874–1964;

served 1929–33) pressured the U.S. Treasury Department to spearhead a campaign to bring down Capone on tax evasion (failing to pay income taxes) charges. Capone joked that he had no idea taxes were due on his illegal activities. Uncertain whether the tax evasion charges would be enough to imprison Capone, Hoover ordered Prohibition agents to collect proof of Capone's Prohibition violations. Meanwhile, Capone, on his way back home from a crime organization meeting, was arrested in May 1929 on the streets of Philadelphia for carrying a concealed deadly weapon. He was sentenced to a one-year jail term. Released from jail early due to good behavior, Capone returned to his Chicago home in March 1930.

On his return Capone found a far different place than the vibrant city he had left almost a year earlier. The U.S. economy had collapsed, and the plight of American people worsened with every day as unemployment rose rapidly. Capone observed ragged, half-starved men roaming the streets of his beloved Chicago. Within days of Capone's return to Chicago,

Frank J. Loesch, head of the Chicago Crime Commission, dealt Capone another blow. To enlist public assistance and support, Loesch had put together a list of twenty-eight Chicago men, all murderers and hoodlums, and Capone's name was atop the list as Public Enemy No. 1. Angry and humiliated by having his name included with what he considered common criminals, Capone decided to take his case to the court of public opinion. Hoping to gain favorable publicity and help the city's people, he opened a soup kitchen at 935 South State Street. Capone's kitchen fed the hungry three times a day. Capone stated that it was a shame the government was trying to find ways to prosecute him when there were more pressing problems to solve, such as feeding the hungry.

Yet press on the government did. One of the agents assigned to Capone's case was Eliot Ness. Ness and his "untouchables," a fearless group of young men who could not be bribed, wreaked havoc on Capone's bootlegging activities as they uncovered his Prohibition violations. Like many Americans, Capone had long viewed law officials as pesky and inept. But on October 24, 1931, a shocked Capone was sentenced to eleven years in prison on the tax evasion charges alone. At the same time Capone was having his troubles in Chicago, the new American Mafia emerged in New York City.

## The American Mafia is born

The organized gangs in New York City had become so wealthy in the 1920s during Prohibition that they weathered the Depression quite well early in the 1930s. The downturn in the economy actually helped stabilize gang membership: Many young Italians and Jews had made large amounts of money from Prohibition violations, enough that they were ready to leave crime and their poor neighborhoods for a different life. But then the Depression hit, and economic conditions froze them in place; they were trapped, with continued crime their only hope for a decent living. As a result, the ranks of organized crime increased.

Charles "Lucky" Luciano (1897–1962) and his allies, including Jewish boss Meyer Lansky (1902–1983), sat at the top of the New York City crime world by September 1931. They were the victors of the Castellammarese War, a gangster war against the old-line Mafia bosses. The Italian and Sicilian Mafia had existed in Southern Europe for centuries and by the early twentieth century still controlled economic activities in certain areas of Italy and Sicily. They often made their money through smuggling and through extortion, such as being paid by shop owners through threats of violence to provide the businesses protective services from other criminals or gangs. As immigration of Italians and Sicilians to the United States took place in the late nineteenth and early twentieth centuries, the Mafia began to emerge in a new setting. These old-line Italian Mafia bosses had required that Mafia members be Italian and had focused on settling vendettas (bitter, prolonged, violent feuds) among themselves rather than making money. However, the prevailing Luciano–Lansky faction, after 1931, concentrated solely on making money and killed those who stood in their way. With the highly profitable bootlegging period over in 1933, they focused on gambling, loan-sharking (loaning money at very high interest rates and using threats to receive repayment), narcotics distribution, and prostitution. They would invest some of their illegally gained profits into legitimate businesses such as hotels, restaurants, and nightclubs. Luciano also reenergized the "Commission," an organized body of representatives from various crime groups. The "Commission" guided the operations of organized crime. This change of direction away from the old Italian Mafia reign, along with the reestablishment of the "Commission," is known as the Americanization of the Mafia.

Lucky Luciano, center, is escorted into court by two detectives on June 18, 1936. Convicted of running a prostitution ring, Luciano was sentenced to thirty to fifty years in prison.
*AP/Wide World Photo. Reproduced by permission.*

# End of Prohibition

It was clear to most Americans by 1932 that Prohibition would soon end. Prohibition was a social experiment that

By the start of the 1930s, it was clear that the American public was in favor of repealing the Eighteenth Amendment, known as Prohibition. *Courtesy of the Library of Congress.*

had failed. First it took jobs away from thousands of honest people employed in the brewery, distillery, and wine industries. Then it created widespread disrespect for the law. Organized crime had become incredibly wealthy. Many Prohibition agents, police, and innocent citizens had lost their lives in shoot-outs over illegal trafficking of alcohol. Furthermore, bootleg alcohol containing poisonous chemicals had caused physical harm, blindness, and sometimes death in over ten thousand people. Prohibition overburdened the court system, and it cost massive amounts of money to enforce. And perhaps most important, many Americans believed that the Eighteenth Amendment was an infringement of personal rights. For all these reasons, Prohibition was doomed.

By 1930 an unlikely group of organizations banded together to form the Prohibition repeal movement: the Association Against the Prohibition Amendment, predominantly businessmen; the Women's Organization of National Prohibition Reform, a large contingent of women headed by Pauline Sabin; intellectuals, writers, critics, and journalists who had always opposed Prohibition; and organized labor, a group that had long been dismayed that the wealthy could afford to purchase illegal alcohol and keep on drinking while common laborers could not afford an illegal beer. A new constitutional amendment would have to be crafted to repeal the Eighteenth Amendment. This had never been done before, and anti-Prohibitionists were not certain that outright repeal would even be possible.

In attempting to repeal the Eighteenth Amendment, anti-Prohibitionists took a practical approach. They laid part of the blame for the Depression on Prohibition. Legalizing alcohol, they claimed, would bring back jobs, generate tax revenue for the government, and stop expensive attempts to enforce Prohibition. Under intense pressure from the public,

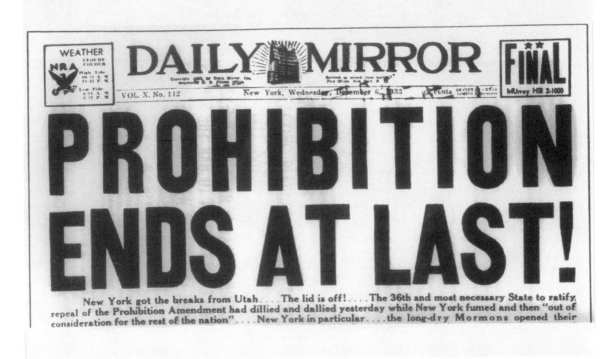

# DAILY MIRROR

FINAL
★★

Copyright, 1933, by Daily Mirror, Inc.
Registered U. S. Patent Office

Entered as second class matter
Post Office, New York, N. Y.

VOL. X. No. 112          New York, Wednesday, December 6, 1933          2 Cents IN CITY
LIMITS · Elsewhere          MUrray Hill 2-1000

# PROHIBITION ENDS AT LAST!

New York got the breaks from Utah. . . . The lid is off! . . . . The 36th and most necessary State to ratify repeal of the Prohibition Amendment had dillied and dallied yesterday while New York fumed and then "out of consideration for the rest of the nation". . . . New York in particular. . . . the long-dry Mormons opened their

Congress agreed to draft a constitutional amendment ending Prohibition. The Twenty-First Amendment was written by Congress and submitted to the states for ratification (approval) in February 1933.

As soon as President Roosevelt took office on March 4, 1933, he issued an executive order drastically reducing the appropriations (funds) used to enforce Prohibition. Knowing it would take the rest of the year to ratify the Twenty-First Amendment, he urged Congress to pass a bill legalizing 3.2 percent alcoholic content, so that at least beer could be legally produced. The bill passed and went into effect on April 7, 1933. Over two hundred breweries immediately hired workers and produced real beer. Speakeasies suddenly became legal beer houses. In cities nationwide, parades, sirens, and cowbells marked the first day of legalized beer.

On December 5, 1933, Utah became the thirty-sixth state to ratify the Twenty-First Amendment, and Prohibition

The front page of the December 6, 1933, *Daily Mirror* sums it up: With the passage of the Twenty-First Amendment, Prohibition came to an end. *AP/Wide World Photo. Reproduced by permission.*

came to an end. That evening Roosevelt issued a proclamation that ratification was complete and that not only beer but liquor was again legal.

## New ventures for organized crime

The repeal of Prohibition put an end to the bootlegging business. Gangsters had to find new business ventures in the midst of the economic crisis. These new ventures included loan-sharking, labor racketeering, and drug trafficking. Loan-sharking became a major source of steady income for organized crime. Typically loan sharks required that for every five dollars borrowed, six dollars had to be paid back each week. That amounted to a loan rate of over 1,000 percent per year.

Labor racketeering was another popular venture. Gangsters worked their way into positions of authority in regular labor unions and then took money from the union's pension and health funds. Drug trafficking was a natural extension of bootlegging: Organized crime again supplied an illegal substance desired by the public. By the twenty-first century drug trafficking remained organized crime's biggest business.

## The outlaws

By 1933 another lawless group had appeared on the American scene: the midwestern outlaws. These outlaws were rural bandits who operated in the Midwest and South in 1933 and 1934. Toting Tommy guns (an automatic weapon with shortened barrel; more formally known as Thompson submachine gun) or sawed-off shotguns and driving fast cars, they robbed banks and gasoline service stations in isolated areas. Before roaring away, they shot up the building and frequently injured or killed people in the way.

The outlaws operated individually or with a partner or family members. Unlike the members of organized crime, outlaws were not unified in any way. The most famous outlaws were John Dillinger (1903–1934), Bonnie Parker (1911–1934) and Clyde Barrow (1909–1934), George "Machine Gun" Kelly (1895–1954), "Ma" Barker and her boys,

George "Baby Face" Nelson (1908–1934), and Charles "Pretty Boy" Floyd (1901–1934). Their total take from robberies was tiny compared to the money organized crime amassed through Prohibition violations. Organized crime considered the outlaws freaks and small-time thrill seekers. However, the organized gangsters and the freewheeling outlaws had at least one thing in common: They both made a mockery of the hapless and often corrupt local police forces.

The Depression-weary public tended to romanticize the gangsters and the outlaws. Americans identified with the outlaws, who were portrayed in newspapers as Robin Hood figures—stealing from the banks where so many Americans had lost their life savings. John Dillinger became a sort of folk hero, leaping over barriers to grab money bags from bank tellers. Newspapers followed his every move just as they followed the movie stars. Although the public was aghast when Dillinger killed innocent people, they were fascinated by his ability to break out of jails and elude police.

# WANTED

## JOHN HERBERT DILLINGER

On June 23, 1934, HOMER S. CUMMINGS, Attorney General of the United States, under the authority vested in him by an Act of Congress approved June 6, 1934, offered a reward of

## $10,000.00

for the capture of John Herbert Dillinger or a reward of

## $5,000.00

for information leading to the arrest of John Herbert Dillinger.

### DESCRIPTION

Age, 32 years; Height, 5 feet 7-1/8 inches; Weight, 153 pounds; Build, medium; Hair, medium chestnut; Eyes, grey; Complexion, medium; Occupation, machinist; Marks and scars, 1/2 inch scar back left hand, scar middle upper lip, brown mole between eyebrows.

All claims to any of the aforesaid rewards and all questions and disputes that may arise as among claimants to the foregoing rewards shall be passed upon by the Attorney General and his decisions shall be final and conclusive. The right is reserved to divide and allocate portions of any of said rewards as between several claimants. No part of the aforesaid rewards shall be paid to any official or employee of the Department of Justice.

If you are in possession of any information concerning the whereabouts of John Herbert Dillinger, communicate immediately by telephone or telegraph collect to the nearest office of the Division of Investigation, United States Department of Justice, the local addresses of which are set forth on the reverse side of this notice.

Outlaw John Dillinger was seen by many as a hero during the early Depression years, even though he was a ruthless criminal. *Corbis-Bettmann. Reproduced by permission.*

# The Lindbergh kidnapping

As America continued its love/hate relationship with crime in the early 1930s, one incident jolted the entire nation. Charles Lindbergh (1902–1974), a fearless pilot, had completed the first solo transatlantic flight in 1927. The "Lone Eagle" was America's foremost hero. He married Anne Morrow in 1929, and together the couple flew on tours across the United States to promote air travel. On March 1, 1932, the country was stunned by the news that the Lindberghs' first child, twenty-month-old Charles Jr., had been kidnapped from his bedroom. The body of the toddler was found in May, a short distance from the parents' home. Eventually Bruno Hauptmann (1899–1936) would be convicted of the murder. Although he maintained his innocence, he was executed on April 3, 1936. For many Americans the abduction was overwhelmingly disturbing. In mid-1932 Congress quickly moved to pass the Federal Kidnapping Act, popularly known as the "Lindbergh Law," which made kidnapping a federal crime. This law was the first allowing federal officers to chase criminals, at least kidnappers, across state lines.

## A New Deal response to crime

The stories of gangsters and outlaws had captured Americans' curiosity, but the brutality of these criminals together with the horror of the Lindbergh kidnapping case made some people wonder whether the United States was in the middle of a moral crisis as well as an economic one. Crime was not an issue in the 1932 presidential race. However, by the time Franklin D. Roosevelt assumed the presidency in March 1933, Americans hoped that he could solve both the economic crisis and the crime problem. Local law enforcement had been unsuccessful in dealing with the lawlessness. The local agencies were hampered by restrictive laws and often were riddled with corruption.

President Roosevelt chose Homer S. Cummings (1870–1956) as his attorney general—the person in charge of the Department of Justice. Cummings would lead the New Deal war on crime. The Justice Department included the Bureau of Investigation, headed by J. Edgar Hoover (1895–1972). With his superior organizational skills, Hoover had put together a top-notch corps of special agents. However, the corps was by law limited to carrying out dreary chores such as trailing prostitutes and checking on violations of obscure laws. The corps could neither make arrests nor carry guns.

On June 17, 1933, special agents and unarmed police officers were escorting bank robber and prison escapee Frank Nash back to prison. Suddenly, three men armed with machine guns ambushed the group, killing three of the police officers and one of the special agents. The nation was outraged. Attorney General Cummings used the incident, called the Kansas City Massacre, to spur the development of an anti-

crime package, which was approved by Congress in May 1934. The package included provisions that made almost any crime that involved crossing a state line a federal offense and fair game for federal agents. Robberies of national banks, illegal use of telephone and telegraph wires, and attacks on federal officials were all made federal offenses. Congress also allowed J. Edgar Hoover's special agents to carry guns and make arrests.

Cummings knew that restoring the public's confidence in law enforcement was key to winning the war on crime. He decided to commit federal agents to raids that would offer the biggest publicity payoff. J. Edgar Hoover and his special agents would play the key role. Cummings and Hoover focused on celebrity criminals who were the symbols of America's crime problem. Hoover and his agents, including Agent Melvin Purvis (1903–1960) who was chief of the bureau's Chicago office, went after the infamous midwestern outlaws. Working with local law officers, they gunned down Bonnie and Clyde in May 1934, John Dillinger in July 1934,

**Melvin Purvis, right, is congratulated by FBI chief J. Edgar Hoover, left, and attorney general William Stanley, center, for ending the career of John Dillinger.** *AP/Wide World Photo. Reproduced by permission.*

"Pretty Boy" Floyd in October 1934, "Baby Face" Nelson in November 1934, and "Ma" Barker and son Freddie in 1935.

Cummings was the supreme symbol of law and order by the end of 1934. By 1935, in the eyes of the public, J. Edgar Hoover was a larger-than-life hero. This image was cemented in the public's mind with the release of the 1935 megahit movie *G-Men*. The film traded the old gangster myth for a new story: a tough lawman bringing criminals to justice and credibility back to law enforcement. Americans welcomed this New Deal on crime. J. Edgar Hoover and his G-men—with some help from Hollywood—had redeemed U.S. law enforcement.

## Organized crime continues to grow

In 1935 the Bureau of Investigation changed its name to the Federal Bureau of Investigation (FBI), and Hoover's G-men became known as FBI agents. Hoover and his men had demolished the midwestern outlaws, but the now-national organized crime syndicate (a network of groups) encountered almost no resistance from the FBI. Organized crime continued to grow and prosper but kept a low profile. Hoover chose not to battle organized crime. He did not want to risk a poor showing against the underworld. To preserve the respect the FBI had gained, Hoover continued to go after easier, high-profile targets that would bring lots of favorable publicity to him and his agency.

In 1936 President Roosevelt ordered Hoover to make national security the FBI's top priority. The FBI was to keep the president informed of any foreign-influenced subversive activities in the United Sates. The FBI's focus remained in this arena for years to come. The agency's failure to pursue the gangsters of the organized crime syndicate left one of the Depression era's legacies—a well-established and wealthy underworld network of crime.

## For More Information

### Books

Behr, Edward. *Prohibition: Thirteen Years That Changed America*. New York, NY: Arcade Publishing, 1996.

Bergman, Andrew. *We're in the Money: Depression America and Its Films.* New York, NY: New York University Press, 1971.

Bergreen, Laurence. *Capone: The Man and the Era.* New York, NY: Simon & Schuster, 1994.

Kelly, Robert J. *Encyclopedia of Organized Crime in the United States: From Capone's Chicago to the New Urban Underworld.* Westport, CT: Greenwood Press, 2000.

Kennedy, Ludovic. *The Airman and the Carpenter: The Lindbergh Kidnapping and the Framing of Richard Hauptmann.* New York, NY: Viking, 1985.

Kobler, John. *Capone: The Life and World of Al Capone.* New York, NY: G. P. Putnam's Sons, 1971.

Kyvig, David E. *Repealing National Prohibition.* Chicago, IL: University of Chicago Press, 1979.

McWilliams, Peter. *Ain't Nobody's Business If You Do: The Absurdity of Consensual Crimes in a Free Society.* Los Angeles, CA: Prelude Press, 1993.

Milner, E. R. *The Lives and Times of Bonnie and Clyde.* Carbondale, IL: Southern Illinois University Press, 1996.

Pegram, Thomas R. *Battling Demon Rum: The Struggle for a Dry America, 1800–1933.* Chicago, IL: Ivan R. Dee, 1998.

Powers, Richard Gid. *G-Men: Hoover's FBI in American Popular Culture.* Carbondale, IL: Southern Illinois University Press, 1983.

Powers, Richard Gid. *Secrecy and Power: The Life of J. Edgar Hoover.* New York, NY: Free Press, 1987.

Rose, Kenneth D. *American Women and the Repeal of Prohibition.* New York, NY: New York University Press, 1996.

Ruth, David E. *Inventing the Public Enemy: The Gangster in American Culture, 1918–1934.* Chicago, IL: University of Chicago Press, 1996.

Severn, Bill. *The End of the Roaring Twenties: Prohibition and Repeal.* New York, NY: Julian Messner, 1969.

Toland, John. *The Dillinger Days.* New York, NY: Da Capo Press, 1995.

## Web Sites

*The Crime Library.* http://www.crimelibrary.com (accessed on August 17, 2002).

*Federal Bureau of Investigation.* http://www.fbi.gov (accessed on August 17, 2002).

"Rum, Riot, and Reform." *The Maine Historical Society.* http://www.maine history.org/rum-riot-reform/main.html (accessed on August 17, 2002).

"Temperance and Prohibition." *Ohio State University Department of History.* http://prohibition.history.ohio-state.edu (accessed on August 17, 2002).

# 16 | End of the Great Depression

The 1930s were a troubled decade, economically and politically, throughout much of the world. In the United States the stock market crash in 1929 and the economic depression that followed brought widespread unemployment reaching up to 25 percent of the workforce (over twelve million workers) by early 1933. Most other workers experienced pay cuts. President Herbert Hoover (1874–1964), who served during the early years of the Depression (1929–33), made only a limited response. As economic conditions worsened, Americans lost faith in Hoover, and there was considerable social unrest. Franklin Roosevelt (1882–1945) was elected as president in 1932, and when he took office in early 1933, he brought hope with his massive New Deal social and economic recovery programs. But even with Roosevelt's aggressive approach, the depression did not significantly improve. In Europe, the economic hard times led to radical politics, including the rise of Adolf Hitler (1889–1945) and the Nazi Party in Germany. Germany and Italy as well as Japan began programs of military expansion, forcefully taking control of other nations.

Finally in September 1939 another world war erupted in Europe, only two decades after the end of World War I (1914–18). This new global war would pit the Allies—primarily the United States, Britain, China, and the Soviet Union—against Germany, Japan, and Italy, the Axis powers. After the surprise Japanese attack on Pearl Harbor on December 7, 1941, the United States entered World War II. The U.S. entry into the war started a full industrial mobilization effort in 1942 and 1943. (Industrial mobilization involves the production of massive amounts of war goods, including ships, tanks, arms, ammunition, and warplanes.) Roosevelt had had strong differences with business interests over New Deal policies through the 1930s, but he had to seek cooperation from business for the war mobilization effort. As a result, many policies and programs introduced by Roosevelt to combat the effects of the Great Depression, including regulation of industry, would come to an end. Funded by large military contracts, industry provided millions of new jobs, and wages were higher than the pay offered during the Great Depression. The increase in jobs and pay finally brought the Great Depression to a close. With increased military spending for production of war materials, optimism over the national economy returned.

## The Cost of War

Wars are expensive, and the U.S. government was willing to spend whatever it took to win World War II. The federal budget grew from less than $9 billion in 1939 to over $95 billion in 1945. A total of $290 billion was spent on the war effort. The United States raised half of the money through general taxes and the rest by selling war bonds and obtaining loans. The Revenue Act of 1942 established a national tax system that would continue into the twenty-first century. The gross national product (total value of all goods and services produced by a nation's workers) jumped from $90 billion in 1939 to $212 billion in 1945. The total amount of war materials produced by 1945 was staggering. U.S. factories had made almost 300,000 warplanes, 86,000 tanks, 64,000 landing ships, 6,000 navy vessels, millions of guns, billions of bullets, and hundreds of thousands of trucks and jeeps. By itself, the United States produced more war materials than the Axis powers (Germany, Italy, and Japan) did as a group.

## A reluctant nation

In Europe the end of World War I (1914–18) had brought peace but not prosperity. Dire economic problems arose in Germany after its defeat in the war, and these difficulties opened the door for Adolf Hitler and the Nazi Party.

U.S. involvement in World War II required massive production of war materials. Here, a woman loads powder into bullet cartridges at a Pennsylvania arsenal. *AP/Wide World Photo. Reproduced by permission.*

Hitler promised to return Germany to power through military expansion. At the same time, a weak civilian government in Japan was replaced by the Japanese military, which harbored desires to expand into China and other East Asian areas. Poor in natural resources, Japan wanted control over resources located in neighboring countries. In the United States, President Roosevelt kept a watchful, worried eye on the gathering international storm. He had little support to prepare for another war: The American public, for the most part, had no desire to become involved; World War I had been enough. It had been called the "war to end all wars."

Meanwhile, German forces under Hitler began storming through Europe. When Germany invaded Poland in September 1939, Britain and France declared war on Germany, and World War II formally began. For the United States involvement in the war would require massive production of war materials, and a large military force would need to be raised. Though the United States remained officially neutral, Roosevelt proclaimed to the nation that it was time to plan for possible war. Roosevelt feared that if Europe and Britain fell to Germany, the United States would be the next nation to face Germany's fearless and well-armed military.

# Industry and government at odds

Private industry and Roosevelt disagreed on how the nation should mobilize for war. For a successful mobilization effort the United States needed to convert privately owned industries from domestic production to war production; increase the mining and processing of raw materials used in manufacturing; control distribution of the raw materials; and oversee the military purchase of war goods. The military had always relied on the nation's largest corporations to be their primary contractors. However, the New Dealers under Roosevelt wished to end this reliance on big business by directing wartime contracts to small businesses as well. They especially wanted to get military contracts to the smaller companies located in parts of the country still suffering from the effects of the Great Depression. They thought that mobilization efforts should be centralized in strong government agencies that could plan the overall war effort and direct contracts to a wide range of businesses in various parts of the country.

Most industries, on the other hand, did not want to interrupt their production of domestic goods or have the government interfere with their economic markets. They believed the war would be brief, and they did not want to convert to a short-term project and give up the profits that they were currently enjoying as the nation was gradually recovering from the Depression. They wanted military production to

When France fell to Germany in June 1940, the United States began providing shipments of arms and other provisions, such as this tank, to Britain. *Courtesy of the Franklin D. Roosevelt Library.*

occur only in plants built with public funds or through special financial arrangements in the government contracts guaranteeing they would receive substantial profits. They also wanted to be as free as possible of New Deal social reforms and labor laws. Businesses feared increased wartime regulation and the creation of new, permanent federal agencies that would control war mobilization and perhaps even the U.S. economy after the war. They insisted that mobilization should rely on corporate volunteerism organized through temporary government agencies that could be easily dismantled following the war.

Given that the nation's business leaders opposed creation of any large New Deal-like agencies to oversee industrial mobilization, Roosevelt had to rely on a set of small temporary agencies heavily staffed with private business advisers, industry advisory committees, and military personnel. Roosevelt first created the War Resources Board (WRB) in late 1939 to plan how to mobilize the nation's industries. The

WRB was the first in a series of mobilization agencies. It developed a plan based on voluntary industrial cooperation. However, the plan to convert industry from domestic to military production was never fully put into use because industry was still reluctant to convert and the public still did not fully support mobilization.

When France fell to Germany in June 1940, the United States began providing shipments of arms and other provisions to Britain. Roosevelt was reelected in November 1940, and he established the Office of Production Management (OPM) in January 1941 to finally get industrial production of war materials under way. The head of the OPM was William Knudsen (1879–1948), former chairman of General Motors. Like the WRB, the OPM had little success in convincing industry to replace their production of civilian goods with military production.

## A new relationship between industry and government

As in the First World War, the United States entered World War II late. The Japanese attack on Pearl Harbor on December 7, 1941, was the trigger for full U.S. mobilization. The surprise air attack on the U.S. Pacific Fleet by more than three hundred warplanes was intended to keep the United States from challenging Japan's continued military expansion in the Far East—especially in the Philippines, where strong U.S. interests existed. The United States suffered thirty-seven hundred casualties, and the American public was shocked and enraged. The United States declared war on Japan the following day, December 8. Three days later Germany and Italy declared war on the United States.

The following month, January 1942, President Roosevelt established the War Production Board (WPB) to assume control over wartime mobilization. The urgency of declared war now brought public support much more strongly behind government efforts to mobilize industry. Industries were now required to convert to military production. The WPB sought to distribute workers and raw materials to those industries most crucial for the buildup. The manufacture of certain domestic goods, such as refrigerators, cars, and toasters, became

The U.S.S. *Shaw* explodes
during the Japanese raid on
Pearl Harbor, December 7,
1941. The United States
declared war on Japan
the following day.
*National Archives and
Records Administration.*

limited, or completely stopped, so that raw materials such as steel and aluminum would be available for manufacturing war materials. Industry began working around the clock, using several shifts through the day.

In addition to stopping passage of any more New Deal reforms designed to regulate industry, such as labor laws regulating wages and maximum hours worked, Roosevelt also offered financial and legal incentives to businesses to conform with the mobilization requirements. Although industry was "required" to mobilize, Roosevelt had limited legal power to actually enforce conversion. Therefore, incentives were used to help avoid confrontations with industry leaders. These incentives included major tax breaks for building new plants to produce war materials, suspending certain laws so that competing companies could instead cooperate, and issuing military war production contracts that guaranteed good profits. Roosevelt essentially turned the wartime economy over to the country's business leaders to ensure more effective cooperation by industry.

Acknowledging the influence of industry in shaping U.S. mobilization policies and seeking to unify the nation, Roosevelt appointed Republican Henry L. Stimson (1867–1950) as secretary of war. Stimson, a strong big-business advocate, took the lead in working on war preparations with industry leaders.

Under Stimson's leadership, manufacturing contracts were primarily awarded to the largest corporations, which had research departments, established assembly lines, and large numbers of workers. Business advisers in government contended that these large companies could most readily convert from domestic to military production. As a result, the ten largest corporations received one-third of all war contracts; smaller companies were largely left to seek smaller contracts from the big companies. What followed was unprecedented in the number of ships, tanks, planes, guns, and ammunition produced. The roles of government and business had suddenly changed. During the Great Depression the federal government had taken the

To meet the ever-growing need to expand the U.S. workforce during the war years, industry began attracting new workers, including racial minorities and women. *Archive Photo. Reproduced by permission.*

lead with great public support in stabilizing the shaky economy. However, government assistance in the economy brought with it certain regulations unpopular with business. The war put the U.S. government in urgent need of industrial production—in other words, it put businesses in a good bargaining position. They were able to dictate their own terms, shed New Deal restrictions, and turn their sights to bigger profits with minimal government intervention.

## Mobilization progresses

In dramatic contrast to the massive unemployment of the 1930s, labor shortages quickly appeared as over five million Americans joined the military services. Industry began attracting new workers, including racial minorities and women. Competition between industries over the available labor supply grew. To help with labor shortages, the War Manpower Commission (WMC) was created in April 1942. This agency directed laborers to the most critical jobs. In February 1943, to further ease the labor shortage, President Roosevelt relaxed some labor standards that had been established by the New Deal in 1938. He set a minimum forty-eight-hour workweek for workers in some critical industries and in certain areas of the nation where labor shortages existed. The WMC identified which industries and areas would be affected. These changes added greatly to workers' earnings, especially in industries producing aircraft, automobiles, ships, steel, and electrical machinery.

As mobilization progressed in 1943, disputes continued to occur between industries over access to raw materials and labor and over other production issues. To resolve the disputes Roosevelt created another small temporary agency, the Office of War Mobilization (OWM), in May 1943. Led by former U.S. Supreme Court justice James F. Byrnes (1879–1972), the OWM helped coordinate activities among industries.

By July 1943 the conversion to a wartime economy was substantially completed. Less than a year later a massive Allied force would land at Normandy, a region in France. This successful invasion to reclaim Western Europe signaled a major turning point in the war as Allied forces clearly gained an upper hand over German forces. Though months of hard fighting remained, it was just a matter of time before Germany would collapse. Germany finally surrendered in May 1945, ending the war in Europe. Japan surrendered in September 1945 after the United States dropped atomic bombs on Hiroshima and Nagasaki.

## Effects of mobilization

After more than ten years of economic depression, war mobilization dramatically revived the U.S. economy. The rate of production of goods and services in the United States more than doubled during the war years, with employment eventually reaching 98 percent of the workforce. Nine million workers had been jobless in 1939, as the nation struggled to make its way out of the Great Depression. By 1945, just six years later, that figure dropped to one million. Many new jobs had been created in private business and industry, and the federal government had grown substantially larger during the war. Already on the rise during the Depression, the number of federal civilian employees grew by 400 percent between 1941 and 1945. In all, seventeen million new jobs were created in private business and government sectors.

With so many new jobs available, more Americans than ever were taking home paychecks. Their hourly pay rates increased 22 percent through the war years. By mid-1943 about 60 percent of factory wage earners, or over eight million workers, earned between 50 cents and $1 an hour, and 3 percent of the workers made over $1.50 an hour. These rates were well above what they received during the Depression. Debts that had built up during the Depression were paid, and savings began to grow. Through war mobilization, corporate leaders regained prestige and political power lost during the Great Depression. By 1943 factory towns, quiet since 1929, were suddenly prosperous.

Farms recovered as well. Prices for crops more than doubled during the war as the demand for food to feed the Allied armies grew and farm production in Europe was greatly disrupted. Farmers' profits soared. After twenty years of economic problems, farmers once again enjoyed prosperity. Farm income rose from $5.3 billion in 1939 to $13.6 billion

**Students at Washington High School in Los Angeles, California, construct model planes to U.S. Navy specifications for use by military personnel.** *Courtesy of the Library of Congress.*

in 1944. Farm communities prospered, and some became economic leaders in their regions.

The New Deal programs introduced after 1933 had helped relieve some of the economic hardships brought on by the Great Depression, but it took massive war mobilization to actually end the Depression. As the nation's economy gained strength, the New Dealers largely faded to the background.

## New Deal Programs Wind Down

By 1940 Roosevelt's push for social and economic reform was largely over. A conservative Congress and numerous business leaders, who strongly believed that New Deal programs inappropriately intruded in private business, had gained sufficient political strength to stall war mobilization until Roosevelt changed his domestic policies. In order to prepare the nation for war, Roosevelt had to decrease federal commitment to social reform. Disappointed, many loyal supporters began leaving government. Over the next few years many New Deal programs were closed.

Social Security, the Securities and Exchange Commission, farm programs, and other New Deal programs would live on beyond World War II, but other key programs came to an end during the war. For example, the Civilian Conservation Corps (CCC), one of the more popular New Deal programs and one of Roosevelt's personal favorites, was ended in 1942. The CCC was originally established in 1933 to employ young men on projects that would improve public lands. When World War II began, the CCC began teaching enrollees how to read blueprints and do other tasks that would be useful in the military. As many CCC enrollees began joining the military services, Roosevelt promoted the CCC as a beneficial agency for youths below the military age. However, Congress cut its funding, believing the CCC was too much in competition with private business.

Similarly, the Works Progress Administration (WPA), another New Deal program, lost most of its workers to the war industry, where pay and jobs were better. Created in 1935, the WPA was closed out by the end of 1943. The National Youth Administration (NYA), also created in 1935, lasted until 1943, primarily because it was teaching youths vocational skills that would be useful in the war industry.

## The New Deal ends

With industrial mobilization complete by 1943, Roosevelt began thinking about the postwar U.S. economy. The president asked the National Resources Planning Board (NRPB), a New Deal organization created in 1933, to devise a postwar plan. The NRPB was originally created to coordinate industrial recovery during the early years of the Depression. In planning for the nation's postwar economy, the board expected that the war industries would reduce their number of employees while shifting back to production of domestic goods. Therefore, board members proposed expanding Social Security for the needy and creating public works projects for veterans returning from the war who could not readily find a job. Business leaders and conservatives in Congress quickly opposed the proposals, fearing that government programs would once again exert their influence in private business. Congress cut off funds to the NRPB, and the board ceased operation.

Not only had the New Deal ended during the war, but its leader was lost as well. President Roosevelt died suddenly while relaxing at his Warm Springs, Georgia, retreat on April 12, 1945. Vice President Harry Truman (1884–1972) took over the presidency as military victory in World War II was in sight and America was poised to enter a new era as a world superpower.

# For More Information

## Books

Doenecke, Justus D., and Allan M. Winkler. *Home Front U.S.A.: America during World War II*. Wheeling, IL: Harlan Davidson, 2000.

Eiler, Keith E. *Mobilizing America: Robert P. Patterson and the War Effort, 1940–1945*. Ithaca, NY: Cornell University Press, 1997.

Gilbert, Martin. *The Second World War: A Complete History*. New York, NY: Henry Holt, 1989.

Heale, Michael. *Franklin D. Roosevelt: The New Deal and War*. New York, NY: Routledge, 1999.

Ketchum, Richard M. *The Borrowed Years, 1938–1941: America on the Way to War*. New York, NY: Anchor Books, 1991.

O'Brien, Kenneth P., and Lynn Hudson Parsons, eds. *The Home-Front War: World War II and American Society*. Westport, CT: Greenwood Press, 1995.

Roosevelt, Franklin D. *The Public Papers and Addresses of Franklin D. Roosevelt*. New York, NY: Random House, 1950.

Waddell, Brian. *The War against the New Deal: World War II and American Democracy*. De Kalb, IL: Northern Illinois University Press, 2001.

Wiltz, John E. *From Isolation to War, 1931–1941*. Arlington Heights, IL: Harlan Davidson, 1991.

## Web Sites

"World War II." *About.com*. http://history1900s.about.com/cs/world-warii (accessed on August 17, 2002).

# Where to Learn More

## Books

Badger, Anthony J. *The New Deal: The Depression Years, 1933–1940*. New York: Hill and Wang, 1989.

Bowen, Ezra. *The Fabulous Century: 1930–1940*. New York: Time-Life Books, 1969.

Britton, Loretta, and Sarah Brash, eds. *Hard Times: The 30s*. Alexandria, VA: Time-Life Books, 1998.

Buhite, Russell D., and David W. Levy, eds. *FDR's Fireside Chats*. Norman: University of Oklahoma Press, 1992.

Burns, James McGregor. *Roosevelt: The Lion and the Fox*. Norwalk, CT: Eaton Press, 1989.

Cochran, Thomas C. *The Great Depression and World War II, 1929–1945*. Glenview, IL: Scott, Foresman, and Company, 1968.

Federal Writers Project. *These Are Our Lives*. New York: W.W. Norton & Company, Inc., 1939.

Horan, James D. *The Desperate Years: A Pictorial History of the Thirties*. New York: Bonanza Books, 1962.

Kennedy, David M. *Freedom From Fear: The American People in Depression and War, 1929–1945*. New York: Oxford University Press, 1999.

Leuchtenberg, William E. *Franklin D. Roosevelt and the New Deal, 1932–1940*. New York: Harper & Row, 1963.

Martin, George. *Madam Secretary: Frances Perkins*. Boston: Houghton Mifflin, 1976.

McElvaine, Robert S. *The Depression and the New Deal: A History in Documents*. New York: Oxford University Press, 2000.

McElvaine, Robert S. *The Great Depression: America, 1929–1941*. New York: Times Books, 1993.

Meltzer, Milton. *Brother, Can You Spare a Dime? The Great Depression, 1929–1933*. New York: New American Library, 1977.

Pasachoff, Naomi E. *Frances Perkins: Champion of the New Deal*. New York: Oxford University Press, 1999.

Perkins, Frances. *The Roosevelt I Knew*. New York: The Viking Press, 1946.

Phillips, Cabell. *From the Crash to the Blitz, 1929–1939*. New York: Macmillan, 1969.

Rogers, Agnes. *I Remember Distinctly: A Family Album of the American People, 1918–1941*. New York: Harper & Brothers Publishers, 1947.

Roosevelt, Eleanor. *The Autobiography of Eleanor Roosevelt*. New York: Da Capo Press, 2000.

Roosevelt, Franklin D. *The Public Papers and Addresses of Franklin D. Roosevelt*. 5 vols. New York: Random House, 1938–1950.

Schlesinger, Arthur M., Jr. *The Age of Roosevelt*. 3 volumes. Boston: Houghton Mifflin Company, 1957–1960.

Schlesinger, Arthur M., Jr. *The Coming of the New Deal: The Age of Roosevelt*. Boston: Houghton Mifflin Company, 1988.

Terkel, Studs. *Hard Times: An Oral History of the Great Depression*. New York: Pantheon Books, 1986.

Thompson, Kathleen, and Hilary MacAustin, eds. *Children of the Depression*. Bloomington: Indiana University Press, 2001.

Washburne, Carolyn Kott. *America in the 20th Century, 1930–1939*. North Bellmore, NY: Marshall Cavendish Corp., 1995.

Watkins, T. H. *The Great Depression: America in the 1930s*. Boston: Little, Brown, & Co., 1993.

Watkins, T. H. *The Hungry Years: A Narrative History of the Great Depression in America*. New York: Henry Holt and Company, 1999.

Winslow, Susan. *Brother, Can You Spare a Dime? America From the Wall Street Crash to Pearl Harbor: An Illustrated Documentary*. New York: Paddington Press, 1976.

## Web Sites

*Franklin D. Roosevelt Library and Museum*. http://www.fdrlibrary.marist.edu

*Library of Congress. American Memory*. http://memory.loc.gov/ammem/fsowhome.html

*New Deal Network*. http://newdeal.feri.org

# Index

**Illustrations are marked by (ill.)**

# J

Jack Armstrong (cartoon character) 208
Japan's role in World War II–268, 272 (ill.)
Japanese immigration to the United States 178
Jazz musicians 204–205, 234
Jigsaw puzzles 200, 200 (ill.), 201
Jitterbug 204 (ill.)
Jobs done by children 194
Jobs, World War II and creation of 15, 127, 140, 179, 274, 275 (*See also* Employment, government agencies providing; Unemployment)
Johnson, Howard 207
Johnson, Lyndon B. 232
Johnson-O'Malley Act (1934) 185
Joint Commission on the Emergency in Education 116
Journalism, newspaper 166, 167 (ill.), 229–231, 232
"Jungles" (transient camps) 216

# K

Kaltenborn, Hans von 233
Kansas City Massacre 262
Kelly, George "Machine Gun" 245, 260
Kennedy, John F. 6, 232
Kennedy, Joseph P. 6
Kent, Frank 230
Kidnapping of Lindbergh baby 261–262
Kilpatrick, William K. 118
Knudsen, William 271
Ku Klux Klan 197
Kuniyoshi, Yasuo 91

# L

Labor (*See also* Child labor; Labor legislation; Labor unions)
New Deal relief for 33–34, 132–133

right to organize recognized by NIRA 132, 135
right to organize recognized by NLRA 135
shortage, during World War II 274
Labor legislation. *See*
Fair Labor Standards Act (1938)
National Industrial Recovery Act (NIRA) (1933)
National Labor Relations Act (1935)
Social Security Act (1935)
Labor unions
AFL and CIO 135, 139
collective bargaining by 33, 132–133, 135
company unions 134
employers' opposition to 130
Franklin Roosevelt supported by 141
government hostility toward 9
membership during Depression 130, 132, 135, 136, 140, 141
membership during the 1920s 128
membership in the 1940s 140–141
Mexican American farm laborers in 181
newspaper reporters in trade unions 229
Prohibition repeal supported by 258
purpose of 127
racial minorities and 173, 174
racketeering in 255, 260
Republican opposition to 128
sharecroppers in 174
teachers in 110, 117 (ill.)
Laissez-faire government 3
Lancaster, Burt 93
Landon, Alfred 34
Lange, Dorothea 74, 75, 77
Language. *See* Slang
Lansky, Meyer 256, 257
Law enforcement officials, corruption and bribery of 252, 254, 261, 262
Law enforcement, image of 239–240, 252, 256, 264
Lawrence, David 230
Laws. *See* Legislation

Mexican Americans 173
   deportation of 179–181
   jobs held by 179
   New Deal effects on 182–183
   unemployment rate for 181
Mexican Farm Labor Union 181
Middle-class and upper-middle-
      class people. *See* Classes, eco-
      nomic
Migrant workers 31, 67, 68, 69,
      180 (ill.), 213, 237
Miller, Arthur 93
Mills, Ogden L. 47
Miniature golf 200, 207
Minimum wage 33, 138, 162,
      168, 181
Minorities. *See* Racial minorities
Mobilization for World War II,
      U.S. 267, 269–271
   cost of 267
   economic effects of 275
   government agencies created
      for 270, 274
   government contracts for man-
      ufacturing 269–270, 273
   Pearl Harbor attack and 271
*Modern Times* (1936) 242, 242 (ill.)
Moley, Raymond 23
Money. *See* Cash, shortage of,
      during nationwide bank hol-
      iday
Moral decay, fear of 243, 250, 262
Morgan, Arthur E. 149
Morgan, John P., Jr. 195
Morgenthau, Henry, Jr. 100, 105
Mortgages, failure to make pay-
      ments on 38, 52–53,
      192–193
Mortgages, payment system for
      50–51, 55–56, 57
Motion Picture Producers and
      Distributors of America
      (MPPDA) 243
Movies
   anarchist comedy 242–243
   attendance 202–203, 229, 235,
      238, 238 (ill.), 239
   comedy and screwball comedy
      242, 245–246
   cost of 203, 238
   double features 238
   gangster movies 203, 239–241

   influence of, on American
      spending habits 4, 7
   law enforcement depicted in
      239, 241, 243
   lotteries at the 239
   moral codes and forbidden im-
      ages for 243, 244
   musicals 203, 244
   Saturday afternoon movies
      207, 239
   shyster movies 241–242
   silent films 4, 235, 242
   socially conscious movies 246
   with sound (talkies) 228–229,
      235
MPPDA. *See* Motion Picture Pro-
      ducers and Distributors of
      America
Murphy, Frank 119, 137
Murrow, Edward R. 233
Music broadcast on the radio 234
Music popular during the 1930s
      204–205
Musicals, Hollywood 244
Musicians. *See* Federal Music Pro-
      ject; Guthrie, Woody; Jazz
      musicians; Radio: popular
      entertainers on
Mydans, Carl 76

# N

NAACP. *See* National Association
      for the Advancement of Col-
      ored People
Nagasaki, U.S. bombing of 275
National Association for the Ad-
      vancement of Colored Peo-
      ple (NAACP) 175, 179
National Broadcasting Company
      (NBC) 233
National Consumers' League
      165, 169
National Education Association
      (NEA) 116
National Employment Act (1933)
      26
National Housing Act (1934) 29,
      38, 55, 56
National Housing Act of 1937
      (Wagner-Steagall Housing
      Act) 35, 55, 57–58

# Y